Power, politics, and organizational change

Winning the turf game

Dave Buchanan and Richard Badham

SAGE Publications
London ▪ Thousand Oaks ▪ New Delhi

First published 1999
Reprinted 2000

SAGE Publications Ltd
6 Bonhill Street
London EC2A 4PU

SAGE Publications Inc.
2455 Teller Road
Thousand Oaks, California 91320

SAGE Publications India Pvt Ltd
32, M-Block Market
Greater Kailash – I
New Delhi 110 048

British Library Cataloguing in Publication data

A catalogue record for this book is available
from the British Library

ISBN 0 7619 6221 2
ISBN 0 7619 6222 0 (pbk)

Library of Congress catalog record available

Typeset by Mayhew Typesetting, Rhayader, Powys
Printed in Great Britain by The Cromwell Press Ltd,
Trowbridge, Wiltshire

For Lesley and June

Contents

List of tables and figures

Tables

Figures

Acknowledgements

This book has benefited from the contributions, advice, criticisms and comments of a significant number of practising managers, personal friends and academic colleagues. These include Helen Bevan, David Boddy, Lesley Buchanan, Paul Chapman, Ian Clark, Tim Claydon, Patrick Dawson, Mike Doyle, Pelle Ehn, Martin House, Andrzej Huczynski, Bill Johnson, Sven Kylén, Brian Moran, John Neath, Rosemary Nixon, David Selden, Derek Staniforth, Paul Steadman, David Webster, Yehudi Webster, David Weir, Michael Zanko – and many others too numerous to mention, including hundreds of managers who have taken part in analyses and discussions of their own political behaviour as participants on our management development programmes in recent years. Richard is particularly grateful to June, Alec, Max, Christian and Mallory, who put up with a disrupted and somewhat grouchy Christmas 1997 and New Year. For all their individual and collective inputs, we are extremely grateful. The flaws and errors in this book, however, remain the sole responsibility of the authors.

We hope that you will find this book interesting and enjoyable. However, we would welcome critical feedback. We would be particularly interested to hear from readers whose experiences of organizational politics are consistent with the argument set out here – and also from those who feel that we have misrepresented these issues. Our email addresses are:

In Britain:	d.buchanan@dmu.ac.uk
In Australia:	richard_badham@uow.edu.au

Introduction

The relatively stable, ordered, bounded, predictable, rule-based hierarchical organization today seems an anachronism. The so-called 'postmodern' organization is characterized by fluidity, uncertainty, ambiguity and discontinuity. Job security is replaced with 'employability security'. Organization boundaries are blurred with the development of partnerships and joint ventures, sub-contracting and peripheral workforces, and social and technology-based networks. Hierarchy is replaced by reliance on expert power; those with the best understanding of the problems take the decisions. In this (stereotyped) 'postmodern' context, individuals are stripped of the conventional resources of a relatively stable organizational position, and are deprived of a meaningful, predictable vision of their own future. This fluid and shifting context implies an increased dependence on personal and interpersonal resources, and on political skills to advance personal and corporate agendas. There is clearly enhanced scope for political manoeuvring in a less well-ordered and less disciplined organizational world. There is also clearly a greater need for a critical understanding of the shaping role of political behaviour in such a context.

The purpose of this book is to offer a theoretical and practical guide to the politics of organizational change. Our focus lies primarily with the *internal* change agent. Much existing commentary concentrates on external agents and consultants (Ginzberg and Abrahamson, 1991; Hartley et al., 1997). However, change is a key element in the roles of most functional and general managers, at all levels, who typically combine change responsibilities with their regular day job. We aim to combine analytical and theoretical frameworks, with empirical evidence, with practical guidance – with a fresh perspective. The exercise of organizational politics can be conceived as a game in which the players compete for different kinds of territory – for turf. What kind of game is this? How is it played? What are the rules? What ethical issues are raised? How does one play this game to win?

Our purpose reflects four beliefs:

The reality of politics

The first is that political behaviour plays a more significant role in organizational life than is commonly recognized – or than is openly admitted. We perhaps like to think of our social and organizational cultures as characterized by order, rationality, openness, collaboration and trust. The reality is different. Competition sits alongside co-operation. Informal 'backstaging' supports public action. We see self-interest, deceit, subterfuge and cunning, as well as the pursuit of moral ideals and high aspirations. It is uncommon to hear decisions defended in terms of political motives and behaviours. Reason and logic must be seen and heard to prevail. To suggest otherwise is to risk censure and ostracism. But initiatives are pursued, decisions are taken, and changes are introduced to preserve and extend the power bases and influence of individuals and groups. Major decisions, and significant changes, are particularly liable to heighten political activity. Organizational behaviour cannot, therefore, be understood without a knowledge of the role of political behaviour.

The repression of politics

The second is that the academic management literature does not adequately explore the shaping role of political behaviour in organizational change. Three broad positions are current: 'denial', 'acceptance without engagement', and 'recognition without advice'. Some commentators refuse to accept that organization development and change, on the one hand, and political behaviour, on the other, have any connection; conflict is the result of poor communications, to be resolved with openness and mutual trust. Others accept the reality of politics, note that the change agent must understand this domain, but argue that personal involvement in political behaviour is ethically unsound. And there are others still who accept both the reality of political behaviour, and the need for the change agent to intervene in this domain, but remain theoretically remote and offer little or no practical guidance.

The two faces of politics

The third concerns the observation that political behaviour presents both positive and negative, 'nice and nasty' faces to the observer – and to recipients or victims. We will argue, therefore, that not all 'tricks' are 'dirty tricks', although clearly some ploys in some contexts should be labelled as such. An adequate treatment must explore both dimensions. A reluctance to address this topic can therefore be seen as naïve, in not recognizing positive aspects of political behaviour, and can also be regarded as dishonest, deceptive and manipulative by suggesting that our attention would be better focused elsewhere, thereby marginalizing this domain. Those whose interests are served by political behaviour benefit from the argument that their actions do not deserve critical scrutiny. A wider understanding of political behaviour may thus both advantage those who would deploy such strategies and tactics, and support those who would seek to challenge and counter such behaviours.

Confronting the challenges

The fourth is that management development should help managers in general, and change agents in particular, to deal with the realities, the complexities, the challenges, the satisfactions and the dilemmas of political behaviour in organizations. Denial is unrealistic. Acceptance without engagement is naïve. Recognition without advice is unhelpful. The link here between understanding and prescription deserves clarification.

Does this lead to a prescription in which all change agents are politicians, all politics is about self-interest and manipulation, and the resulting management stereotype is a self-consciously devious Machiavellian? No. Organizations have social, technical, economic and cultural aspects as well as a political dimension. In a text such as this, political behaviour is taken aside or bracketed for 'special treatment' because the topic is omitted or misrepresented elsewhere. The conventional toolkits of change, in project management, in socio-technical system analysis and design, in organization development, and in planned change methods remain valuable, but are adequately dealt with elsewhere. Political behaviour must be set firmly in context. We can use a motoring metaphor to illustrate this point. The vehicle requires a traditional engine, wheels, seats, a shell and a chassis – but the driver will find the journey easier with *power-assisted steering*.

What does the phrase 'political behaviour' mean? We offer working definitions of power and politics in Chapter 1. We explore in more detail in Chapter 2 the ways in which these terms have been defined. Chapter 3 offers a series of illustrations of political behaviour from practising managers. In the meantime, can we ask you, the reader, to consider what you mean by political behaviour? How would you define and understand this term? What illustrations would you bring from your experience to describe the nature of political behaviour? Thus armed with your own experience-based perceptions, you will be in a better position to evaluate the approaches and examples discussed later.

The readership for whom this text is primarily intended is a practising management one, probably following a post-experience Masters degree programme. Our experience suggests that the tools, techniques, methods and approaches of organizational politics are broadly familiar to this readership. An understanding of political behaviour in organizations seems to be part of the tacit, taken-for-granted 'recipe knowledge' of most practising managers. The 'added value' in the treatment here, therefore, lies in providing a conceptual and theoretical overview of the field, in focusing on the shaping role of political behaviour in organizational change, and in the advocacy of a creative, reflective and critical approach to the use of political strategies and tactics. While this book will be of particular value on Masters level modules in the management of change, human resource management and organizational behaviour, we also expect the text to be of interest to senior undergraduate modules in those subjects, and to a general management readership as well.

Given this readership, the selection of materials raises problematic issues. There is now an extensive literature on the management of change. There is also an extensive and historical literature on power and politics (dating back, for example, to Thomas Hobbes and Niccolò Machiavelli; see Clegg, 1989), much of it written for audiences far removed from the contemporary day-to-day realities of implementing organizational change. Some conceptualizations and analyses of power and politics are more concerned with global, social, national and community affairs than with the problems of the business organization, public or private sector. And some of the power and politics literature is couched in a highly arcane and abstracted language, creating problems of access and interpretation for the uninitiated.

Given these difficulties, our selection of material is based on a view of the field of organizational politics from the standpoint of the internal change agent. The term 'change agent' is used here loosely to refer to anyone involved in initiating or implementing change, whether or not they have an official job title recognizing that responsibility. (While concentrating on internal agents, much of the argument here probably applies to external change agents as well.) The crude notion of 'relevance' is not much help. Some of the more esoteric and generalized analyses of power shed useful light on the shaping role of politics. Some of the more readily accessible conceptualizations of power and politics come close to oversimplifying and trivializing the issues. We have therefore sought to survey the field from the standpoint of the internal change agent, exercising an authors' privileged politics of inclusion and exclusion from that particular perspective. Academic readers familiar with the wider literature of this field will doubtless note major gaps.

This begs the question: who is the mythical 'change agent' whose perspective is being adopted? We will answer this question in Chapter 1, but two comments may be helpful here. First, the concept of *change agency* is of considerably more value than the notion of the singular change agent (Buchanan and Storey, 1997). Change is typically driven by what Hutton (1994) describes as a 'cast of characters'. Our 'change agent' is thus any member of that cast of characters, formally appointed by the organization, or a self-appointed promoter or saboteur seeking to drive an alternative agenda in addition to subverting officially sanctioned initiatives. Second, the change agent is viewed here as a *political entrepreneur* (Laver, 1997), deploying political tactics when necessary to advance combinations of personal and organizational change agendas, potentially in the face of opposition and resistance. This should not be taken to imply that change agency is an exclusively political activity, merely that political skill is a key element in the wider behaviour repertoire of the change agent.

The term *political entrepreneur* has been chosen with particular care, given the options. The label 'political activist' seems inappropriate for two reasons, being drawn from the domain of national party politics, and implying a highly visible, ruthless and self-serving approach. The term 'political operator' appears to be in more widespread use to describe the politically aware, astute and skilled manager. However, the term 'political entrepreneur' has the advantage of emphasizing the risk-taking and creative dimensions of the role of the change agent, and also the personal commitment, extending on occasion to passion, toward the change agenda. The term 'political entrepreneur' thus implies a behaviour repertoire, of political strategies and tactics, and a reflective, self-critical perspective on how those political behaviours should be deployed.

The change agent who strives to be politically neutral or 'squeaky clean' faces double jeopardy:

Squeaky clean and outmanoeuvred

First, the 'squeaky clean' approach is likely to be ineffective in the face of self-interested and sophisticated resistance tactics, or 'counter-implementation' measures. The change agent who is not equipped, or not willing, to deal with political issues and power plays is thus likely to be outmanoeuvred – and will probably fail. This argument is based on the presumption that organizational politics are pervasive, and cannot be 'wished away' or 'managed away'. It is necessary to confront circumstances as they are, and not as one would wish them to be. In colloquial terms, management in general, and change management in particular, is a 'contact sport'. Those who do not wish to get bruised should not play.

Squeaky clean and unprofessional

Second, the 'squeaky clean' approach which ignores, avoids or otherwise denies the political realities of organizational life could be viewed as unskilled, incompetent, unprofessional and unethical. And, as we shall argue later, advocates of ostensibly 'squeaky clean' management perspectives obscure the contentious political dimensions and implications of their positions. It may be more ethical and professional to deal effectively with the political dimensions of change management than simply to observe the political realities from some remote moral high ground. Change generally stimulates both support and resistance. Some resistance may be self-serving, while some may be based on a sincere belief that change is misguided. A committed change agent inevitably becomes a 'guardian' of the change agenda. This can warrant a politically entrepreneurial approach to conducting that protective function in the face of public challenge and 'backstage' tactics. Again in colloquial terms, if you confront a 'bodyguard', you presumably know what to expect.

We offer no simple contrast between, on the one hand, a politically neutral or ethical stance, and, on the other, an unprincipled approach in which 'anything goes' in the pursuit of change. The judgements that one may need to bring to this domain must be contingent and situational. The popular notion that 'power corrupts' must be balanced against the observation that power also helps in the pursuit and achievement of valuable social and organizational objectives. The politically entrepreneurial actions of the change driver will invariably be defensible, on some criteria and for some constituencies, while being wholly unacceptable on other grounds and for other players. We hope to demonstrate the integrity (personal, and organizational) of consciously undertaking political behaviour in an organizational change context.

The text is constructed in an accessible, if sometimes demanding, writing style, assuming a readership (practising managers and senior under-graduate) with organizational experience. Our aim has been to make the text entertaining and engaging for the reader, and also to reflect the non-linear, untidy character of change, and the sometimes devious character of much of the subject matter.

The structure of the book is as follows.

Chapter 1, 'How far are you prepared to go?', explores the broad nature of power and politics, the heightened significance of political behaviour in organizational change, and the problems of finding and defining 'the change agent'. Typical political tactics, drawn from practical managerial experience, are also introduced. The chapter concludes with a model of political behaviour in organizational change in which the concepts of 'warrant' (for particular types of behaviour) and 'reputation' (how a change agent is perceived by other organizational actors) are central.

Chapter 2, 'The terminology game', examines the literature of power and politics in search of competing definitions of these terms. Power can be conceived as a property of individuals, a property of relationships, or as a property of social and organizational structures and procedures. The problems of defining political behaviour are also examined. The ways in which we use conversation controls, influencing tactics and impression management methods are explored to illustrate that it is possible to conceive of every social interaction in political terms. This definition problem can be resolved by adopting a constructivist stance; the ability to define behaviour as political, or to reject such a definition, is itself a political act.

Chapter 3, 'Sit in judgement', presents a series of 'incident reports' from managers describing instances of political behaviour in their own experi-ence. These narratives are prefaced by a decision guide which can be used to determine whether political behaviour is ethical and thus appropriate in particular circumstances. Readers are thus invited to sit in judgement on these accounts, and to evaluate that 'ethics test' applied to real cases.

Chapter 4, 'Men behaving badly', addresses the issue of how to behave politically in the face of the manipulative, coercive and self-interested politics of others. The chapter reviews critiques of Machiavellian political behaviour from the 1960s onwards. It shows how concerns raised at that time about Machiavellian managers, 'gamesmen', 'narcissists' and 'fixers' have continuing relevance. While these concerns may appear dated today, particularly in the context of the 'new leadership' which encourages team-work and empowerment rather than autocratic manipulation, the chapter argues that the 'new leadership' can be regarded as equally devious and manipulative. Many of those earlier concerns are thus relevant to contemporary views of the 'male politics' of 'men behaving badly'. The politically incorrect chapter title and content reflect the fact that writers in the 1960s and 1970s were mostly male, and were writing about men, for men.

Chapter 5, 'The entrepreneurial hero', details contemporary prescriptive models of risk-taking 'champions of innovation' and the creation of a distinctive approach to 'positive' politics. The power tactics of 'entrepreneurial heroes' and 'new leaders' are contrasted with the 'negative' politics of traditional hierarchical bureaucracies. This chapter demonstrates that a sharp distinction between 'positive' and 'negative' politics is far from clear in practice. The change agent seeking ethical guidance is advised to abandon universalistic historical rationales and ethical principles, and to adopt instead a situational ethic.

Chapter 6, 'The politics of failure and the failure of politics', considers evidence from studies of change which supports the view that problems can often be attributed to organizational and managerial factors, and not to the substance (new technology, software, hardware, procedures) of change. Two related arguments are explored. First, that some 'organization-related' failures are due to a failure, or an unwillingness, to address political issues. Second, that the change agent who addresses these issues needs to manage complex political interdependencies and should be sensitized to, aware of, and perhaps trained in Machiavellian methods.

Chapter 7, 'Power-assisted steering: maxims for Princes and Princessas', considers the array of practical advice available to the change agent in the deployment of political strategies and tactics. Much of that advice is couched in 'simple recipe' terms. Missing is any notion of the frame of reference, or perspective, which the change agent might bring to translate this advice into action. The change agent is faced with a choice of strategies and tactics, based on an understanding of the context. Practice cannot simply follow a recipe. Practice is creative, judgement-based and improvisatory. The change agent will thus typically deploy 'complicating strategies' which are multi-dimensional, multi-faceted, complex and evolving through time, based on whatever opportunities and resources come to hand. This is also known as '*bricolage*'; the change agent is thus a '*bricoleur*'.

Chapter 8, 'The triggering factors', explores the individual, decisional and structural roots of political behaviour. A brief account of the substance and implications of Michel Foucault's perspective on power is also provided. This emphasizes the pervasive and productive aspects of power, and challenges the notion of 'triggers' in a controversial, but enlightening, manner. The value of being able to conceptualize power from different perspectives is considered, rather than an attempt to decide 'which is correct'. Although accounts of change initiatives from the 1950s and 1960s do not often confront the topic, political factors have probably been pervasive. It has perhaps been unfashionable, until more recently, openly to admit and discuss these issues. That fashion trend probably has little to do with real trends in organizational political behaviour. More significant is the argument that emerging organizational trends will put political skills at a premium in the new millennium.

1 How far are you prepared to go?

CONTENTS

"You're an evil bastard, Gilroy. I like that."

The turf game

Interviewer: But many managers argue that organizational politics are a distraction, it's not what they're paid for, not part of the job?

Manager: I would say b******* to that. I would say that people who get to those jobs only get to that level because, first, they are reasonably good at playing these games, and second, actually enjoy playing them. The people who fail at that level are, by and large, people who aren't particularly good at playing and don't understand.

This quote from an interview with a practising and experienced manager can be interpreted in two ways. First, this may represent a cynical view of organization and career, in which only the 'shrewd wheeler-dealers' get to the top, and in which those who ignore the politics game, and who do not enjoy it anyway, are destined to fail. Alternatively, this may represent a realistic view of organizational life and managerial career, and of the significance of power and political behaviour both to the effectiveness of the organization and to the individual. This text supports the second position, while accepting without reservation that political behaviour can also be both individually self-serving and organizationally damaging – on occasion. Ferris and Kacmar (1992, p. 113) note that:

A fundamental issue in work on organizational politics concerns its largely negative interpretation. Most people perceive only the dark side of politics, and indeed there is a dark side, characterized by destructive opportunism and dysfunctional game playing. However, politics can be positive as well, for organizations and for individuals.

Political behaviour thus presents both an ugly and deplorable face as well as a positive and beneficial one. It is more realistic and appropriate to seek out the positive and to confront the negative, than to deny altogether the significance of the topic.

Defining power and politics

Defining the terms 'power' and 'politics' is not straightforward. These are broad and vague concepts that have proved difficult either to define or to measure, with precision, and without ambiguity. The term 'power' has become a 'contested concept' (Astley and Sachdeva, 1984), giving rise to endless disputes about how it should be defined and about its 'proper' or acceptable use. We will consider in Chapter 2 how other commentators have addressed the language of this topic. For the moment, we will use these working definitions:

- *power* concerns the capacity of individuals to exert their will over others;
- *political behaviour* is the practical domain of power in action, worked out through the use of techniques of influence and other (more or less extreme) tactics.

Power is thus an ability 'to produce intended effects' in line with one's perceived interests (Pettigrew and McNulty, 1995), to 'overcome resistance on the part of other social actors in order to achieve desired objectives or results' (Astley and Sachdeva, 1984). *Political behaviour* concerns the ability to 'get things done your way'. It is 'the observable, but often covert, actions by which executives enhance their power to influence decisions' (Eisenhardt and Bourgeois, 1988, p. 737). Power can thus be viewed as a latent capacity, as a resource, or a possession, while politics can be viewed as power in action. Mintzberg (1983, p. 25) argues: 'But having a basis for power is not enough. The individual must act.'

As Pettigrew and McNulty (1995, p. 870) point out, the social and political dynamics vary from one organization to another, and thus the skilful and wilful player has to use to best advantage the resources to hand in that context:

Awareness and perspective is necessary to know when to intervene and how. There is, therefore, a premium on matching a constellation of power sources to a particular issue, situation by situation, and then drawing upon the right mixture of analysis, persuasion, persistence, tact, timing, and charm to convert potential power into actual influence.

The power one has thus depends on the organizational context as well as on the skill, will and other resources (funds, position, credibility) of the individual.

The roots of political behaviour

Why does political behaviour occur? Its roots lie in personal ambition, in organization structures that create roles and departments which compete with each other, and in major decisions which cannot be resolved by reason and logic alone but which rely also on the values and preferences of the key actors involved. These 'triggers' are explored in Chapter 8.

Power, politics and change are inextricably linked. Change creates uncertainty and ambiguity. People wonder how their jobs will change, how their workload will be affected, how their relationships with colleagues will be damaged or enhanced. Change in one organizational dimension can have knock-on or 'ripple' effects in other areas. As organizations become more complex, the ripple effects become harder to anticipate. Managing change can thus be a challenging, exhilarating and creative activity. The more uncertain and ambiguous the setting, the greater the scope for creative input.

The American diplomat Henry Kissinger once wrote,

> Before I served as a consultant to Kennedy, I had believed, like most academics, that the process of decision-making was largely intellectual and all one had to do was to walk into the President's office and convince him of the correctness of one's view. This perspective I soon realized is as dangerously immature as it is widely held. (cited in Pfeffer, 1992b, p. 31)

In conditions of high uncertainty, when decisions are unstructured, or 'unprogrammable', difficult choices are typically resolved by political means. Why? Because rational arguments and empirical evidence may be lacking given the uncertainties surrounding such decisions, or because reason and 'facts' are not compelling on their own (Drory, 1993; Schilit, 1986).

As Mangham (1979) argues, where there is a degree of choice concerning the direction of a large and complex organization, reasonable people are likely to disagree about means and ends, and reasonable people are also likely to fight (figuratively speaking) for what they believe to be the appropriate line of action. Most significant organizational decisions are thus the outcome of a social and political process that is only partly influenced by evidence and rational argument – shaped by 'the pulling and hauling that is politics' (Mangham, 1979, p. 17). Kakabadse and Parker (1984, p. 182) note that:

> Change is not about one truth or an open sharing of views. Change is about renegotiating certain dominant values and attitudes in the organization in order to introduce new systems and subsystems. Under such circumstances, visions and values are not likely to be shared, with the likely result being a clash of wills. Successful change involves one person or group influencing the organization according to their values.

Change and uncertainty heighten the intensity of the politics which are part of the fabric of all complex organizations. Uncertainty can be exploited by those who have the appropriate skills and knowledge, and who are able and willing to deploy their expertise at the right time. In other words, the uncertainty generated by change creates room for manoeuvre.

Although there are individual differences when it comes to tolerating uncertainty, most of us prefer order and predictability most of the time. Those who have the ability to reduce uncertainty can gain significant reputations and positions of considerable influence. They achieve this by offering clear definitions of problems, and by specifying solutions, thereby restoring order to otherwise confused situations.

The effective change agent is thus someone with what Mintzberg (1983) calls the 'will and skill' to engage in the political processes of the organization. Another American commentator, Pfeffer (1992b, p. 30) argues that, 'unless we are willing to come to terms with organizational power and influence, and admit that the skills of getting things done are as important as the skills of figuring out what to do, our organizations will fall further and further behind'. This means abandoning the notion, popular in the field of organization development, that the change agent is merely a 'neutral facilitator' deploying appropriate techniques to foster open information sharing, joint problem solving and collaborative action planning among an organization's willing membership. There may, of course, be occasions when the change agent can most effectively function in such a role, but this is only one dimension of a wider behaviour repertoire.

Writing from practical management experience, Wallace (1990, p. 59) describes how his large-scale information systems project was 'characterized by rapid activity and forward thinking but, above all, by a series of activities associated with influencing the actions of others in order to achieve organizational objectives'. He describes how the uncertainties surrounding the project opened opportunities for politically skilled managers:

> A significant issue appeared to be the considerable state of turbulence in the organization as a whole. A large and very complex amalgamation was occurring. There were frequent changes of staff, staff responsibilities and reporting relationships. In some senses, these changes created information and power 'vacuums' resulting in people being unclear and confused about the events occurring about them. One effect of this was that people were distracted from concentrating on the project, which suggests that managers may well be able to take advantage of such circumstances in order to achieve change . . .
>
> Also from the managerial perspective, it appeared that there was a need to be able to exercise personal influence rather than rely on the authority of management position. This implies that in complex situations with a high potential for conflict, managers need to adopt diffuse and innovative strategies rather than to attempt to inflict mechanistic and structured approaches. (p. 60)

The positive dimensions of political behaviour

How can an organization claim to be effective when managers either feel that they have to, or actively want to spend time, energy and creative effort playing the politics game? Surely such behaviour detracts from the business of providing services and making products? Eisenhardt and Bourgeois (1988), for example, argue that organizational politics in a top management team are associated with poor organizational performance. Political behaviour, they point out, can be damaging because it creates inflexibilities, throws up communication barriers, restricts information flows, and consumes time – thus endorsing a compellingly negative view of power and politics. In a subsequent publication, however, Eisenhardt et al. (1997) appear to contradict their earlier position, arguing that conflict can be constructive and beneficial after all.

In the same way that conflict can be constructive, as well as damaging, we will argue that organizational politics can have advantages both to the organization and to individual managers. Many change agents find themselves working with individuals and groups whose co-operation is necessary, but over whom they have no formal organizational authority. Political tactics may be legitimately used to recruit allies and form coalitions to exert influence in current initiatives and into the future. Political skill may be required to protect the change agent (who, we will argue, is often in a personally vulnerable and risky position) from threat, challenge or attack. Pfeffer (1992a) argues that the financial and social costs of attempting to eradicate organizational politics are extremely high (assuming that eradication is a realistic option to begin with). He notes that competition and disagreement are sources of energy and creativity, and that the quality of debate in the 'politics-free' organization with the 'strong culture' is likely to be poor.

Harrison (1987) argues that political behaviour can complement 'legitimate' management actions in a number of ways:

1   Such tactics can be used to counter the use of otherwise legitimate means to non-legitimate ends, such as the unreasonable assertion of authority by a manager.
2   The political system makes visible those members of the organization with the skills in dealing with the power-plays and the intrigue, and helps them to develop their political capabilities.
3   Political debate helps make explicit all the dimensions of an argument, perhaps including issues that would not be readily recognized or encouraged by the legitimate system.
4   Political action may be required to remove (bureaucratic?) blockages raised by the legitimate system.
5   Political tactics can be used to facilitate the implementation of decisions reached by legitimate means.

Interviewer: You think some managers enjoy playing the politics game?
Manager: Absolutely, I think most do. I think if you took that out of management, then it would in effect become a very sterile kind of technocratic activity. That may reflect the fact that I enjoy it, and that I see it as being part of the natural state of things. People are naturally competitive. I suppose the thing about building a successful team is not about eradicating that competition but in being able to harness it and focus it, therefore the competitiveness can be a force of good. I think people argue that politics is a destructive process when they're losing. Normally, if you lose, you vow to get them next time, don't you? There's always a rematch.

Hardy (1996) argues that political forces provide a critical source of dynamic energy for strategic organizational change. To shut down the political action is to turn off this source of creative energy. Politics may be a distraction, but this is part of organizational reality – a political 'game' which the change agent has to play – and perhaps even enjoy.

The nature of the turf game

To refer to this aspect of management behaviour as some kind of game is to highlight the creative and enjoyable elements involved, and not to discount its significance. The language of games is useful because it allows us to discuss what kind of game this is, and to identify the strategies and tactics that are involved. Various commentators have found this terminology useful. Bardach (1977) discusses 'implementation games'. Mintzberg (1983) describes a series of organizational political games. Riley (1983) found in her research that the game metaphor was a common feature of organizational political imagery. At least some managers seem to enjoy playing this game, at least some of the time. Political processes can be a source of creative energy. Organizational politics can thus be a key motivator for some managers, and a factor in keeping individuals committed and energetic.

Organizational change thus triggers, or more likely intensifies, the *turf game*. The turf game can be defined simply as a game in which individuals and groups seek to defend and to extend their turf. This goal can also extend to avoiding sections of turf that are 'of poor quality' in that they are undesirable for some reason (personal or organizational). Turf comes in a wide range of different varieties. It may concern areas of influence and power, and these are the resources on which most commentators focus when discussing politics. However, turf can also concern status and reputation in the organization and perhaps also in the wider community. Turf often concerns access to and control over resources such as people, space and money. Sometimes, the turf that matters can be nothing more complex than an individual's desire to keep doing what they enjoy doing – to preserve and perhaps to enlarge their personal 'comfort zone'. Turf can thus be personal, and it can also be collective. Individuals act to protect their personal turf; groups act to protect their collective turf.

Like any metaphor, this one breaks down when pursued too far. There are at least three respects in which the game imagery can be misleading. First, this is a 'long game' concerning exchanges between players over extended periods, and not one which can readily be resolved into 'single plays' around specific change projects. Second, the action is not confined to a well-defined arena or pitch but is worked out on an ill-defined, undulating and unpredictable organizational terrain. Third, the metaphor implies 'playing hard always to win', whereas in many situations one may consciously decide to lose, perhaps in the interests of maintaining long-term relationships, or in the context of anticipated future events.

Our aim in this book is to explore the nature of the turf game, and to expose its strategies and tactics in the context of shaping organizational change processes. One outcome is to identify advice and guidance in an area that many still regard as unethical, or 'off limits', both to professional managers and to academic commentators (who may be expected to maintain higher levels of ethical integrity). Another outcome is to expose the realities of the organizational politics game to wider scrutiny and assessment.

This aim is underpinned by three major arguments:

Emancipation through exposure

First, to the extent that the shaping role of organizational politics in change processes has been overlooked, exposure of the strategies and tactics involved can serve an emancipatory function. Anyone, at any level in an organization, can be a player in the turf game, although some groups and individuals are better placed with regard to resources and power bases than others. It is, however, useful to remember that even low-skilled, low-status and ostensibly powerless employees can bring many organizations grinding to a halt through determined collective action. The power bases, sources and resources of individuals and groups are important, but so is the skill with which such resources are deployed. Knowledge of strategies and tactics can thus compensate for weaker power bases. Brass and Burkhardt (1993, p. 466) argue that:

> [S]trategic action can be used to compensate for relatively weak resources. Skilful political activity is one tool for overcoming a lack of resources or making less valuable resources more potent. Actors in powerful positions, who control ample resources, are less dependent on their capabilities to use resources strategically than are actors who lack ample resources.

Opening political behaviour to scrutiny potentially widens access to the mechanisms involved. The behaviour of others can be more readily diagnosed and, if appropriate, questioned and challenged. The strategies and tactics involved are not copyright and can be deployed by anyone familiar with them, and possessing the requisite skill and will. Political behaviour can be used effectively to subvert, block and redirect change as well as to drive it.

The professional political response

Second, let us consider the particular case of an individual pursuing a change agenda that has broad organizational support for its potential benefits (restructuring to reduce hierarchy and bureaucracy; a new computerized information system which will inform decisions more effectively). In other words, the change agent has a more or less formal organizational mandate or warrant to act in fulfilment of that agenda. It does not matter in the context of this argument that the change agent also expects personal career gain from the success of the venture (as self-interest is often regarded as a defining feature of political behaviour). With major, complex, strategic, unstructured, uncertain organizational change, resistance and challenge can be expected. Such challenge is predictable, and is potentially beneficial with respect to the maintenance of constructive and creative debate. Some resistance may be supported by genuine organizational concerns, and some by perceived threats to the self-interest of particular individuals and groups.

How might the change agent respond to a covert politically motivated challenge? To walk away from such challenge, and to avoid engagement in political activity, will in many circumstances damage the organizationally sanctioned agenda. The change agent may thus have a tacit, personal warrant to respond politically. It may thus be argued that the competent, professional, ethical response is to deal with political challenge on its own terms.

Reflexive improvisation: more jazz than symphony orchestra

Third, political behaviour seems to form part of the taken-for-granted 'recipe knowledge' of most managers. This suggests that such behaviours are used habitually and without prior analysis. It is particularly appropriate in this domain, therefore, to recall the value of adopting the stance of the 'reflective practitioner' first described by Schon (1983). The reflective practitioner, or 'practical theorist', has a repertoire of theory and experience which is deployed to meet changing circumstances as required. The reflective practitioner thus develops his or her own underpinning theories and practical interventions in a consciously considered and self-critical manner. In this perspective, management practice is *improvisatory* – but this does not suggest 'making it up as you go along' (as many managers, particularly with the use of political behaviours, appear to do). This implies that decisions and actions are informed by a combination of theoretical frameworks, past experiences and personal assumptions and values. Collin (1996, p. 74) draws a useful analogy with the jazz idiom in music:

> A more appropriate metaphor might be that of playing jazz. Jazz players improvise, but are not anarchic. They are disciplined, skilled, creative and intuitive. They make music in relational, collaborative and non-hierarchical ways.

Thomas (1993, p. 202) also speaks of the importance of 'intuitive artistry' for the manager faced with unique circumstances in which 'technical rationality' is unlikely to be an effective problem-solving approach. Each case is unique, prompting reflection. Making sense of one's circumstances requires a combination of general knowledge, previous experience and an appropriate conceptualization of the problem in hand. What is required, therefore, is not technical knowledge but 'workable knowledge' – decisions and solutions that will work in these unique circumstances and that are both socially and practically acceptable. Our aim, therefore, is to reinforce the perspective of the reflective practitioner, particularly in the context of choosing, deploying and justifying political strategies and tactics to shape, influence and drive significant organizational change.

The autonomy of organizational politics

The central proposition of this book is that *the change agent who is not politically skilled will fail*. This implies that it is necessary to be able and willing to intervene in the political processes of the organization, to push particular agendas, to influence decisions and decision makers, to deal with (and potentially silence) criticism and challenge, and to cope with resistance. This also implies the ability to intervene in ways that enhance rather than damage one's personal reputation. It may also be necessary – and this is also a political stance – at times deliberately to avoid or to play down such activities. Some managers regard such calculations and activities as distasteful. Some textbooks in this field advise the change driver to avoid involvement in the turf game.

What is the current management view of organizational politics? We surveyed a group of 90 middle and senior managers in England during the first quarter of 1997, to identify trends in organizational change, and to establish current opinion about aspects of the organizational change process. (See Appendix I for details.) One of the four survey questionnaire sections dealt with political issues. Respondents were presented with a series of statements about the politics of change, and were asked to rate their agreement or disagreement with each of those items on a five-point (Likert) scale. The results of that survey are summarized in Table 1.1.

The unskilled will fail

The first interesting result was that 67 per cent agreed with the statement reflecting the argument of this book: the politically unskilled agent will eventually fail. This item attracted only 13 per cent disagreement.

Change intensifies the politics

A second interesting result is in the 70 per cent agreement that complex change intensifies organization politics, suggesting that this is a domain that change agents seek to ignore or to avoid at their peril.

Stakeholders and their turf

A third notable result concerns the 86 per cent agreement with the statement that managing change is about managing stakeholders. This characterizes the turf game primarily as one of interpersonal influence, dealing with the needs, interests and perceptions of a range of individuals and

Table 1.1 **Survey results 1997 (%): change management and political factors**

		Strongly agree	Agree	Neutral	Disagree	Strongly disagree
(1)	The change agent who is not politically skilled will eventually fail.	11	56	20	12	1
(2)	The more complex and wide-reaching the change, the more intense the politics become.	16	54	20	9	1
(3)	Managing change is really about managing the stakeholders who will be affected by changes in different ways and to different degrees.	24	62	9	4	0
(4)	The change agent today needs well-developed negotiating, persuading and influencing skills.	62	37	1	0	0
(5)	One of the main current sources of resistance to change in my organization is people trying to defend their personal territory or 'turf'.	21	60	12	6	1
(6)	Employees at any level can be influential players in the politics of the organization.	18	63	6	12	1
(7)	Most middle managers enjoy playing the organizational politics game.	3	34	34	25	5
(8)	Most senior managers enjoy playing the organizational politics game.	10	26	43	21	0
(9)	To be effective, the change manager has to be a highly skilled political activist in the organization.	14	42	14	28	1
(10)	It is unethical and unprofessional to get involved in the organizational politics when planning and implementing change.	8	20	21	43	8
(11)	The effective change agent needs to be politically sensitive, but must not get directly involved in the political 'action'.	19	56	14	11	0
(12)	What really matters is organizational performance; politics is a distracting side-issue.	21	58	9	11	1
(13)	Organizational politics is usually damaging, is a sign of incompetent management, and needs to be eradicated wherever possible.	16	37	23	21	3
(14)	Change always creates winners and losers, and the losers just have to accept this.	3	13	21	53	9
(15)	Organization politics can have beneficial outcomes.	4	42	38	14	1

constituencies both inside and outside the organization. Note also the support for the item which read, 'The change agent today needs well-developed negotiating, persuading and influencing skills' – 99 per cent. One reason for this lies with the 81 per cent agreement with the statement that resistance to change is based on people trying to defend their territory or turf. Another reason lies with the 81 per cent agreement that employees at any level can be influential players in the politics of the organization. This is not a game played exclusively in the offices and corridors of middle and senior management.

The pleasure principle

To what extent do managers enjoy playing the turf game? The survey findings suggest that about one third of senior and middle managers enjoy the experience, with one third neutral, and the rest critical.

Contradictions and ambivalence

Other items revealed a much wider spread of views, reflecting the contested nature of the notions of power and politics, and also the organizational and personal disputes which these issues generate. Some of these responses appear to contradict responses to items already discussed. What do these contradictions reveal?

Only 56 per cent agreed that the change agent has to be a skilled political activist, and almost 30 per cent disagreed with this statement. Is this finding inconsistent with earlier responses? We were able to discuss this point with respondents at a feedback meeting. The explanation for the apparent contradiction lies with the use of the term 'activist'. This term was felt to imply a highly visible – and perhaps blatantly self-serving – role in the organization, the despised 'corporate Machiavellian' (see Chapter 4). This was regarded by respondents as unacceptable, and that potentially explains why this item did not attract a higher level of agreement. The term 'political activist' also has connotations of national party politics.

There was also a spread of views with respect to whether it is unethical and unprofessional to get involved in politics as an organizational change agent. While 28 per cent of respondents agreed with this statement, only 51 per cent disagreed (taking the stand adopted in this book). Of even greater damage to the argument set out here, 75 per cent agreed that the change agent needs to be politically sensitive, but must not get directly involved in the political 'action'. This is the 'acceptance without engagement' position mentioned in the Introduction and adopted by some commentators on organizational change.

A further 79 per cent agreed that politics is a distraction from the main business of achieving organizational performance. These views contradict the arguments of Pfeffer and Hardy, set out briefly above, and the central argument of this text. Finally, while 53 per cent agreed that politics is a damaging sign of management incompetence and should be eradicated, 46 per cent felt that politics can have beneficial outcomes for the organization. Moreover, 62 per cent voted to support the losers in change rather than simply leave them to their fate.

A survey of over 400 American managers by Gandz and Murray (1980) revealed similar ambivalence about organizational politics. Over 90 per cent of their respondents agreed that politics was commonplace, 89 per cent said that successful executives had to be skilled politicians, but 55 per cent said that politics interfered with efficiency, and almost 50 per cent argued that management should try to eliminate organizational politics.

In summary, these results imply widespread agreement concerning the realities of political life in organizations, particularly in the context of change, and over the need for the change driver to confront these realities. However, the results also highlight disagreements over how the game is to be played, and about the intended outcomes of the play.

There's no escape

One reason why the change agent must develop political antennae and deploy some level of political skill concerns the inevitability of the political dimension of organizational life. Organizational politics is a 'naturally occurring phenomenon'. Reasonable people can be expected to disagree on major, uncertain and ambiguously defined issues, and to argue strongly for their personal convictions. Organizational politics can thus be viewed as an *autonomous* phenomenon, not simply derived from weak organization structural design, the (warped and devious) psychology of (some) organization members, or the incompetence of management. All of those factors – structural, personal, managerial – exacerbate, mollify and otherwise colour or texture the organization's political activity. But to regard organizational politics as autonomous is to accept that it cannot be eradicated or 'designed away' simply through systematic changes in those factors. The concept of autonomy here draws partly from the work of Wight (1978), who claimed the same status for international politics, and from Parry (1972, p. 115), who credits Machiavelli with first depicting an autonomous political domain which obeys its own laws, rules and dictates.

This autonomy argument does not lead to the conclusion that politics cannot be managed. On the contrary, the fact that politics can be managed is central to the purpose of this book. However, this argument does lead to the proposition that organizational politics *cannot be managed away* in some utopian or idealistic sense. That is unrealistic, if not naïve, and denies the lived empirical reality of past and contemporary organizational experience. Our concern should thus lie, not with somehow attempting to eradicate this unwanted pest, but with how this domain should be addressed. This central aspect of managerial practice must take into account a range of possibly conflicting considerations – social values, ethical norms, personal integrity, individual effectiveness and organizational performance.

The political 'variant' is the norm

A second reason why the change agent must have political skill concerns the differences in views that arise across an organization's stakeholders – and with how those differences get resolved.

> *Interviewer*: So in your experience, political behaviour is widespread, across sectors?
>
> *Manager*: I said this is a naturally occurring phenomenon, and you were saying this is difficult to sell to people. I think that's people being somewhat dishonest, but that is the conventional wisdom of the day. Or perhaps they haven't worked in organizations. I've worked across a number of private and public sector organizations, and in all of those experiences, it seems to me there's been the same competition of ideas. I've worked in a couple of management services departments in the private sector, usually led by somebody who believes that they knew better than most other people how the organization should be run. If only the other buggers would move out of the way, if the sales and production directors would only listen to the management services department, the whole thing would be more profitable – and what we needed was more people in management services to prove that point. It's the same set of conflicts about how to do things. Most people have a reasonably high degree of conviction about that.

Markus (1983) identifies what she describes as the triggers of the political variant in terms of organizational behaviour. Triggers include competition for resources and power bases, and the inevitable disputes about objectives, values, the nature of the problem, the 'best' solution.

Considering these triggers in relation to conditions in most organizations, political activity would seem to be the norm, not a variant. The 'competition of ideas', and the combination of personal interest and genuine conviction underpinning that competition, appears to be commonplace. The range of stakeholders – individuals and groups – in most organizations is wide and diverse, and most disputes and disagreements cannot be resolved by rational argument and evidence alone. Needs, perceived interests, values and preferences come into play. Decisions are thus typically the result of a combination of rational argument supported by effective lobbying, trading, influencing, coalition formation, and other approaches. The change driver needs to be accomplished in this 'fixer–facilitator–wheeler-dealer' mode, while perhaps ensuring that there is also a rational, logical, reasoned and accepted business case for decisions reached and changes implemented.

If the 'political variant' is indeed the norm, there are profound implications for the 'politics damaging – politics beneficial' argument. One voice can claim that these conflicts consume time and energy and attention, thus harming organizational performance. Another voice can equally claim that these disagreements, disputes, arguments, uncertainties, doubts and conflicts can be a valuable source of creative energy, supporting positive change and innovation and raising individual and organizational effectiveness.

Change agency

The literature consistently advocates the need for what Schon (writing about radical military innovations) calls a 'champion of the idea'. Schon (1963, pp. 84–5) argues that:

> Essentially the champion must be a man [*sic*] willing to put himself on the line for an idea of doubtful success. He is willing to fail. But he is capable of using any and every means of informal sales and pressure to succeed. No ordinary involvement with a new idea provides the energy required to cope with the indifference and resistance that major technical change provokes. It is characteristic of champions of new developments that they identify with the idea as their own, and with its promotion as a cause, to a degree that goes far beyond the requirements of their job. In fact, many display persistence and courage of heroic quality. For a number of them the price of failure is professional suicide, and a few become martyrs to the championed ideas.

This notion of *the* singular change agent is deeply embedded in modern consciousness. Echoing Schon, Maidique (1980, p. 59) argues that,

> At all stages of development of the firm, highly enthusiastic and committed individuals who are willing to take risks play an important role in technological innovation. In the initial stages . . . these entrepreneurial individuals are the focus that moves the firm forward. In later stages, they absorb the risks of radical innovation, that is, of those innovations that restructure the current business or create new business.

Heroic entrepreneurial figures are thus sought and praised for successes; scapegoats are hunted and punished for failures.

Major change is rarely dependent on the actions of lone individuals, although some players may have more influential parts than others. Change is typically shaped by the actions and interactions among what Hutton (1994) calls 'the cast of characters', including different varieties of 'champion'. Change agents – internal and external – often play a number of different roles, each making different demands on the behaviour repertoire. Buchanan and Storey (1997) argue that the notion of the singular 'change agent' is thus unhelpful, because change normally involves a plurality of actors or players. The notion of *the* change agent can be a misleading fiction. They argue instead for the concept of 'change agency', identifying for analytic purposes a number of potentially distinct roles (Table 1.2).

We will use the term *change driver*, recognizing that this is only one of the change agency roles that individuals can assume in the course of

Table 1.2 **Change agency roles**

Initiator	The ideas person, the heatseeker, the project or process 'champion'
Sponsor	The main beneficiary, the focal person, the project or process 'guardian'
Driver	Promotes, implements, delivers – often the process or 'project manager'
Subversive	Strives to divert, block, interfere, resist, disrupt
Passenger	Is carried along by the change
Spectator	Watches while others change
Victim	Suffers from changes introduced by others
Paramedic	Helps others through the traumas of change

promoting or subverting a range of change initiatives. However, *all* of these roles potentially have a political dimension.

This division of change agency roles is something of a fiction, but has considerable analytical value. Clearly, individuals may find themselves playing more than one of these roles at the same time. Some role combinations may appear 'obvious', such as 'initiator–sponsor' or 'sponsor–driver' – although the combinations of required behavioural competences may not always belong to the same individual. Some role combinations may indeed be awkward, such as 'driver–victim', where the person responsible for delivering the change feels that they personally will suffer in some way from that implementation. Also, the same individual may find that they move from one role (or role combination) to another as a change process unfolds. The initiator may become the driver and may become victim or paramedic also.

Two key points emerge from this analysis:

Different roles, different skills

First, the behaviours and skills involved in each of these roles are different. The behaviours of the initiator concern inciting enthusiasm for new ideas and projects, infecting others with that enthusiasm, stimulating the desire for change. This is quite different from the behaviours of the sponsor, a formally identified and senior position in some organizations, who typically serves in a monitoring capacity. The sponsor often chairs a steering or review group, and acts as 'protector/guardian' for change, perhaps negotiating or fighting for additional resources when a project falters, and dealing with challenge and resistance from other senior players in the organization. The behaviour repertoire of the driver concerns a combination of change and project management skills, interpersonal skills in negotiating, persuading and influencing, and political skills, combined possibly with knowledge of the substance of the change itself. The behaviours of the subversive mirror those of the driver.

Role taking, role switching

Second, a key element in the skill of the change driver lies with what Buchanan and Storey (1997) call 'role taking and role switching'. One critical element of political skill in particular lies with conscious decisions concerning which of these roles to occupy and play at a given point in the change implementation process, and when to switch from one role or role combination to another. The political skill of 'positioning' is discussed in Chapter 7. Some change agency positions are formally recognized in some organizations as full-time roles, albeit temporary. But the majority of managers who would claim to hold change responsibilities combine these with their regular managerial day job, in line and support positions. In other words, the position or location of the individual in relation to the change process is often a matter for personal choice and shaping, within the wider constraints of the organization's structure. While it may be advantageous to be seen to be an initiator in some settings, it may be more advantageous in other circumstances to be viewed as a driver, or as a paramedic, or even as a subversive. Whatever the skill demands of a particular change agency role, one of the key capabilities is chameleonic flexibility (Ferris and King, 1991).

The desirable subversive

A word about the role of the subversive, which, like 'politics', carries negative connotations. The subversive role should be viewed in a positive light in many settings, for at least two reasons. First, subversives keep the debate alive, maintain a challenge to the dominant arguments in the organization, and ensure that those who would be in the 'driving seat' for change are clear about their position, their case, their arguments and their objectives. Without challenge, criticism and debate, our thinking can become sloppy. Subversives counter this tendency. Second, it is useful to be aware of the strategies and tactics of the subversive, so that these can be identified and countered, and also so that these behaviours can be deployed to block and divert changes which may be assessed as damaging when they are being driven by others. This returns us to the argument about the emancipatory value of the agenda of this book. To understand the political skills of the change driver is to be able to use those skills both to drive and to subvert change in the organization.

Turf game tactics

What does it mean to be engaged in the organizational politics of a change process? What are the strategies, tactics and ploys of the turf game? How far are you prepared to go to achieve your ends? In this section, we explore provisional answers to these questions, by considering how contemporary managers and change drivers address these issues in practice, and by relating their perceptions to some of the literature dealing with this topic.

Interviewer: Is this an ethical issue, or are we simply talking about effective management?

Manager: It's probably naïve, but I believe that you can't be an effective manager unless you understand the politics and the processes that go on. If you don't believe that's going on, then you are operating almost in an ivory tower. And there are some managers who operate in an ivory tower, and wonder why they are never successful, why they don't get that extra quarter . . . hundred thousand or whatever it is they want. Unless you can read that political situation, you are in the s***.

If you've got naïve people at the top who believe that the facts alone will sell the idea, and you don't realize you need to wheel and deal, then you don't delegate and you end up wondering why you don't get what you want. In any organization, I mean, you have to know how to play the managing director, don't you? If you didn't know that, then somebody else usually walks all over you.

You have to know how to play the game, and you have to understand what kind of game this is in the first place. Working with managers on a range of development programmes covering this topic over the 1990s has allowed us to explore perceptions of the nature of the turf game from the practitioner perspective. How do managers describe the turf game and its strategies and tactics?

Table 1.3 presents a sample of the answers managers provide to the question: what are the moves and tactics of the 'turf game' in the context of organizational change? These examples of political behaviour were collected between 1993 and 1997 from discussions with a number of management groups, mainly in Australia, Britain and Scandinavia (Sweden and Finland). Experienced managers typically have no difficulty in answering this question. One typical joking response is that, 'these are of course not based on personal actions, but on close observation of the behaviour of others'. The ease with which such responses are usually forthcoming, and the fact that management groups from different countries identify many of the same tactics, suggest that this is part of the taken-for-granted 'recipe knowledge' of many experienced managers.

Many of these tactics relate to a summary from Gray and Starke (1984, p. 519), whose seven headings organize our list: 'image building', the use of 'selective information', 'scapegoating', the creation of 'formal alliances', 'networking', 'compromise' and 'rule manipulation'. The management experience from which these examples are drawn suggests an eighth category of more covert and ruthless tactics.

Table 1.3   **Turf game tactics**

Image building	Actions which enhance reputation and further career; appropriate dress, support for the 'right' causes; adherence to group norms; air of self-confidence.

- 'You have got to be seen to be successful at all costs.'
- 'Seek to be associated with success: seek the spotlight.'
- 'Be perceived to be acting in the best interests of the organization.'
- 'Manage the way in which you are perceived.'
- 'Give the right signals – the ideas you express, the way you dress.'
- 'Be politically correct – watch my legs, not my lips.'
- 'Wait until it has been successful – then claim the credit.'
- 'Your reputation comes first.'

Selective information	Withhold unfavourable information from superiors; keep useful information from your competition; offer only favourable interpretations; overwhelm others with complex technical data.

- 'Exclude others as appropriate from your plans and activities.'
- 'Withhold information and dispense misinformation to maintain control.'
- 'Never disclose your full hand.'
- 'Control information; exclude people, release information selectively.'
- 'Slant information, deny knowledge, reveal nothing.'
- 'Don't be tempted to be frank; you become vulnerable when exposed in this way.'
- 'Keep critical items of information up your sleeve.'
- 'Use misinformation to keep others on the defensive.'
- 'Manipulate others by exclusion, misleading, withholding.'
- 'Create an illusion by excluding information and mystifying concepts.'
- 'Abuse your expertise; make it difficult for others to question and challenge.'

Scapegoating	Make sure someone else is blamed; avoid personal blame; take credit for successes.

- 'Blame others when things go wrong.'
- 'Blame a predecessor.'
- 'Pick your timing to discredit people.'
- 'Make people look stupid in front of their boss.'
- 'Always find someone else to blame if things go wrong.'
- 'Highlight your successes – exaggerate your successes.'
- 'Wait until it has been successful, then claim the credit.'
- 'Identify a scapegoat, a whipping boy.'
- 'Attempt to undermine colleagues and promote yourself.'

Formal alliances	Agree actions with key people; create a coalition strong enough to enforce its will.

- 'Gain access to key players and information.'
- 'Seek the support and affiliation of those in power.'
- 'Know who the key players are and exploit them to your own ends.'
- 'Make alliances with others.'
- 'Align yourself with powerful mentors.'
- 'Be on the side of the power brokers.'
- 'Associate with power bases, i.e. creep.'
- 'Establish alliances for personal gain.'
- 'Find a powerful supporter, a champion.'

Table 1.3   *continued*

Networking	Make lots of friends in influential positions.

- 'Be mobile – out and about, talking, networking.'
- 'Invite the "right" managers to social events.'
- 'Build the right contacts and networks.'
- 'Get out there and actively campaign.'
- 'Develop wide networks.'
- 'Exploit the key players to your own ends.'
- 'Lobby allies and potential supporters.'
- 'Find out about the thinking of other managers; drop in for casual conversations.'

Compromise	Give in on unimportant issues to create allies for subsequent, more important issues.

- 'Give up a token battle, if necessary, to win the war.'
- 'Concede minor issues, but attack when necessary.'
- 'Decide how much you are prepared to lose.'
- 'Be flexible and adaptable; roll with the flow.'
- 'Build contingency plans, use damage limitation tactics.'
- 'Be ready to change your opinions quickly.'

Rule manipulation	Refuse requests on the grounds of, 'against company policy', but grant identical requests from allies on grounds of 'special circumstances'.

- 'Ask yourself – what can I get away with?'
- 'Know the boundaries of what you can get away with.'
- 'The rules are judgemental.'
- 'Anything goes (almost); there are no rules, make up your own.'
- 'Break the rules, if you can get away with it; don't get caught breaking the rules.'
- 'Rules are for breaking.'
- 'Never get caught playing the game.'
- 'Stay clean – don't get caught playing the game.'

Other tactics	These items do not 'fit' the Gray and Starke headings, and seem to be concerned with the apparently more covert and ruthless aspects of political infighting. Note that 'other tactics' turns out to be a large category here:

- 'The best players are not always obvious.'
- 'This game is played covertly, not much out in the open.'
- 'This can be a rough, tough game – no holds barred.'
- 'Be bold and prepare to be ruthless.'
- 'When all else fails, don't be afraid to use coercion.'
- 'Use diversionary tactics: retaliate first, attack others.'
- 'You need to act ruthlessly, be single-minded.'
- 'Be prepared to play dirty.'
- 'Keep a "dirt file".'
- 'Recognize that coercion may sometimes be necessary.'
- 'Undermine the expertise of others.'
- 'Undermine opponents through "whispers in the corridors".'
- 'Play one person or group off against another.'
- 'Capitalize on the weaknesses of others.'
- 'Use "subversives" to plant ideas with other managers.'
- 'Use other people to "fire the bullets".'
- 'If losing, use delaying tactics.'
- 'Do it to them before they do it to you.'

Table 1.3   *continued*

- 'Avoid confrontation when that could damage your position.'
- 'Trash the deal in the details; nit-picking can be an effective blocking tactic.'
- 'If all else fails, make sure you have a bolt hole.'

One of the most extreme (and ruthless, if not downright brutal) characterizations of political tactics can be found in the work of von Zugbach, whose book *The Winning Manager* (1995) identifies 13 'winner's commandments':

1   Me first. Nobody else will put your interests before theirs.
2   There are no absolute rules. Other people's ideas of right and wrong do not apply to you.
3   The organization is there to serve your interests, not the other way round.
4   You are on your own. Nobody is going to help you become a winner.
5   Be paranoic. Watch out, the bastards *are* out to get you.
6   Suck up to those who matter and suck up well. Identify the key people in the system who will help you.
7   Say one thing and do another. You need to pay lip-service to the organization's cherished notions of how things should be done.
8   Be a team player, but make sure you beat your fellow team members.
9   Remember that the truth is not always to your advantage. Those who control your future do not necessarily want to hear the bad news.
10   Manipulate the facts to suit your interests. Even when things are bad you should come up smelling of roses.
11   Get your retaliation in first. When there is blood on the organization's carpet, make sure it's not yours.
12   Blow your own trumpet – or better still, get someone else to do it for you.
13   Dominate your environment or it will dominate you. (von Zugbach, 1995, pp. 1–2)

These commandments are based on the argument that:

> Winning the organization game is about overcoming the barriers, human and organizational, to gaining power in the organization with the minimum of effort and the maximum rewards. Let's be clear what I mean by power. While this word can be used to describe wealth, status and influence, it can also mean an individual's ability to maintain control over his activities with the minimum of interference from others. Power in the organization is about deciding what you want and making sure that you get it. (von Zugbach, 1995, pp. 1–2)

For those who might find these commandments difficult to follow, von Zugbach lists examples of the behaviour of 'the losing manager'. Do you attend meetings where no political decision will be made? Do you regard the organization's rules with sanctity rather than contempt? Do you perform tasks that could have been delegated? Do you do things for which the team gets the credit? Do you make yourself available and allow others to interrupt you? Do you regularly volunteer when asked? Do you read carefully every memo, letter, report and every other document which lands in your tray?

The political entrepreneur: warrant and reputation

But of course, the effective conduct of organization politics, whether from a general management perspective, or from the viewpoint of the change driver, is not about learning the lists of tactics and commandments sampled here. Choice of appropriate action in particular circumstances is a matter of *informed improvisation*. Knowledge of the context and of the other players must lead to a *creative* choice of strategy. Using advice from the literature and from the experience of other managers can open the perpetrator to accusations of misconduct or unethical behaviour (keep a dirt file? discredit others? make others look stupid before superiors? exploit key players for your own ends?). At face value, to follow such advice would seem to involve the change driver in some considerable personal risk.

> And it should be realised that taking the initiative in introducing a new form of government is very difficult and dangerous, and unlikely to succeed. The reason is that all those who profit from the old order will be opposed to the innovator, whereas all those who might benefit from the new order are, at best, tepid supporters of him. This lukewarmness arises partly from fear of their adversaries, who have the laws on their side, partly from the sceptical temper of men, who do not really believe in new things unless they have been seen to work well. The result is that whenever those who are opposed to change have the chance to attack the innovator, they do it with much vigour, whereas his supporters act only half heartedly so that the innovator and his supporters find themselves in great danger.
>
> In order to examine this matter thoroughly, we need to consider whether these innovators can act on their own or whether they depend on others; that is, whether they need to persuade others if they are to succeed, or whether they are capable of establishing themselves by force. In the former case, they always fare badly and accomplish nothing. But if they do not depend on others and have sufficient forces to take the initiative, they rarely find themselves in difficulties. Consequently, all armed prophets succeed whereas unarmed ones fail. This happens because, apart from the factors already mentioned, the people are fickle; it is easy to persuade them about something but difficult to keep them persuaded. Hence, when they no longer believe in you and your schemes, you must be able to force them to believe. (Machiavelli, 1988, pp. 20–21)

This is one of the most well-known quotations from Machiavelli, whose ideas on political strategy and tactics – about five hundred years later – still divide opinion. The contemporary relevance of Machiavellian thinking is reinforced, for example, by Pfeffer (1992b, p. 29), who points out that, 'organizations, particularly large ones, are like governments in that they are fundamentally political entities. To understand them, one needs to understand organizational politics, just as to understand governments, one needs to understand governmental politics.'

The question which Machiavelli seems to pose for the change driver dealing with the politics of the change process is: how far are you prepared to go to achieve your objectives? Machiavelli put moral scruples at a discount, regarding them as a handicap. He was, of course, writing for the leaders of principalities in southern Europe in the sixteenth century, not for contemporary change drivers. However, a stream of commentators has consistently argued for the continuing relevance of his ideas, and his practical advice.

Research in this area was inspired by Christie and Geiss (1970). One of their main contributions was to design a questionnaire assessment of an individual's Machiavellian tendencies. This questionnaire is known as the Mach IV, because it went through a number of development stages, and is included in Appendix II. Readers can use that questionnaire to identify whether they are High Mach or Low Mach personality types. The Mach IV has been used in many investigations, correlating scores with age, gender, career success and job performance. Graham (1996), for example, reports a study which suggests that Machiavellian project managers do not have more successful careers than low scorers. The implications of that research tradition are explored in Chapter 4.

Are we going to argue that the effective change driver must be a Machiavellian? Is a warrant for introducing change also a warrant for cunning, devious, manipulative and underhand behaviour – a warrant for 'anything goes'? Clearly, this is not the case. Ferris et al. (1992), exploring how political factors affect promotion decisions, note that the 'pure organizational politician' will hit an early promotion ceiling through inability to display a balance between 'political savvy' on the one hand, and 'solid past performance and demonstrated ability' on the other.

The argument here is not that only High Mach change drivers can be effective and successful. On the contrary, the behaviours which this implies may be perceived in negative terms, which can damage the individual's credibility and status, thus reducing their managerial performance in general and their ability to drive change in particular. The argument, however, is about the extent to which change drivers must develop their *behaviour repertoire* to deploy appropriately in context the tactics, ploys and manoeuvres discussed in this chapter, whether these are labelled 'dirty tricks', 'office politics', 'Machiavellian' or not. Just as national politicians justify their actions with the traditional claim, *raison d'état* (for the good of the state), so change drivers acting as political entrepreneurs can justify their behaviour in terms of benefit to the organization. This crude 'means justify ends' argument is explored in detail later, when we examine the ways in which change drivers give accounts of and justify their political behaviour. This argument can be summarized by contrasting the position

Table 1.4 **Perspectives on politics**

The puritan	Does not get involved at any level because politics means 'dirty tricks', and is unethical and damaging.
The street fighter	The 'pure politician' for whom playing the game, to win, by whatever means, is the end in itself – and is enjoyed.
The sports commentator	Understands the game and can pass appropriate comment and judgement, but does not become personally involved in the play.
The political entrepreneur	Adopts a creative, committed, reflective, risk-taking approach, balancing conventional methods with political tactics when the circumstances render this necessary, appropriate and defensible.

of the political entrepreneur with three other perspectives on the use of political tactics in organizational change (Table 1.4).

The position of puritan, denying the relevance and value of political behaviour, is unrealistic and unsustainable in practice. The position of street fighter is similarly unsustainable. This is the negative face of power – blundering, self-serving, damaging. The sports commentator position equates to the 'acceptance without engagement' perspective found in the organization development literature. This position too, we suggest, is naïve and unsustainable. The only credible posture is that of the political entrepreneur. This position might also be described as 'acceptance with skilled, reflective, creative engagement'.

What factors might usefully inform the creative, reflective perspective of the change driver towards political action? Figure 1.1 offers an overview of these factors, in a framework which links the main elements of the turf game. This framework provides a platform for explanation, for systematic reflection, and for the consideration of practical guidance. It is not a causal model, and does not point to any rigid set of rules or principles. The central elements in this framework concern the concepts of 'warrants', 'accounts' and 'reputation'.

Context: the pitch

The change agent is not a 'free agent'. Any actor in any organizational position can be seen both to work within existing structures, and to attempt to change them, but is at the same time influenced, facilitated and constrained by those structures. The sociologist Anthony Giddens captures this reflexive relationship in the term 'the duality of structure'. The actions of the change driver thus have to be seen in the context of the formal authority structure of the organization, the prevailing culture in terms of norms, values and expectations with respect to behaviour, the availability of resources (people, information, budgets), and past experiences – positive and negative – of change. These factors determine the organization's 'readiness for change', can shape the ease or difficulty of a change initiative, and can shape appropriate implementation processes, including the degree and forms of political behaviour encountered.

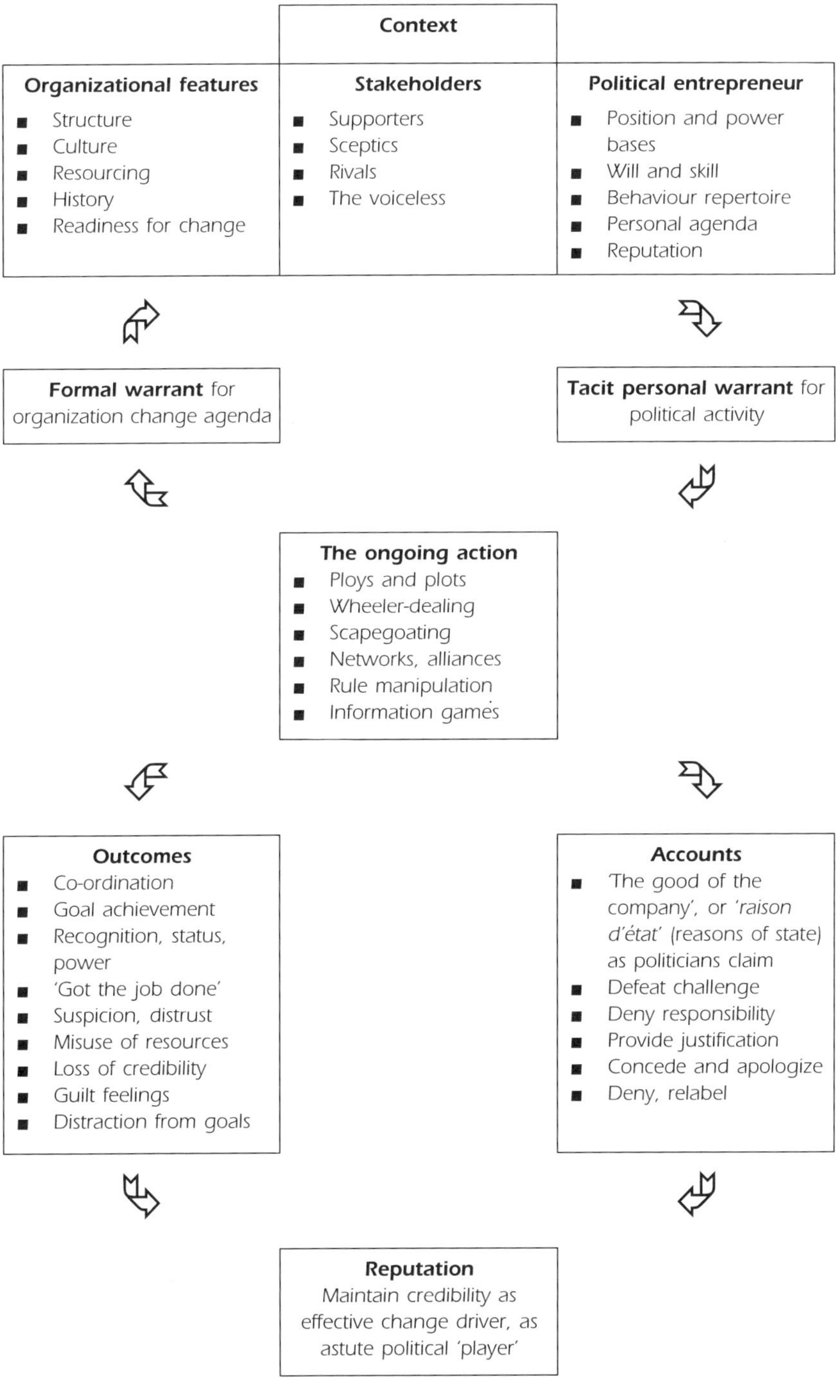

Context

Organizational features	Stakeholders	Political entrepreneur
■ Structure ■ Culture ■ Resourcing ■ History ■ Readiness for change	■ Supporters ■ Sceptics ■ Rivals ■ The voiceless	■ Position and power bases ■ Will and skill ■ Behaviour repertoire ■ Personal agenda ■ Reputation

Formal warrant for organization change agenda

Tacit personal warrant for political activity

The ongoing action
- Ploys and plots
- Wheeler-dealing
- Scapegoating
- Networks, alliances
- Rule manipulation
- Information games

Outcomes
- Co-ordination
- Goal achievement
- Recognition, status, power
- 'Got the job done'
- Suspicion, distrust
- Misuse of resources
- Loss of credibility
- Guilt feelings
- Distraction from goals

Accounts
- 'The good of the company', or 'raison d'état' (reasons of state) as politicians claim
- Defeat challenge
- Deny responsibility
- Provide justification
- Concede and apologize
- Deny, relabel

Reputation
Maintain credibility as effective change driver, as astute political 'player'

Figure 1.1 **Warrants, accounts and reputation**

Political entrepreneur: the change driver

The framework also has to take into account the characteristics and resources of the change driver. Formal organizational position has a determining influence on factors such as perceived authority, access to senior management, and access to information and other resources. These factors and individual personality influence the power bases of the change driver, their behaviour repertoire, and their expertise or 'will and skill' with respect to change implementation. There are two further critical factors here. The first concerns *agenda*: what is the change driver attempting to achieve in this context? This is typically a complex combination of personal desires (satisfaction, achievement, career progression) and organizational goals (cost cutting, profitability, customer service). A second critical factor is *reputation* – the measure of esteem which the change driver enjoys in the assessment of other members of the organization. The change driver with a strong reputation carries more weight and influence than one held in low regard. Reputation is both an 'input' to this framework, and also one of the main 'outputs'. While some forms of political behaviour are likely to damage the change driver's reputation, some forms of political behaviour will strengthen it.

Stakeholders: the other players

The other players on the pitch – the stakeholders in change – are clearly elements in the context, but deserve separate attention. It has become commonplace to advocate stakeholder analysis when planning change. This simply involves identifying key stakeholders, clarifying their needs and interests, and establishing an appropriate management strategy for winning their support, accommodating their desires, or marginalizing their concerns. The change driver can expect to find supporters, sceptics and 'subversives' or rivals in the organization, along with those who lack power and other resources to establish a voice with respect to what is being proposed. However, as Egan (1994) argues, 'the voiceless' also require active management, because they can be recruited by rivals and turned into challengers.

Warrants: do the right thing

The concept of warrant concerns 'knowing that you are doing the right thing', and concerns the degree of confidence that the change driver has in being able to offer a convincing explanation and justification for their actions in pursuit of particular goals. Warrants have two related dimensions. The first concerns *formal sanction* for particular change initiatives. The second concerns *personal conviction* that one's actions – political and otherwise – are appropriate. The fortunate change driver has a clear senior management remit and adequate resources to drive a particular initiative.

That remit or warrant may even be in writing. However, life for the change driver is not always thus charmed. An initiative may be based, for example, on a mix of personal commitment and some limited managerial support. In this case, the 'ongoing action' comes into play to obtain the senior management sponsorship and resourcing required. In other words, the change driver may have to act (politically) without a formal warrant in order to obtain one.

The change driver is never going to receive any formal written warrant to act politically. That judgement must always rely on personal conviction and circumstance. A warrant to act politically can be based on a number of interacting factors: the benefits to be derived from change; personal career goals; reactions to past changes; the anticipated responses of other stakeholders, particularly those seeking to block, disrupt or subvert all or part of the agenda. Personal and organizational agendas are not as clearly distinguishable as these remarks imply. The perceived success or failure of a change initiative can influence the perceived effectiveness of the change driver responsible.

The ongoing action: ploys and plots

The change driver may thus feel mandated not only to adopt a conventional change implementation posture (open, participative, supporting, joint problem solving), but also to engage in political tactics. Here we are concerned with recruiting support, forming alliances, anticipating and immobilizing resistance – with what Kanter (1983) describes as the 'change architect' deploying 'power skills' and 'coalition forming'. So, here are the ploys of wheeler-dealing, image building or impression management, scapegoating, networking and coalition building, rule manipulation (and rule breaking), the 'tactical' use (and misuse) of information, and other perhaps more brutal tactics.

Outcomes: positive, negative, personal, organizational

We argued earlier that the exercise of organizational politics can have both damaging and constructive consequences, a view now widely accepted (Kumar and Ghadially, 1989). The positive consequences may include improved co-ordination of effort behind change, the achievement of organizational goals or objectives, recognition, status and career enhancement for the change driver responsible, feelings of personal achievement, and increased influence and power. Possible negative consequences include the creation of a climate of suspicion and distrust in the organization, distraction from organizational goals, the unproductive allocation of resources (skilled management time as well as money), feelings of personal guilt, faltering change implementation, and a loss of credibility.

Accounts: justification and defence

This framework assumes that the change driver may be required to justify his or her actions, and particularly political actions. If so challenged, a satisfactory defence may require appeals to 'the greater good of the organization', or to the damaging actions of other stakeholders. But 'accounting', as we will explore in more detail in Chapter 7, has other dimensions (McLaughlin et al., 1992). When faced with challenge or accusation in this domain, the change agent may deny responsibility, offer some other form of justification, concede the point and apologize, or deny that the behaviour was 'political' in the first place. The change driver who is able to account effectively for their actions will clearly enhance their public reputation as well as reducing feelings of personal guilt. Although accounts and political ploys are distinguished here, it is clear that accounting is a special, and indeed critical, type of political skill, deserving separate treatment. Accounts can also be regarded as the 'public' face of the change driver's warrant. The warrant to act politically is based in part on the question, 'Am I doing the right thing here?'; a satisfactory account has to persuade others that you were justified in those actions.

Is there a danger in this perspective? The need to be seen to be successful is often now equated with success itself. Form and substance, reality and the illusion of reality, become confused. As in national party politics, virtuosity in 'spin', or in presentation (of people, of policies, of actions, of events and outcomes), has become increasingly significant. Management 'skill' becomes the ability to simulate appropriate attitudes, values, beliefs and emotions in an opportunistic manner to suit the circumstances. This perceived need to 'manufacture appearances' at the expense of substantive change and improvement, is what Ferris and King (1991) describe as 'the dark side' of political behaviour.

Reputation: maintaining credibility

This framework invites the change driver to consider the question: 'what sort of reputation do you want to develop', in this organization and in the wider community? Kotter (1985) argues that the change driver who combines personal credibility with an established track record obtains resources for change more easily and quickly. Laver (1997) defines reputation as a 'socially defined asset', dependent on one's behaviour, and on the observations, interpretations and memories of others. Reputation is part of the 'stock in trade' of the political entrepreneur. Will you do what you say? Have you done that before? Are your threats and promises reliable? Do you have a reputation for fair dealing, for keeping your word, for sidelining frustrating opposition, for the careful and sophisticated building of support for initiatives and ideas, for the tactful removal of opponents? What initiatives, policies, ideas and styles do you wish to be associated with?

Table 1.5 **Machiavellian FAQs**

So, do we all need to become Machiavellians now?	No. But as a change driver, you may need to be able to use those kinds of behaviours in particular circumstances.
Are you telling me I have to change my personality?	No. But do you want to consider widening your behaviour repertoire of political tactics?
Are some organizations 'politics-free'?	No. But some may be more political than others, and change makes the political issues more intense and visible.
Will it not be chaos when everyone is a skilled political player?	No. Skilled players have a more interesting 'high performance' game – and this can also be a team game as well as individuals against individuals; that's not chaos.
Can management control and stop political behaviour?	No. This is a naturally occurring phenomenon, an inevitable aspect of organizational reality.
Should management try to control and stop political behaviour?	Not necessarily. Natural social controls usually shut down the 'political activists' who are causing damage by their blatant behaviour.
Surely politics is always damaging?	No. Dealing effectively with political issues can bring several personal and organizational benefits, particularly to the change process.
Do I have to abandon the values of trust and openness in communications and relationships generally?	Absolutely not. Constant changes may have made people resistant to further organizational changes, and these traditional social values become even more important. But do a stakeholder analysis; are you going to manage all your stakeholders with the same approach?
It has to be unethical to get directly involved in political games, even in change?	No. If you are a change driver, you could be seen as unprofessional and incompetent if you ignore the political issues blocking the implementation of your project.
I will be accused of being inconsistent if I am open and honest today, and devious and Machiavellian tomorrow.	You have to use the management approach that is consistent with your diagnosis of the situation; what is inconsistent about that?

Laver (1997, p. 26) points out that reputation is tediously and painstakingly constructed while desperately fragile:

> One of the interesting things about a reputation . . . is that it can take a very long time to build a reputation that can be effectively destroyed in seconds. A reputation for utter ruthlessness with the spiky club, for example, may be built painstakingly, even painfully, over the years on the basis of relentless repetition of ruthless acts. A reputation for honourable behaviour may take years of honourable behaviour to develop. But a single act of pointless mercy when utter ruthlessness was expected, a single dastardly deed when 'doing the right thing'

was anticipated, can destroy these carefully crafted reputations at a stroke. Such reputations, viewed in these terms, represent huge but very fragile instrumental investments for the people who own them.

These considerations defeat the accusation that what is on offer here is a simple 'ends justify the means' argument. The change driver who uses political tactics and emerges with their personal reputation in tatters (even if change is seen to be successful) will have future career difficulties. We are looking at a set of means in a particular context, in relation to a diverse agenda of personal and organizational goals and outcomes, and with respect to the effect that a set of change implementation actions will have on the reputation of the change driver, now and into the future. Reputation is thus one critical 'output' from this framework, and is also a critical 'input'. The change driver with a weakened reputation will have problems launching and moving any further significant change initiatives. We will revisit this framework and its elements at various points throughout the text, and particularly at the end of Chapter 7 in considering the development of an appropriate perspective on political behaviour.

The arguments of this chapter may give readers the impression that this book offers an uncompromisingly brutal stance with respect to organizational politics. Subsequent chapters will attempt to qualify that perception. Table 1.5 summarizes the most 'frequently asked questions' (FAQs) taken from the various discussions (occasionally heated) which we have conducted with management groups on this subject, along with the answers that sketch the overall position that we wish to advance.

2 The terminology game

CONTENTS

"Son, of course there's more to life than just money – it's power."

The necessary and desirable politics of change

This chapter explores a number of contrasting perspectives on power and politics. Rather than seek to establish which of these views is correct, it is argued that there is value in being able to view this field from a range of different perspectives. The main division in current thinking seems to lie between 'episodic' and 'pervasive' views.

Episodic and pervasive perspectives on power

Episodic perspectives consider 'the ability of A to make B do something'. Power is an obvious resource, and the effects of political behaviour are visible. Those who regard power as pervasive, on the other hand, point to the ways in which behaviour is controlled by non-obvious features of organization structures and procedures. The argument that power lies deeply embedded in taken-for-granted social practices leads to the view that such practices are more powerful and effective because they are discreet and non-obvious, and are thus less easily challenged. However, one's definition of power or politics (within an organization, or within academic debate) is in itself a political act, in attempting to 'impose' one's views of these phenomena on others. Inevitably, therefore, the argument of this book can be seen as a political statement. This chapter thus argues for a socially constructed view of these issues, in which definitions derive from the meanings and interpretations of those involved in the action.

Interviewer: What was the political dimension of the reorganization?

Manager: We started a restructuring of [the whole organization], 3,000 people, services to about a million people, essentially with what amounted to little more than a blank sheet of paper. The aim of the reorganization was to improve the quality of the services we provide to the community. And it was, basically, go away and tell me how you can do that – develop proposals for how we could do that. There were some difficulties with that from the outset. I think there may have been a political decision not to define more clearly the terms of reference for that review. And I think part of that may well have been due to a couple of issues. One I think was allowing you generally to be creative in your thinking before management had judged the outcomes of that. I think there was another one which was largely about senior managers being able to take one step back from the proposals that were being developed, so, instead of being seen as attaching their allegiances to the proposals that were coming out, they were able to stand on the sidelines and just gauge the reaction of others in the organization. And leave it for us to work them out. And I also think there may have been – and as the process went on you pick up these things – maybe tensions among the senior management team about what the outcomes should perhaps have been. And I think maybe the decision was to leave that to a later date before they more clearly defined the type and nature of the change.

Chapter 1 claimed that organizational change intensifies political issues and behaviours. Schon (1963, p. 82) argues that 'champions of change' can expect to encounter resistance to new ideas, and that political behaviour by implication is desirable:

> Resistance to change is not only normal but in some ways even desirable. An organization totally devoid of resistance to change would fly apart at the seams. It *must* be ambivalent about radical technical innovation. It *must* both seek it out and resist it. Because of commitments to existing technology and to forms of social organization associated with it, management must act against the eager acceptance of new technical ideas, even good ones. Otherwise the technical organization would be perpetually and fruitlessly shifting gears.

Our organizations are not always the happy, harmonious, collaborative communities that many management texts imply, but are more appropriately viewed from a '*negotiated order*' perspective (Strauss et al., 1973). This means that decisions are typically the result of processes of influencing, trading, bargaining and compromise, to secure the best deals for the players involved in a series of 'competitive tactical encounters' (Bacharach and Lawler, 1981, p. 7). The players may, of course, call on empirical evidence and rational argument in support of their cause, but such appeals are rarely enough to make a particular case stick in the face of the competing demands of other players. The organization structures which we see around us develop from the resolution of the political tensions between individual members and groups or coalitions. Among the first things one learns on joining a new organization are, for example:

- who is friendly with whom, who are sworn enemies, the secret liaisons (in and out of work);
- the 'real' (not always well hidden) agendas of key resource holders;
- who controls 'discretionary' resources, and therefore who to 'reach' if you want something done;
- past and current 'hot' issues and arguments;
- whom to befriend, and whom to avoid.

Commenting on organization decision making, Tushman (1977, p. 212) observes that:

> Political processes arise not because of individual or group perversity, but because of the nature of organizational processes and decision making under uncertainty. If decisions must be made without enough information or in the face of diverse goals, then non-bureaucratic methods must evolve to attend to the differences in preferences, values, and beliefs about cause and effect relations. If even the most objective issues are open to multiple interpretations, and if organizational participants often derive different meanings from the same information base, then bureaucratic decision making procedures will unambiguously decide only a limited set of organizational decisions.

Change thus triggers a debate – a competition – between ideas, suggestions, proposals and counter-proposals, each struggling for attention and support. It is reasonable to expect people to disagree under such circumstances, particularly where some see themselves as 'losers' in relation to what is being proposed. Such disagreement is surely desirable, in the interests of exposing contrasting arguments to public scrutiny.

The processual perspective on change

In other words, organizational change is an intrinsically politicized process as, for example, Frost and Egri (1991, p. 231), echoing Schon's argument, explain in the following terms:

> [P]olitics is often the inevitable consequence of self-interested contests between and among actors which are engendered by the inherent ambiguity of issues, ideas and things. In that innovation *at its core* is about ambiguity and is replete with disputes caused by the differences in perspectives among those touched by an innovation and the changes it engenders, we believe that innovation often becomes a very political process. Rather than viewing these struggles for ascendancy in a negative light, we propose that politics serves both a natural and necessary role in the course of human interaction. Judging political actions and outcomes as good or bad, right or wrong, is to a large extent a function of the perspective, the values and the interests of the evaluator.

Frost and Egri regard political action in change as 'natural and necessary'. This view is reflected in theories of organizational change drawing on the 'processual/contextual' perspective.

The processual perspective derives primarily from the work of Pettigrew (1973, 1985, 1988), who argues that change can only be understood by considering the interactions between the substance, context and process of change in the organization. Pettigrew also argues that the change agent must be willing to intervene in the political systems of the organization, the main task being to *legitimate* change in the face of competing proposals. The management of change, in the words of Bennis (1984), is thus equated with 'the management of meaning', or with attempts to establish the credibility and legitimacy of particular definitions of problems and solutions with others, and to gain their consent and compliance.

This processual perspective has been developed more recently by Dawson (1996), who argues that, to understand the process of change, we need to take into consideration:

1 the past, present and future *context* in which the organization functions, including external and internal factors;
2 the *substance* of the change itself (new technology, new payment system, new structures) and its significance and timescale;
3 the *transition process*, tasks, activities, decisions;

4 *political activity*, both within and external to the organization;
5 the *interactions* between these factors.

The external context often suggests or dictates or shapes the substance of change (for example, new health and safety regulations, product innovation by competitors). Internal context factors often facilitate or constrain particular change proposals (for example, availability of adequate expertise and technology, culture which supports risk taking, budgetary slack). In turn, the substance of change shapes both the form and possibilities of political activity. Consider the differing implications of change which is of marginal significance, on the one hand, and change which is central to the success of the organization, on the other – or change which is slow and incremental, on the one hand, and rapid, on the other. Actors can draw upon evidence from the context and substance of change to support and legitimate their own proposals (the straightforward, 'we must do this because . . .' argument). It is therefore, as Dawson emphasizes, the *interaction* between context, substance and political factors which shapes the process of organizational change.

This argument presumes that we can view the exercise of power and politics positively, and that we have a clear understanding of what the terms 'power' and 'politics' actually mean. Both of these assumptions are open to serious challenge.

You take the high road

The survey results reported in Chapter 1 revealed an ambivalence in management attitudes towards organization politics and the exercise of power. This ambivalence is reflected in the wider literature of power and politics, with commentators taking contrasting views.

More power to ya

A positive view of politics and political skills can be seen in articles whose titles include terms such as 'more power to ya!' (Matejka et al., 1985), 'playing the game' (Conklin, 1993), 'politics: a key to personal success' (Coates, 1994), and 'navigating the waters of organizational politics' (Buhler, 1994). The negative view is reflected in articles on 'politics – the illegitimate discipline' (Thompkins, 1990), and by references to 'a walk on the dark side' (Ferris and King, 1991), and the 'black arts of the whipping boys' (Cockerell, 1996). Voyer (1994) demonstrates how coercive political behaviour can reduce employee satisfaction and organization effectiveness.

This ambivalence is reflected in some of the theoretical literature on power and politics, in an interesting 'two-dimensional' manner. Several commentators have distanced themselves from 'politics as dirty tricks' by

identifying two different aspects of power deployment. McClelland and
Burnham (1976; reprinted 1995) distinguish between the 'institutional
manager' and the 'personal power manager'. The latter seek advancement
at the expense of others and 'are not disciplined enough to be good
institution builders' (p. 130). The personal power manager, they claim, has
other undesirable features:

> [They] exercise their power impulsively. They are more often rude to other
> people, they drink too much, they try to exploit others sexually, and they collect
> symbols of personal prestige such as fancy cars or big offices. (p. 129)

The institutional manager, on the other hand, who combines power motivation with self-control, represents 'the socialized face of power':

> Above all, the good manager's power motivation is not oriented towards per-
> sonal aggrandizement but toward the institution that he or she serves. [They] are
> more institution minded; they tend to get elected to more offices, to control their
> drinking, and have a desire to serve others. (p. 129)

The 'good' or 'institutional' manager thus has the following profile:

- feels responsible for developing the organizations to which they belong;
- believes in the importance of centralized authority;
- enjoys the discipline of work, and getting things done in an orderly
  way;
- is willing to sacrifice self-interest for organizational welfare;
- has a keen sense of justice, concerning reward for hard effort. (p. 133)

In other words, the good manager is one who deploys power in the interests
of others and in the interests of the organization, rather than in pursuit of
self-advancement. The use of power can therefore be effective, as long as it
is subject to appropriate discipline, control and inhibition. The uninhibited
and uncontrolled use of power makes for ineffective management. This
perspective does not readily permit the proposition that institution building
and personal career enhancement can be pursued simultaneously.

This dichotomy between 'socialized' power and personal gain is reflected
elsewhere. Egan (1994) bases his prescriptions for 'working the shadow
side' of organizational life on a distinction between institution-building and
empire-building politics, once again arguing for the potential benefits of the
former and the damaging consequences of the latter. Greiner and Schein
(1988) appear to offer a contrasting perspective from within the organization development (OD) movement, emphasizing the effective deployment
of power in implementing change. However, their argument also rests on
the distinction between positive and negative uses of power. They contrast
'the high road', in which power brokers deploy their resources and tactics
in ways that are 'open and above board', with 'the low road', where deceit,

manipulation and 'political games' are used to further self-interest. The low road, they suggest, is not appropriate for the professional, ethical, OD practitioner.

The silver-tongued hustler

In what may be considered a leading 'mainstream' OD text, French and Bell (1995, p. 318) devote over 20 pages to an overview of power and political issues. Here, the OD practitioner is 'encouraged to learn as much as possible about bargaining, negotiations, the nature of power and politics, the strategy and tactics of influence, and the characteristics and behaviours of powerholders'. However, they also emphasize the 'normative-re-educative' and 'empirical-rational' bases of OD, and deny the relevance of 'power-coercive' strategies. In contrast to their remarks about the significance of this topic, they also state that: 'The role of the OD practitioner is that of a facilitator, catalyst, problem solver, and educator. The practitioner is not a political activist or power broker' (French and Bell, 1995, p. 313).

Ward (1994, p. 143) argues with an air of finality that:

> To ignore organizational politics when managing change is to fail. What then is the alternative? Should one be political? The short answer is no. You should not be political. If you do become political, then professional integrity is sacrificed. You are just another silver-tongued hustler parading your wares while seeking to manipulate. This is the road to disaster. Politics does not add value.

This distinction between socialized and uninhibited, between institution building and personal empire building, between the high road and the low road, can be seen as an attempt to bracket a legitimate domain of the 'political', allowing these authors to claim that their perspective addresses organizational realities, while dismissing the acceptability of 'dirty tricks', 'wheeler-dealing', 'backstaging' and other equally dubious and damaging tactics. This is the 'sports commentator' position from Chapter 1: acceptance without engagement, able and willing to understand the turf game and pass judgements on it, but not prepared to become actively and personally involved. This appears to be an attractive position, legitimating a style of political operation, and establishing a threshold of acceptability.

What are the practical and moral implications of the 'sports commentator' position on the role of politics in organizational change?

Practical implications

The single main practical implication concerns the risks of avoidance. Assume that the change driver faces covert or 'backstage' resistance and subversion from other players in the organization, concerning a change agenda which has attracted broad support. It may not always be possible or credible to deal with those threats by ignoring them or by refusing to

engage in appropriate counter-measures. In many circumstances the effective and professional approach will involve appropriate backstage activity
to counter such threats. The sports commentator position may thus have
damaging implications for the change agenda *and* for other organization
members expecting to benefit from the change *and* for the reputation and
career advancement of the change driver.

The next layer of practical difficulty potentially arises where the 'street
fighters' – the 'pure' politicians or Machiavellians seeking only personal
advantage and satisfaction – establish control over an organization's change
agenda. Such a situation will clearly cause significant damage, sooner or
later, unless other players have the will and skill to challenge them.
Avoidance may lead not only to the abandonment of a current initiative,
but to the pursuit of a series of alternative projects of dubious long-term
organizational advantage.

Moral implications

The moral implications are more subtle. Here we have a compelling voice
which says, 'Don't get involved, keep it clean, remain open, honest and
collaborative.' This attempt to defend the moral high ground unfortunately
runs into the argument that politics is an inevitable and even desirable
companion of change. This lofty position sidelines the right of challenge and
protest, by appealing to shared goals and 'common purpose'. The insistence
on co-operation and openness, as opposed to backstage manoeuvring, shuts
down opportunities to press an individual's or a group's ideas, proposals,
criticisms, counter-proposals and claims through whatever creative,
forceful, socially acceptable means they feel appropriate.

One moral implication of the 'squeaky clean' imperative is thus to stifle
the expression of dissent. And that is not a liberating or emancipatory
stance. This may instead be viewed as an extreme and rigid authoritarian
position, which we feel obliged in the context of the argument of this book
to reject. The emancipatory view, in contrast, involves recognizing the
political reality of organizational functioning, exposing political behaviour
to scrutiny, legitimating intervention in political processes, and dissemi-
nating more widely an understanding of effective intervention strategies
and tactics – which can of course be used to block and subvert change
initiatives as well as to promote and drive them.

The cost of maintaining the high road

Before accepting the 'dirty politics' argument, it is instructive to assess the
potential costs, to the change driver, and to the organization, in keeping
to 'the high road'. As Egan (1994) points out, even though you may be
unwilling to use political tactics, others are. False sentimentality can thus
be damaging, in offering advantage to adversaries. Pfeffer (1981, p. 93)
offers a summary of common strategies for avoiding the use of political

Table 2.1 **The costs of controlling politics**

Strategies	Costs
Introduce slack in budgets, and create extra posts, to reduce competition for resources	Overhead, inventory, excess capacity, additional staff
Establish a strong culture, with shared beliefs, values and goals, to reduce conflict and disagreement	Fewer points of view, less diversity of opinion and information brought to decision making, lower quality of decisions
Make decisions appear less important to reduce levels of challenge and dispute	Decision avoidance, critical analysis missing, important information not used
Reduce complexity and uncertainty, factors which encourage political activity for personal gains	Creation of rigid rules and procedures, reduce the organization's capacity for change

Source: Based on Pfeffer (1981: 93)

behaviour in decision making, and of the damaging costs of those approaches (Table 2.1).

The view taken here is that the political process cannot be 'managed away', and that it needs therefore to be managed in some way. The 'high road' is not a realistic long-term option. However, the process of 'managing politics' is not a technical matter of 'pulling levers' and applying the 'right techniques'. Considerably more contextual awareness, judgement, creativity and risk taking is involved than that.

Power: what is it, and how can I get more?

Power seems to be a straightforward concept. We know what it is when we see it, and can differentiate with relative ease between those members of the organization who have it, and those who do not. The concept is clearly related to control, and to the ability of individuals to achieve their preferred outcomes. Power is often regarded as a kind of latent property of the individual, as a capability exercised through a range of social and interpersonal skills. This conception of power is useful, but can also be regarded as narrow and oversimplified. Defining the concept of power turns out to be more difficult than it may at first appear.

Hardy (1995, pp. xx–xxi) notes 'the many different voices which have spoken on the subject' and the confusing range of perspectives adopted:

Power has been both the *independent variable*, causing outcomes such as domination, and the *dependent variable*, usually the outcome of dependency or centrality. Power has been viewed as *functional* in the hands of managers who use it in the pursuit of organizational goals, and *dysfunctional* in the hands of those who challenge those goals and seek to promote self-interest. It has been viewed as the means by which *legitimacy* is created and as the incarnation of *illegitimate* action. Power has been equated with *formal* organizational arrangements and as the *informal* actions that influence outcomes. It has been seen as *conditional on conflict* and as a means to *prevent conflict*. It has been defined as a resource that is *consciously* and deliberately mobilized in the pursuit of self-interest, and as a system of relations that knows no interest, but from which some groups *unconsciously* and inadvertently benefit. It has been seen as an *intentional* act to which causality can be clearly attributed and as an *unintentional*, unpredictable game of chance. The study of power has created a *behavioural* focus for some researchers and *attitudinal* and ideological factors for others. Power has been berated for being repressive and lauded for being productive. Small wonder, then, that there is little agreement.

Power as an individual property

The most popular conception of power concerns the 'latent property' notion. Power is something you possess. This leads to questions such as: how much power does an individual have, where did it come from, and how can an individual acquire more power? If power is a capacity to exert one's will, we must be able to identify the source of this capacity. Pfeffer (1992a) lists a series of structural and individual sources of managerial power:

Structural sources of power include:

- formal position and authority in the organization structure;
- ability to cultivate allies and supporters;
- access to and control over information and other resources;
- physical and social position in the organization's communications network;
- the centrality of your unit or section to the business;
- role in resolving critical problems, in reducing uncertainty;
- degree of unity of your section, lack of internal dissent;
- being irreplaceable;
- the pervasiveness of one's activities in the organization.

Although not all of these structural properties can be expected to apply in every instance, this list helps to explain why accountants tend to be more powerful and influential in most organizations than, for example, personnel and training managers.

Individual sources of power include:

- energy, endurance and physical stamina;
- ability to focus energy and to avoid wasteful effort;
- sensitivity and an ability to read and understand others;
- flexibility and selecting varied means to achieve goals;
- personal toughness; willingness to engage in conflict and confrontation;
- able to 'play the subordinate' and 'team member' to enlist the support of others.

Pfeffer (1992a, p. 166) notes that, 'Some of these characteristics may bring one more social approval than others, but all seem to be displayed by people who are able to acquire and wield substantial power'. The manager who can draw from both structural and individual sources of power has an enviable position. These cannot be regarded as exhaustive lists of structural and individual power bases or power sources. As Hardy and Clegg have pointed out (Clegg and Hardy, 1996; Hardy, 1995), one's power base will depend on whatever resources are available and appropriate in the circumstances, and a list of potential power bases is thus infinite. Even being downtrodden, voiceless and marginalized is to possess a power source which can be exploited, if and where the circumstances allow.

Power as a relational property

There is, however, a second and related view which treats power not as a property of the *individual*, but as a property of the *relationship* between an individual and others. This perspective is normally attributed to the work of French and Raven (1958), who identified the five main bases of power summarized in Table 2.2. Bacharach and Lawler (1981, p. 34) distinguish between *bases* of power (factors that you control) and *sources* of power (how you come to control those bases). Pfeffer deals with sources. The bases which French and Raven identify have a number of significant features.

First, they depend on the beliefs of others. Beliefs and perceptions shape our behaviour as much as whatever constitutes reality. Beliefs may be influenced by the abilities and behaviour of the change driver, and it is the perceptions of others that count. A change driver may be able to control rewards and penalties, have superior knowledge and so on, but if others do not believe that he or she has these attributes, then they may be unwilling to comply with requests. Similarly, change drivers may be able to manipulate others into the belief that they do possess power which they in fact do not have. Compliance may then be forthcoming even though the change driver does not have access to, say, the rewards, sanctions, expertise, or friends in high places, that others believe he or she commands. Power is not merely a property of the individual, to be acquired and accumulated. Power is a *relational* construct.

Second, these power bases are interrelated. The exercise of one may affect one's ability to use another. The change driver who resorts to coercive power may, for example, lose referent power. Clegg (1997, p. 489), for example, argues that, 'Coercive power should be the refuge of last resort for the diplomatically challenged and structurally secure, not the hallmark of management's right to manage.' The change driver may be able to use legitimate power to enhance referent and expert power. Power and influence are not static concepts.

Third, the change driver can operate from multiple bases of power. The same person may be able to use different bases, in different combinations,

Table 2.2 **Five power bases**

Reward power	is based on the belief of followers that the change driver has access to valued rewards which will be dispensed in return for compliance with instructions.
Coercive power	is based on the belief of followers that the change driver can administer penalties or sanctions that are considered to be unwelcome.
Referent power	is based on the belief of followers that the change driver has desirable abilities and personality traits that can and should be copied.
Legitimate power	is based on the belief of followers that the change driver has the authority to give instructions, within the boundaries of his or her formal position or rank within the organization.
Expert power	is based on the belief of followers that the leader has superior knowledge relevant to the situation and the task in hand.

Source: Based on French and Raven (1958)

in different contexts, and at different times. Few change drivers may be able to rely on a single power base but need to be able to draw appropriately on several.

The framework of French and Raven has been developed by Benfari et al. (1986), who identify the eight power bases set out in Table 2.3. Their three additional power bases are information, affiliation and group power. Emphasizing its relational nature, Benfari and colleagues note that the exercise of power can be perceived by the targets or recipients as either positive or negative, depending on the circumstances. This is denoted in the table by either a 'P+' or a 'P–' respectively. Reward power and referent power are typically regarded favourably by those on the receiving end, while coercion and information power are usually seen in negative terms. But perceptions of the other four power bases largely depend on how they are exercised. The abuse of authority to bully and control others is usually scorned, but the exercise of strong leadership in a crisis is typically welcomed. Allowing others access to the thinking of senior figures through affiliation power may be regarded favourably, while inflexible appeal to 'what senior management or policy demands' may not. There are, therefore, clear choices, with differential implications for the change driver's reputation, concerning the use of power.

Benfari et al. (1986, p. 16) also argue that referent power is both important and under-utilized in organizational settings, observing that:

> Because of multiple programs and limited resources, conflict is an everyday occurrence. The key to conflict resolution is the ability to negotiate workable psychological contracts with colleagues who have no formal reporting obligations. The use of threats (coercive power) or appeals to upper authority can lead to long-term conflict. The party under siege can, at some time in the future, make use of affiliation power to retaliate. Acquiring and using referent power effectively is important not only to managers in matrix organizations but to all managers at any level in any organization.

Table 2.3　**The effective use of power**

Power base	Explanation	Perceived as
Reward	Positive strokes, remuneration, awards, compliments, other symbolic gestures of praise	P+
Coercion	Physical or psychological injury, verbal and non-verbal put-downs, slights, symbolic gestures of disdain, physical attack, demotion, unwanted transfer, withholding of needed resources	P–
Authority	Management right to control, obligation of others to obey, playing 'the boss' and abusing authority	P–
	Exercise of leadership based on authority in times of crisis or need	P+
Referent	Identification based on personal characteristics, sometimes on perception of charisma; or reciprocal identification based on friendship, association, sharing personal information, providing something of value to the other, and on common interests, values, viewpoints and preferences; creation of reciprocal 'IOUs'	P+
Expert	Possession of specialized knowledge valued by others, used to help others, given freely when solicited	P+
	Unsolicited expertise, seen as unwarranted intrusion; continual use can create barriers; expertise offered in a condescending manner can be seen as coercive; withholding expertise in times of need	P–
Information	Access to information that is not public knowledge, because of position or connections; can exist at all levels in the organization, not just at the top; those at the top may know less about what is going on; secretaries and personal assistants to senior executives often have information power, and can often control information flows to and from superiors	P–
Affiliation	'Borrowed' from an authority source with whom one is associated – executive secretaries and staff assistants act as surrogates for their superiors; acting on the wishes of the superior	P+
	Acting on their own self-interest; using negative affiliation power by applying accounting and personnel policies rigidly	P–
Group	Collective problem solving, conflict resolution, creative brainstorming; group resolution greater than the individual contribution	P+
	A few individuals dominating the proceedings, 'groupthink'	P–

Source: Based on Benfari et al., 1986

They offer a series of suggestions for building your referent power:

- get to know the motives, preferences, values and interests of your colleagues;
- build relationships using shared motives, goals and interests;
- respect differences in interests and don't attack another person's style;
- give 'positive strokes', use reward power, confirm others' competence;

- invite reciprocal influence, show that you respect the opinions of others;
- share information, give your expertise, particularly where you stand to benefit;
- minimize concerns with status, put signs of office aside – people relate to equals;
- develop communication skills – people value clear and consistent messages;
- get to know how people react to stress and crisis – it can be difficult or impossible dealing with someone under stress;
- get to know the informal political structure of your organization, as the formal structure does not display this.

The construction and development of referent power, following these guidelines, is neither particularly time-consuming nor is it costly. Benfari and colleagues describe the use of 'positive strokes', for example, as a 'cheap and easy way to build a relationship'.

There are at least two problems with these 'property' and 'relational' concepts of power. First, they do not distinguish power-related behaviour from other forms of organizational behaviour. Some commentators regard power as a pervasive phenomenon, and see power manifested in every nuance of social and organizational life – from clothing to motor car, from size of office to size of salary, from family name to job title, and in male–female relationships. A generic concept of power with such extensive connotations can have limited analytical appeal. Second, these conceptions tend to present a surface view of power, as something that can be neatly categorized (five or eight types of sources or bases). These tidy schemata ignore the less readily visible, hidden or 'embedded' elements of power relations and power distribution in the organization.

The 'distinctiveness' problem

Many commentators in this field equate power with influence, with cause and effect, with the ability of A to make B do something they might not otherwise do. While some have defined power as a potential to act, Dahl (1957) argues that unused potential cannot be realistically regarded as power. In Dahl's view, power is exercised episodically, whenever one party influences and changes the behaviour of another.

There is a difficulty here. We ask you the time, you raise your wrist, you tell us the time. We have controlled your behaviour in this brief episode, albeit in a relatively trivial manner. Every social encounter involves ongoing mutual influence of this kind, affecting attitudes and behaviour, in more or less significant ways. And many social encounters are characterized by power imbalances, in which one party has more ability and resources than the other, and is able to maintain a higher degree of control over the interaction and its outcomes. It is thus possible to argue that all social interaction involves the exercise of power in some form. As Mangham (1979, p. xi) claims (in what today might be regarded as politically incorrect language):

> I consider nearly all behaviour to be fundamentally political in the sense that when one individual interacts with another, more often than not he is motivated so to do because the encounter provides him with some benefit, even if that benefit may be nothing more than a reduction of uncertainty.

Adopting a similar position, Astley and Sachdeva (1984, p. 104) argue that:

> [I]t is possible to interpret every instance of interaction and every social relationship as involving an exercise of power, because actors clearly affect one another all the time they are interacting. But this very pervasiveness tends to make the concept of power elusive and redundant, for it begins to have no meaning apart from the ideas of social interaction and organization.

A term that covers such a broad spectrum of behaviour, and does not enable us to make useful distinctions, is thus potentially redundant, as this latter statement indicates. Consequently, we are not able to tell when somebody is utilizing a power-based approach and when they are not, or when they are engaged in organizational politics or not. We will return to this particular definitional problem when we explore in more detail what the term 'political behaviour' might mean in practice, and where the same issue of differentiation arises.

The 'embeddedness' problem

The second problem concerns the preoccupation with the visible aspects of power, and the relative neglect of its 'hidden' dimensions. The quotes around the term 'hidden' imply that these elements *are* detectable, as long as one knows what to look for. Power and its distribution are visibly designed into the hierarchical structure of the organization, giving privileged individuals access to decision making, information sources and budgetary responsibility, for example. This is also known as formal authority or legitimate power.

Hickson et al. (1971) argue that the power of a sub-unit or group or department depends on its centrality in the workflow of the organization, its relative independence from other sections, the uniqueness and non-substitutable nature of its expertise, and its ability to cope with and handle uncertainty. The most powerful groups are those which cope independently and effectively with the greatest uncertainty using expertise not available elsewhere in the organization. These factors are also designed into or embedded in the organization structure. This 'strategic contingencies' explanation of relative power and powerlessness also helps to explain the differing levels of influence of, say, accountants and human resource professionals in many organizations (you usually have to employ a 'professionally qualified' accountant, but 'anyone' can do personnel work).

Formal organization charts, however, rarely reveal the full picture of power and its pervasive distribution in an organization. Power is also embedded in other less visible features. The issue is, that which is hidden or latent is less easily detected, analysed and challenged, but is not necessarily less potent. Some examples may help to clarify this point.

Consider the pay review and promotions game in a university. On the one hand, promotion procedures are driven by a range of identifiable actors. This includes staff seeking promotion and pay rises, heads of departments, faculty deans, personnel officers, and committees populated with members drawn from around the organization. Where does the power reside in this game? One can look first at the relative status of the key players and likely coalitions, and reach a judgement concerning their potential impact on decisions. Behind the interactions of these players lies a set of paperwork, which requires completion, signature and counter-signature. There is in addition a set of regulations concerning the timing of submissions and the hearing of cases, the style and nature of cases that are presented for promotion and advancement, and the timing and conduct of committee meetings.

The regulations also usually cover the nature of the arguments that are appropriate; are we evaluating the job, or are we assessing the individual, for example, where different considerations might apply? To confuse matters further, there are subtly different procedures, paperwork and committees for different categories of (professorial, other academic, academic-related and non-academic) staff. An individual seeking promotion can find their case blocked by a powerful individual (a dean, say, or a head of department), simply making the bald claim that 'this person should not in my view be promoted'. Powerful individuals, when they wish, can advance cases rapidly in the same manner.

Players in this game can also call upon the rules and regulations surrounding the procedures to interfere with, delay or permanently block a promotions case. It may be possible to claim, for example, that while an individual fully merits recognition, the case has unfortunately been submitted in the wrong format, at the wrong time, to the wrong committee, counter-signed by an inappropriate person, or has adopted inappropriate arguments. The point at issue, of course, appears to concern the degree of rigidity or flexibility with which the regulations are to be applied. When formal regulations and unwritten rules converge in the notion of precedent, it is always difficult to counter the argument that, 'we must apply our rules consistently', and to avoid accusations of wanting to make 'special cases' to suit particularly favoured individuals by bending the rules. In this way, relatively less powerful individuals (personnel officers, or 'lay' members of a committee) can exploit regulations to block or delay a case, while at the same time proclaiming that person's merits, and otherwise sounding positive and publicly supportive.

Power as an embedded property

Moving beyond the more or less obvious rules and regulations, and the subtle ways in which they can be exploited, there are in most organizations a number of other unwritten rules (see Scott-Morgan, 1995) concerning 'the ways things are done around here'. Here we enter the cloudy domain of organization culture, concerning values, standards, styles of behaviour, expectations, rituals, procedures and goals. Some of these features may be shared (everybody must use the same investment appraisal format), some may not (the purpose of the organization). But taken together they establish a fabric of norms and expectations that not only shape attitudes and behaviour, but influence the distribution of power across the organization's membership. These norms and expectations can also be exploited in precisely the same way as written, formal procedures, to support an argument or a position, to advance a particular perspective, or to challenge and block an initiative being driven by someone else.

The symbols of power – dress and appearance, the trappings of high office, the support and recognition of high-placed players – can also be exploited in an intimidatory manner. Displays of expertise, connections, access to information, wealth, status, and of the potential to reward or punish can intimidate many into tacit acquiescence. The appropriate manipulation of such symbols, with an eye to the protection of one's reputation, is also a critical dimension of the use of embedded power.

Power can thus be regarded as woven into our acceptance of the 'taken-for-granted' order of things, the social and organizational structures in which we find ourselves, the rule systems that appear to constitute the 'natural' running of day-to-day systems and processes. It can be difficult to challenge 'the way things are' or even to recognize in the first place that what one is presented with is an established pattern of power relations and not some immutable facet of social reality. It is clearly in the best interests of those who possess power if the unequal distribution of power is accepted, taken for granted, not challenged, accepted, invisible.

Bachrach and Baratz (1962) refer to this face of power as 'non-decision-making'. Agendas are restricted to 'safe' issues; controversial issues are excluded from informal conversations and from formal decision-making processes; organizational procedures are invoked to exclude those in subordinate positions from decision processes. Power brokers decide outcomes 'backstage'. Organization structures, rules, systems and procedures are thus not politically neutral, but they may be perceived to belong in that category, and thus go unchallenged. Non-decision-making can take at least three forms:

1   The more powerful may deal with the grievances of the less powerful by ignoring them, by dismissing them as minor, unsubstantiated, or irrelevant, or by subjecting them to endless and inconclusive consideration by committees and enquiries;

2 The less powerful may anticipate that their grievances and demands will be ignored or rejected, and are thus futile, and do not raise them in the first place;

3 The more powerful can control which matters are 'legitimate' and discussible, and the forums and procedures through which such issues are raised, to stifle the articulation of particular issues and demands, while encouraging 'acceptable' topics and themes. (Clegg, 1989, p. 77)

This third mechanism is known as the 'mobilization of bias' in favour of particular groups, interests and topics, and against others. This can lead to a situation in which demands and grievances are not raised because problems are not recognized as such. Individuals and groups may be rendered politically dormant because they accept the 'existing order', or because they lack the understanding or imagination to conceive of a different order, or because they anticipate that their resistance will be ineffective. Concepts of mobilization of bias and non-decision-making lie in the 'context' box in Figure 1.1. Political skill thus resides in the ability to exploit and manipulate and to resist and challenge the use of those contextually embedded characteristics of power in appropriate ways, to achieve results, and to maintain a healthy reputation. Political skill is as much about the manipulation of symbols, structures, procedures, arguments and the perceptions of others as the deployment and manipulation of 'listable' power bases and resources.

Value in diverse conceptualizations

In summary, we have identified three different, but related, concepts of power:

1 Power is a *property of individuals*, defined across a number of identifiable power sources or bases, some structural and some individual, and exercised in attempts to influence others.

2 Power is a *property of relationships* between members of an organization, identified by the extent to which some individuals believe, or do not believe, that others possess particular power bases.

3 Power is an *embedded property* of the structures, regulations, relationships and norms of the organization, perpetuating existing routines and power inequalities.

While each of these diverse conceptualizations is useful, awareness and understanding of all three is essential. The inclusion of the notion of power as an embedded, culturally pervasive construct, lacking a clear and distinctive definition, has three major consequences.

First, it alerts us to the less visible and less tangible dimensions of power, embedded or carried in the taken-for-granted procedures and practices of the organization and of society as a whole. This is important because invisibility and intangibility cannot be equated with insignificance. On the contrary, the apparently insubstantial elements of power can be extremely potent in skilful hands. In addition, that which cannot be readily seen and described can be extremely difficult to question, challenge or resist.

Second, it alerts us to the wide range of methods and techniques available to the change driver as initiator of power politics – and also to the range of potential responses from the targets of such political moves. Early conceptualizations tend to regard power as a 'one-way' resource, something which 'we use on you'. The conceptions of 'non-decision-making' and 'mobilization of bias' suggest that power is a more fluid, dynamic, shifting and malleable resource. One cannot decide one's tactics as a change driver in this domain from a textbook checklist. Determining an appropriate strategy requires personal skill, knowledge of the context, judgement and creativity. A broad understanding of the embedded nature of power, along with the property and relational dimensions, exposes the scope for such creativity.

Third, these conceptions alert us to the notion that what may be defined as 'power' in the tidy pages of a text such as this may not be unambiguously so regarded, or so represented, in practice. Power in the real world becomes a slippery concept when the initiators can simply – and accurately – claim that they are applying custom and practice, or accepted norms, or 'the rules and regulations', or precedent in the interests of consistency. What may be defined as the exercise of power from one perspective may also be defined as commonplace, taken-for-granted practice from another. The acts of defining behaviour in power and political terms, and of challenging such definitions, can themselves be viewed as political behaviours.

We'll take the low road

> Politics refers to individual or group behaviour that is informal, ostensibly parochial, typically divisive, and above all, in the technical sense, illegitimate – sanctioned neither by formal authority, accepted ideology, nor certified expertise (though it may exploit any one of these).

> (Mintzberg, 1983, p. 172)

Mangham (1979, p. 15) observes that, 'each of us has the capacity consciously to *manipulate* our own behaviour and that of others and that many of us fully utilize that capacity, for good or ill'. Traditional organization theory emphasizes co-operation and collaboration and 'chooses to ignore "the darker side of humanity", man's evident capacity, and occasional ardent desire, to screw his fellow man (or, in more polite terms, to achieve his ends at the expense of his colleagues)' (p. 15). Altruism and collaboration thus sit alongside competition, lies, cheating and manoeuvring.

Political behaviour is therefore normally equated with the informal, parochial, divisive, illegitimate, devious, cunning, underhand and unsanctioned – anti-social. Nevertheless, we have tried to construct a reasonable argument in defence of political behaviour in at least some organizational change settings – as potentially pro-social. We have not, however, attempted to define political behaviour with precision. What are the characteristics that distinguish political behaviour from non-political or apolitical behaviour? As with the concept of power, this definitional issue is less straightforward than it first seems.

Negative views of politics

One widely cited approach to the definitional issue comes from the work of Mayes and Allen (1977), whose matrix is presented in Table 2.4. Mayes and Allen base their definition of political behaviour on a classification of the means and ends of influence attempts. The means which one organizational player uses to influence another, to achieve their preferred outcomes, can either be sanctioned by the organization, or not. Similarly, the ends or outcomes being pursued may or may not be organizationally sanctioned. Those behaviours where the goals and the tactics both enjoy organizational sanction are labelled 'non-political' (cell I in the matrix). Whether the tactics are sanctioned or not, and the ends or goals are also not sanctioned (perhaps personal gain), the behaviour is labelled as both political and dysfunctional (cells II and IV). But where the ends are sanctioned and the means or tactics are not, the political behaviour may be organizationally functional.

There are problems with this approach. One difficulty is: who decides what is sanctioned and what is not? Many organizations have rules which identify behaviours regarded as 'illegitimate' or unacceptable; but these rules typically cover the obvious topics of theft of company property, disclosure of sensitive information, and health and safety regulations, for example. Such rules cannot cover every contingency that might arise in interpersonal and group behaviour across the organization over time. Different members of the organization, in different functions and at different levels, often have different views on this issue. Some players may describe as political some behaviours which are in fact sanctioned in some form. Those behaviours which are sanctioned and those which are not in a given setting may, therefore, not always be apparent. Behaviours defined as 'political' may also belong to other categories of action: revenge, returning a favour, incompetence, error, lack of understanding, rigid rule following, and so on. A second difficulty concerns the narrow definition of the terms 'functional' and 'dysfunctional' which seem to concern contribution to 'the greater good of the organization'. Now that is frequently a source of dispute, particularly in the face of rapid and radical change. And the

Table 2.4 **Dimensions of organizational politics**

Influence means	Influence ends	
	Organizationally sanctioned	Not sanctioned by organization
Organizationally sanctioned	I: Non-political job behaviour	II: Organizationally dysfunctional political behaviour
Not sanctioned by organization	III: Political behaviour potentially functional to the organization	IV: Organizationally dysfunctional political behaviour

Source: Mayes and Allen, 1977

concept of influence means and ends being functional or dysfunctional for the change driver is not readily admitted in this approach.

Mayes and Allen remind us that political behaviour is often viewed as covert, and lacking sanction, and as serving personal goals rather than the organization as a whole. It is hardly surprising that, defined in this way, 'politics' in organizational life gets a bad press, is relatively shunned by academic commentators, and is often denied by some managers.

Supporting the negative view of political behaviour, Drory and Romm (1990) offer a definition of organizational politics which seeks to establish common elements across different perspectives found in the literature. They first point out that politics is played at, and can be analysed at, three levels: individual, group and organizational. We are not dealing exclusively with the actions of lone individuals, but also with collective leadership, group norms and values, establishing group consensus, and the formation of coalitions. Organizations also become involved in electoral politics and legislative issues, but this latter aspect has attracted less research and commentary. Table 2.5 summarizes the three main 'definition elements' which characterize organizational politics from their review. These include outcomes, means and situational characteristics.

This definition of organizational politics thus has three strands. First, behaviour can be defined as political if the motivation is self-serving with respect to winning power and resources, counter to the goals of the organization. Second, political behaviour is defined in terms of the informal use of power and influence to achieve hidden objectives. Third, political behaviour arises in situations characterized by uncertainty, conflict and resistance – consistent with the view that organizational change is likely to intensify political activity.

This approach again denies that political behaviour may potentially be deployed with corporate objectives in mind, instead of – or in some instances as well as – personal goals. Drory and Romm suggest that further research is needed to explore the uses of organizational politics in the pursuit of formal organizational goals. While conflict and resistance may trigger political behaviour, particularly on the part of change drivers and those who seek to challenge change initiatives, many organizational change settings are also characterized by at least some degree of support

Table 2.5 **Definition elements of political behaviour**

Outcomes	are self-serving.
	act against the organization's effectiveness and goals.
	are concerned with the distribution of resources and advantage.
	usually involve behaviour linked with the attainment of power.
Means	involve influence attempts or tactics.
	concern the use of power tactics.
	include informal, covert, non-job-related behaviours.
	involve concealing true motives.
Situational characteristics	typically include conflict and resistance in the organization.
	also include uncertainty in the decision-making process.

for change (from senior management, from individuals and groups who perceive benefit from change). In other words, the 'situational characteristics' with respect to organizational change may be better represented by a continuum of co-existing views, from public welcoming acceptance to covert challenge and subversion.

Positive views of politics

One exception to this negative view lies in the work of Kumar and Thibodeaux (1990), who present a model that both acknowledges and advocates the use of political strategies in planned organizational change. Their model offers what can be described as an 'escalation approach' to the deployment of political tactics, depending on the level of significance of the changes being proposed. They identify three levels of change:

- First-level change involves improving unit or department effectiveness.
- Second-level change involves the introduction of new perspectives to organizational sub-systems.
- Third-level change concerns organization-wide shifts in values and ways of working.

They argue that, while first- and second-level changes respectively require political *awareness* and political *facilitation*, third-level change entails political *intervention*. In other words, the more significant the change, and the more widespread the organizational implications, the greater the political involvement required by the change driver. Intervention at this level, they argue, may involve stimulating debate, gaining support from key groups and individuals, and covert manipulation. Kumar and Thibodeaux admit that what they advocate may be regarded as 'ethically objectionable', pointing also to the 'distasteful' reality of organizational politics in their defence (p. 364).

However, 'ethically objectionable' as this may seem, the exercise of power is pervasive in social interaction, and involves our use of behaviours, language and symbols (style of dress, office furniture, motor car) to shape the perceptions and behaviour of others. Kakabadse and Parker (1984, p. 62) go so far as to observe that, 'social order rests on deceitfulness, evasiveness, secrecy, frontwork and basic social conflicts'. We may describe our attempts to exercise power over others in more or less 'acceptable' terminology: as 'normal interaction', or as 'influencing others', or as 'manipulation'. But the end results – shaping, affecting or manipulating others' behaviour – are the same. We achieve this, sometimes consciously, but often unwittingly, through three related mechanisms:

- conversation controls;
- influence tactics;
- impression management.

Conversation controls

We 'manage' our conversations through a range of conscious and unconscious verbal and non-verbal signals and questioning techniques. These signals and techniques tell the parties to a conversation, for example, when one has finished an utterance and when it is somebody else's turn to speak. These signals also reveal agreement, friendship, dispute and dislike – emotions which in turn shape the further response of the listener. When conversing normally, we use these signals unconsciously or habitually. However, an awareness of the methods being used can allow us quite easily to bring these under conscious control. This can be advantageous in many social settings. Therapists and counsellors, for example, use a range of methods to shape conversations in ways that allow their clients to articulate their difficulties and to work towards identifying appropriate solutions. Managers holding employment selection, appraisal or promotion interviews need to understand conversation control techniques in order to handle these particular interactions effectively. We can also use conversation controls to shape or steer the behaviour of others, to achieve our own preferred ends. Conscious command of these methods increases our ability to manipulate and control others. This increases our power. Huczynski (1996, pp. 35–41) offers a useful summary of 'high-power' and 'low-power' conversation tactics. Table 2.6 defines the seven main conversation control strategies used by *powertalkers*.

Huczynski also describes conversation styles that suggest the speaker has low power (Table 2.7).

There are significant gender and culture differences in the use of these conversation control techniques, but a detailed discussion is beyond the remit of this text. Powerful individuals of either sex, or individuals seeking to give others the impression that they are powerful, tend to dominate conversations, offer less personal information and emotional display, and assert status by interrupting, speaking firmly and in detail, and by providing opinions, suggestions, information and disagreement. It is instructive to observe the use of high-power and low-power conversation strategies in a

Table 2.6 **Powertalking strategies**

Positive talk	Powertalkers respond positively, make genuine commitments, have high expectations, are optimistic, avoid conditional phrases, seek creative solutions, look for the benefits.
Give credit	Powertalkers either alter, or ignore, their shortcomings, describe their achievements positively, neither apologize nor justify, praise others for their success.
Learn from experience	Powertalkers say, 'I learned' instead of 'I failed', seek the positive in the face of setbacks, think positive when feeling low, focus on options rather than on regrets.
Accept responsibility	Powertalkers admit their own feelings, accept responsibility for actions, control their use of time.
Persuade others	Powertalkers emphasize benefits, keep options open, seek ways to improve relationships, focus on the positive, accept the ideas of others.
Decisive speaking	Powertalkers commit to specific duties and targets, extract detailed information, set realistic goals, decide what to say and then say it.
Tell the truth	Powertalkers avoid suspicious and misleading phrases, say 'no' when they mean 'no', avoid self-criticism, respect others with whom they interact – remembering and using others' names.

Source: Based on Huczynski, 1996, pp. 35–41

Table 2.7 **Low-power indicators**

Hedges and qualifiers	'Maybe it has some strengths': Qualifications mean avoiding commitment, so you don't have to disagree with someone. You can change your view when you discover theirs.
Irritators	'. . . you know', 'sort of', 'kinda': These suggest you lack confidence in what you are saying, that you feel the need to apologize, that you lack knowledge and ability.
Intensifiers	Redundant adjectives, like 'really', 'awfully' and 'horrendously': These terms lack substance; use more powerful language such as 'remarkably', 'outstanding', 'excellent'.
Tags	Tags are the bits at the end where you say, 'aren't they?', or 'didn't you?' These turn a decisive statement into an unnecessary question, attempting to please, avoiding conflict.
Hesitations	'Um, er, ah, uhh, well . . .': These suggest the need for time to think, or the fear of 'coming over too strong'. Can signal uncertainty, and encourage interruption.
Excessive questions	A speech pattern that can signal uncertainty and a need for attention.
Others	Unnecessary or excessive apologizing, giving irrelevant information, excessive personal disclosure, over-politeness.

Source: Based on Huczynski, 1996, pp. 35–41

real organizational setting, and to check from observations that this categorization of strategies does apply to relatively high- and low-power individuals.

Influence tactics

How do you persuade someone else to do what you want them to do – sometimes against their will? We use a range of influence tactics to achieve this, a topic that has attracted considerable research interest. It is possible to make a distinction between power (drawing on sources, bases and resources) and influence (using interpersonal tactics), but the dividing line is vague. The exercise of influence is also about control – control of someone else's behaviour to achieve your preferred outcomes. The more effective our influencing skills, therefore, the more control and the more power we potentially have.

The best known research into influence attempts is the work of Kipnis et al. (1980, 1984). Kipnis identified eight categories of influence tactic, summarized in Table 2.8.

Kipnis also distinguished four types of manager, based on patterns of use of different influence tactics:

- *Bystanders* rarely use any of these influence tactics, have low organizational power, have limited personal and organizational objectives, and are frequently dissatisfied.
- *Shotguns* use all of these influence tactics all the time, have unfulfilled goals, and are inexperienced in their job.
- *Captives* use only one or two 'favourite' tactics, out of habit, and with limited effectiveness.
- *Tacticians*, however, make high use of rational appeal and average use of the other tactics, are successful in achieving their objectives, have high organizational power, and tend to be satisfied in their work.

It is again interesting to apply these categorizations, of influence tactics and of managerial types, to organizational settings, to establish whether they are supported by experience.

Impression management

Impression management is the process whereby we seek to control the image that others have of us. This concept is founded in the work of Goffman (1959), and it is now widely recognized as a significant aspect of organizational behaviour. Rosenfeld et al. (1995, p. 4) argue that:

> We impression manage in many different ways: what we do, how we do it, what we say, how we say it, the furnishings and arrangement of our offices, and our

Table 2.8 **Influencing tactics**

Assertiveness	Order the person to do it. Point out that the rules demand it. Keep reminding them about what is required.
Ingratiation	Make the request politely and humbly. Act friendly and complimentary before asking. Sympathize with any hardships that may result for them.
Rational appeal	Write a detailed justification. Present relevant information in support. Explain the reasoning behind your request.
Sanctions	Threaten to get them fired. Threaten to block their promotion. Threaten them with a poor performance evaluation.
Exchange	Offer an exchange of favours – mutual backscratching. Remind them of favours you have provided them in the past.
Upward appeal	Get higher-level management to intervene in your support. Send the person to speak to your boss.
Blocking	Threaten to stop working with the person. Ignore the person and stop acting friendly. Withhold collaboration until they do what you want.
Coalition	Get the support of colleagues to support your request. Make the request at a formal meeting where others will support you.

physical appearance – from the clothes and make-up we wear to non-verbal behaviours such as facial expressions or postures. All these behaviours in some way can help define who and what we are.

Effective impression management means being consciously aware of and in control of the cues that we send to others through verbal and non-verbal channels. This suggests that we consciously seek to manipulate and control the impressions or perceptions that others have of us. As with conversation controls, we can use impression management to manipulate the behaviour of others. We do this, for example, by 'giving off' the impression that we are friendly, submissive, apologetic, angry, defensive, confident, intimidating, and so on. The more effectively we manage our impression, the greater the control we can achieve in social interaction, and the greater our power to pursue our preferred outcomes over others.

Gardner (1992) speaks of impression management as 'organizational dramaturgy', and in terms of 'stagecraft': actors, audience, stage, script, performance and reviews. It is not surprising, therefore, that some managers regard impression management simply as a form of acting and as deceit. The problem with this view is that we 'manage' our impression all the time, whether we like this concept or not. It is hardly possible to avoid sending 'signals' to others through, for example, our style of dress, posture, facial expressions, gestures, tone and pitch of voice, and even location in a room. The only useful distinction here is between conscious (and by implication more effective – for the initiator) impression management and unconscious (and by implication less effective, or even misleading) impression management. Conscious control has many advantages. Social interactions run more smoothly when we provide the 'correct' signals to others, who in turn accurately 'decode' these signals of our attitudes and intents. Impression

Table 2.9 **Creating a favourable self-image**

Ingratiation	Use flattery, agree with the opinions of others, do favours to encourage people with power and influence to befriend you.
Intimidation	Convey the image of potential danger to those who could stand in the way of your advancement. Use veiled threats of exposure.
Self-promotion	Win respect and admiration of superiors through embellishing your accomplishments, overstating your abilities, displaying awards.
Exemplification	Create an impression of selfless dedication and self-sacrifice, so those in positions of influence will feel guilty and offer reward or promotion.
Accounting	Distance yourself from negative events, deny personal responsibility for problems, diminish the seriousness of difficulties.
Supplication	Get those in positions of influence to be sympathetic and nurturing, for example through requests for 'mentoring' and other support.

Source: Based on Feldman and Klitch (1991)

management is a critical skill in counselling, and in selection, appraisal and disciplinary interviewing contexts. Candidates are typically trained to manage the impressions they give in employment interviews.

Feldman and Klitch (1991) offer some interesting contemporary advice on how to manage your impression effectively to enhance your career. First, they suggest six techniques for creating a favourable self-image with others (Table 2.9). They also argue that a contemporary 'careerist orientation' to work is based on six key beliefs, incorporating much practical impression management advice:

1 Merit alone is insufficient for advancement in organizations. Creating the appearance of being a winner, or looking 'promotable', is just as important.
2 To advance, it is critical to pursue social relationships with superiors and co-workers. On the surface, these relationships should appear to be social in nature, but in reality they are used instrumentally for job contacts and insider organizational information.
3 Looking like a 'team player' is central to career advancement. However, individuals should still pursue self-interest at work through 'antagonistic co-operation'; that is, appearing co-operative and helpful on the surface while simultaneously seeking information about how to overcome one's competition.
4 In the long run, an individual's career goals will be inconsistent with the interests of any one organization. Therefore, in order to advance, individuals must appear to be loyal and committed to their current employers, while keeping their résumés circulating and otherwise 'keeping their options open'.
5 Dishonest or unethical behaviours are sometimes necessary in order to get promotions to which one feels entitled. However, it is important not to advocate dishonest or unethical behaviour or even acknowledge the existence of such behaviour. Instead, individuals should become adept

at inconsistency, and develop the ability to hold public positions that are either mutually inconsistent or inconsistent with past public positions.

6   Much of the 'real work' of many jobs cannot be tangibly assessed, nor can relative success on those jobs be easily validated. Thus it is important to construct the illusion of success and power socially through symbols such as dress and office design. These props might include locks on file drawers, positioning visitors so the sun is in their eyes, and having visitors' chairs lower than the office occupant's desk.

The value of political skills

Feldman and Klitch are clearly emphasizing the need to maintain the illusion of success, sociability, collaboration, loyalty, integrity and power. This 'careerist advice' can be seen in either evaluative or descriptive terms. On the one hand, we may consider the relevance of this advice in the context of personal and social values and norms, and make a judgement with regard to how moral, ethical, acceptable or legitimate we consider such advice to be. On the other hand, we may note that this 'advice' merely attempts to describe empirically verifiable aspects of contemporary organizational reality, in a way that may or may not match with our own personal values.

An understanding of conversation control, influence tactics and impression management techniques can thus be particularly significant for the change driver for at least five reasons.

First, as we have already established, evidence and rational argument are rarely sufficient to establish unambiguous choices between significant organizational options.

Second, the change driver often has to work quickly to achieve results, to change behaviour, and does not always have adequate time for protracted debate and negotiation. It may be necessary in some circumstances, therefore, to take shortcuts – or to make shortcuts through the organization's political system.

Third, the change driver often has to deal with turbulent and uncertain situations, in which an array of different types of tactics, deployed in a creative manner to fit the circumstances, is more valuable than reliance on familiar past habit. In 'high-velocity' environments characterized by rapid change and unpredictability, one needs a range of 'weaponry' to deal with the range of issues that arise.

Fourth, change drivers often have to work with people over whom they have no formal managerial authority, but whom they still have to persuade to collaborate, co-operate and comply. However, those individuals and groups can legitimately, when asked, say 'no' because their job or their position does not require such compliance. Approaches other than shouting 'Do what I tell you' are thus necessary.

Finally, change agents typically have to deploy an array of tactics which, on the one hand, are effective, but which, on the other hand, will also sustain or enhance the reputation of the change driver and not damage it. Approaches that are effective in this respect in one setting may be wholly inappropriate in another. The change driver thus needs an extensive behaviour repertoire of both political and conventional tactics in order to succeed.

Organization politics: the language game

We have tried in this chapter to demonstrate that the concepts of power and politics are not easy to define with clarity and precision. The popular conception of power as a 'resource possessed' appears narrow when we consider the importance of the perceptions of those subjected to power plays, and when we further consider the extent to which power is embedded in the structures, norms and expectations of an organization. If we accept these wider notions of power, then we also have to accept that those who possess a limited power base may, if they are skilful and willing, exploit relational and embedded resources to their advantage. Similarly, those with a strong power base can skilfully complement that resource through those other channels.

The simple question, 'What is power?', turns out to have a relatively complex answer. The simple request, 'How can I get more power?', turns out to have several different answers, depending on the perspectives one chooses.

The concept of political behaviour also defies unambiguous definition. It is particularly difficult to draw clear distinctions between political and non-political behaviour. Every social interaction combines aspects of conversation control, influence attempts and impression management. This is how we, consciously or unconsciously, attempt to shape the attitudes and behaviours of others. These are interpersonal resources which we use to control our social interactions and to control other people. Some individuals are more skilled at this than others, although most of the skills involved can be learned through training and experience. The exercise of conversation controls, influence tactics and impression management techniques can thus be equated with the exercise of power – and can in turn be regarded as political behaviour. A further problem lies in the observation that some of our manipulation attempts can be pro-social, and may have significant benefits for the other party, in therapeutic, counselling and some other organizational interviewing contexts.

It looks very much as though *everything* we say and do, across the spectrum of our social existence – domestic, leisure and organizational, verbal and non-verbal, substantive and symbolic, consciously and unwittingly – can be described in terms of power and politics, in terms of

Interviewer: How do you mean – the soft side? Politics is usually covert, symbolic, rather than formal visible displays?

Manager: I guess what I'm saying is, if you're asking people to . . . what's power, OK? Power is control, agree with that? If you're talking about fundamental changes which bring about pretty fundamental power shifts, what you're asking people to do is to either give up their control or change the nature of their control. I think that there's aggressive ways of doing that, but there's also ways of doing that which are 'nicer' ways of doing it. Methods of going about things that, because you're creating a context for people and because they have got a bigger picture and understand where they fit in and are part of the process of change, often people are willing to forgo some of that control because of what they get back in exchange. And I've seen that happen a lot with doctors. When you go to doctors and say, 'We want to change your role and we're going to take all your nurses out of your outpatient clinics and swap them for unqualified workers 'cos you don't need a nurse' – they go mad. But if you say, 'We've got a situation here, what do you think the key issues are, how do you think we should go about creating solutions?' Approached in that way, people will change fundamentally, because they've bought into the problem, and also bought into the solution. And they will forgo control.

Interviewer: But this is not politics. This is participative management.

Manager: No, it's different. It's about . . . people talk about participative management, but I'm talking about a dimension on from that. How do I describe it? It involves specific techniques to bring about political changes, and I think this builds on participative management.

Interviewer: We maybe don't have a good enough language to deal with this – but it's about 'supportive manipulation'?

Manager: Yes, that's exactly what it is. And participative management is not enough. It's about finding ways, at the individual level, of implementing the things you want to happen at the corporate level.

manipulation and control, in terms of our attempts to stamp our preferred outcomes on the situation in preference to the outcomes preferred by others. If we drive this point to its logical analytical conclusion, then the concepts of power and politics become useless. Perhaps we should abandon these ambiguous and confusing terms?

The social construction of political behaviour

This conclusion is over-pessimistic, and exaggerated. One value of these terms lies in their ability to allow us to make useful distinctions between different types of behaviour. However, another value lies in their ability to combine and bring together practices which share 'family resemblances'; we will see later how 'participative management' can be placed in the same category as 'Machiavellian politics'. 'Political behaviour' can also be a useful category if it is regarded as *socially constructed*. In other words, how do the players in a given setting distinguish behaviour that is 'political' from 'other' behaviour? The meaning of political behaviour that is important, in a general organizational context, but particularly for the change driver, is the meaning given to the term by the organizational players.

The notion of socially constructed meaning may sound complex, but is easily illustrated.

Let us assume that you have been commissioned to study aggression in Nottingham nightclubs. You surely have to begin by defining what you are going to study. Aggressive behaviour can be defined in terms, let us say, of raised voices, angry language, physical contact, pain and harm, damage to property. Now let us imagine that on your first field visit to a Nottingham nightclub, armed with a notepad, you witness an episode involving two young men at a table near the bar. Voices are raised. Insults are exchanged. One man punches the other on the upper arm. The other retaliates by pushing the first man away. A chair is knocked over. The table is shaken. Beer is spilled. Glasses tumble to the floor and shatter. As this 'fits' with your indicators of aggressive behaviour, you reach for your pad and make notes. But let us now also imagine that, to complete the field notes, you interview the two men in an attempt to establish the cause of this extremely aggressive outburst. Both men are shocked that you have seen their behaviour as aggressive. They are best mates. What you saw was 'a bit of fun', a 'typical knockabout', a regular Friday night joke that got out of hand. The spilled beer and broken glasses were accidental. The episode you witnessed demonstrated the opposite of aggression. This was a display, in their view, of a close and continuing friendship. (And they are not simply trying to mislead the naïve researcher.)

It would take a rigid and inflexible observer to insist, on this evidence, that what was observed was a display of 'aggression' that 'matched' the definition of the term. Surely the 'definition' of the episode that matters in terms of understanding this social drama is the definition of the players. In other words, aggression is a socially constructed concept difficult to define, even in more extreme cases (crimes of passion, for example), outside a knowledge of the meaning attached to the behaviour by those involved.

What has this to do with organizational politics? Attempts to establish a prior definition from the 'neutral' standpoint of an observer can have limited analytical or explanatory power. This problem is apparent with the Mayes and Allen (1977) definition of political behaviour in terms of 'organizational sanction', where consistent arbiters of what is and what is not 'sanctioned' are hard to find. This problem is also apparent in the 'definitional elements' approach of Drory and Romm (1990); on whose definitions or understandings of the outcomes, means and situational characteristics of particular behaviours are we to rely? The definitions which count are the socially constructed definitions used by the players in the game in a particular context. The observer seeking to understand and explain political behaviour has to adopt the standpoint of the players. If the players label some behaviours as 'political', and other behaviours as 'non-political', then those are the labels which will colour their judgements of, and shape their responses to those behaviours irrespective of any external definitions and judgements. We have to abandon our observers' standpoint and use the labels and definitions that apply in the setting under consideration.

Accounting for political behaviour

This argument has a further and more fundamental step. The concept of 'labelling' behaviour in the way that we have been discussing has far more interesting consequences. For example, let us say we 'catch you out' in some devious, underhand, cunning political power play, perhaps, for sake of illustration, to discredit a colleague. If we are able to make this accusation 'stick', then your reputation could be irreparably damaged, other colleagues may never trust you again, co-operation will be withheld, your promotion chances will be marred, and we can make your life in this organization unpleasant for years to come – if you decide to stay. However, if you are able to refute this accusation, then your reputation could not only be saved, but could be immeasurably enhanced. Your counter-claim (if indeed you do not publicize this in advance of a challenge) could run something like this:

> Don't be ridiculous. This was not a power play. This was simply a routine attempt to persuade someone of the logic of the case, to bring someone round to my way of thinking, which, by the way, has general agreement across the organization. And this individual was not only going to damage the change initiative, but also damage the futures of many colleagues who would benefit (through improved job security, quality of working life, and so on). In any case, this individual was acting against the change out of purely personal motives.

The essence of political behaviour thus lies not in the tactics, methods and techniques that we have listed, although these are certainly illustrative of the kinds of behaviours we are considering. The essence of political behaviour lies instead in the ways in which it is represented by the players in the game. Representation involves what has come to be known as the 'management of meaning', which is achieved through symbolic actions, and primarily through the judicious use of language. As Pettigrew (1977, p. 85) argues:

> Politics concerns the creation of legitimacy for certain ideas, values and demands – not just action performed as a result of previously acquired legitimacy. The management of meaning refers to a process of symbol construction and value use designed both to create legitimacy for one's own demands and to 'de-legitimize' the demands of others.

What we are dealing with here, however, is not so much the legitimation of interests as the representation and legitimation of political behaviours used in pursuit of those interests. Power, from this perspective, becomes the ability to impose one's interpretation on events in competition with the meanings offered by others. The quintessential political behaviours thus lie in *labelling* actions as political, in *challenging* such classifications, and in *justifying* such actions when necessary and appropriate with a plausible *account* in the prevailing circumstances. Power is the ability to 'make your account stick'.

The conduct and justification of organizational politics is thus a language game, as well as a game of strategies, tactics and behaviours. It can therefore be described as a representational or impression management activity. Pfeffer (1992a, p. 190) expresses this in terms of the concept of 'framing'. Framing refers to the need to appear reasonable in context. Thus, 'what looks reasonable, or ridiculous, depends on the context – on how it is framed in terms of what has preceded it and the language that is used to present it'.

Play the game

From the standpoint of the change driver, the definitions that one uses for power and politics are of much less interest than how behaviour is perceived and understood by other players in the organization. In Western industrialized cultures, decisions must *appear* to be rational, even though the players involved typically know this is not an accurate representation. As Pfeffer (1992a) observes:

> All organizations strive for the appearance of rationality and the use of proper procedures, which include using information and analysis to justify decisions, even if this information and analysis is mustered after the fact to ratify a decision that has been made for other reasons. (p. 248)

> Thus, in many instances, individuals in organizations do not seek out information in order to make a decision, but rather, they amass information so that the decision will seem to have been made in the 'correct' fashion – i.e., on the basis of information rather than uninformed preferences or hunches. (p. 250)

> Because of the need for the appearance, if not reality, of rational decision processes, analysis and information are important as strategic weapons in battles involving power and influence. In these contests, the ability to mobilize powerful outside experts, with credibility and the aura of objectivity, is an effective strategy. (p. 254)

This argument further reinforces the central role of *accounts* in justifying political action in organizational change. Does this reduce the political dimensions of the work of the change driver to appearances, to surface characteristics, play acting and illusion, or to a potentially sleazy combination of 'frontwork' and 'backstaging'? This may appear to some readers a cosmetic and unethical stance, a mere language game, with negative implications for personal job and career satisfaction. Jackall (1988, p. 198) observes that:

> In such a world, notions of fairness and equity that managers might privately hold, as measures of gauging the worth of their own work, become merely quaint. One fluctuates between a frustrated resentment at what seems to be a kind of institutionalized corruption and systematic attempts to make oneself a beneficiary of the system. Being a 'good soldier' may carry for some the private satisfactions of work well done, of bargains kept, or of organizational goals attained through one's best efforts. But one's dedication may also make one unfit for the manoeuvres that can bring organizational privilege and reward.

In describing earlier the 'careerist orientation' advice of Feldman and Klitch (1991), we noted that this could be seen in either evaluative or descriptive terms, but left the issue unresolved. This advice promotes the maintenance of appearance over the achievement of substance, promotes illusion over reality. Should we regard this as morally reprehensible, or accept this as an accurate account of organizational reality?

It is important to recall in this context the substantive, unavoidable and necessary shaping role of power and politics in change. We are dealing with skilful behaviour that can have positive as well as negative outcomes for the individuals and organizations involved. We are dealing with a range of political styles, from coercion at one extreme, to a considerable variety of less aggressive methods. We are faced with the need to represent goals and behaviours, and the goals and behaviours of others, in a manner that promotes the legitimacy of one and the unacceptability of the other. We are faced with the need continually to slide back and forth across the line between illusion and reality. We are playing a game of symbols and language in which what one says and how (and when and where and to whom) one says it, can be as significant as what one does, and how one does it.

The change driver concerned with implementing a particular initiative or programme, with making a mark, with making a difference, with career advancement, with organizational success, can only escape from this language game by pursuing some other career.

3 Sit in judgement

CONTENTS

Warrants, accounts and reputations

> The means to any end are merely mechanisms for accomplishing some-
> thing. The something can be grand, grotesque, or, for most of us, I
> suspect, somewhere in between. The end may not always justify the
> means, but neither should it automatically be used to discredit the
> means. Power and political processes in organizations can be used to
> accomplish great things. They are not always used in this fashion, but
> that does not mean we should reject them out of hand. It is interesting
> that when we use power ourselves, we see it as a good force and wish we
> had more. When others use it against us, particularly when it is used to
> thwart our goals or ambitions, we see it as an evil. A more sophisticated
> and realistic view would see it for what it is – an important social
> process that is often required to get things accomplished in inter-
> dependent systems.
>
> (Pfeffer, 1992b, p. 35)

As Clegg (1989, p. 67) points out, many writers on power use 'imaginative
vignettes or hypothetical stories' to illustrate a point, cut a distinction,
support an argument. That is the approach of this chapter, but with a
difference. The stories reported here are real, not invented, taken from
interviews with practising managers. The purpose of this chapter is to
invite the reader to test some key aspects of the framework of political
behaviour presented in Chapter 1. We present a series of short 'incident
reports' from change drivers, and ask you to judge the behaviours reported
and their implications.

How do change drivers become engaged in political activity, what forms
does this engagement take, and can these actions withstand public scrutiny?
There are clear difficulties in bringing evidence to such questions, given the
sensitivities of disclosure. Attempts to disguise organizations and actors
can separate accounts from their history and context, making adequate
interpretation problematic. This chapter illustrates a range of political
behaviours in different organizational contexts. The identities of the
organizations and the players involved are disguised for obvious reasons.

These incident reports are based on interviews with managers who were
asked to describe situations in which they became involved in political
behaviour. More detailed accounts would offer significant background and
context information. Each incident is reported from the standpoint of an
individual (male or female) change driver. Obtaining complementary
accounts from other actors in each setting would, clearly, be problematic, if
fascinating.

Two of these incidents will be worked through in detail. The others will
be left to your judgement. A template for recording your judgements on
these incidents, and for comparing judgements with other readers where
circumstances allow, is provided at the end of the chapter. The aims are to
hold our framework against actual political behaviour, and to encourage

readers to reflect critically on the nature and role of political behaviour in organizational change in their own experience, compared with others.

As these are real accounts concerning actual incidents, the reporting is somewhat uneven. Some of these reports are relatively brief, and lack context information which would reveal the organizations, and the players involved. Others are longer and offer deeper insights into the views of the narrator. In some cases the narrator is the key player in the action described. In other cases, the narrator is speaking as a concerned, and involved, observer of events and the behaviour of others. In each case, the narrator disclosed only information that they felt comfortable disclosing, knowing that what they revealed could eventually find its way into a book such as this. The unevenness in reporting thus also reflects the extreme sensitivity, and the legitimate demands of confidentiality, surrounding each incident.

Good guys, bad guys

It would be easy to represent change drivers unambiguously as 'the good guys', and thus to label resistors and subversives as 'baddies'. But as Clegg and Hardy (1996) observe, this distinction would be superficial. Adopting the standpoint of the change driver does not imply taking the side of the change driver, whose behaviour may be controversial.

Henry Mintzberg (1983) defines political behaviour as that which is informal, parochial, divisive, and illegitimate or not officially sanctioned. The main problem with this definition is that it cannot be applied to observable behaviour in a manner that will produce consistent judgements. Much depends on who is doing the judging. One can reasonably expect that the initiators of political behaviour, the targets, the observers on the scene at the time, and readers coming to a written account of the incident, will all produce differing assessments. What does 'informal' imply, given that much behaviour in organizations falls into this category, and that 'informal' behaviour is not necessarily damaging? Why is 'political' equated with 'parochial', and is this not a category into which much of our behaviour falls? Can we say that political behaviour is divisive in the same way that, say, redistributing budget allocations, or giving one person a favoured assignment, are divisive acts? And there are difficulties in defining what is legitimate and what is not in any given setting, as organizational rule books rarely cover more than the most extreme contingencies.

One approach to these dilemmas is to hold examples of questionable political behaviour against a set of guidelines. One template, designed specifically to deal with organizational politics, comes from the work of Velasquez et al. (Cavanagh et al., 1981; Velasquez et al., 1983). Their concern is to establish a structure for ethical decisions that will allow us to distinguish 'dirty politics' from 'responsible political action'.

Table 3.1   **Ethical models for judging political behaviour**

Model	Strengths as an ethical guide	Weaknesses as an ethical guide
Utilitarianism	Encourages efficiency and productivity	Virtually impossible to quantify important variables
	Parallels profit maximization and auditing methods	Can result in unjust allocation of resources
	Goes beyond the individual to consider impact on all constituents	Individual rights may be violated to achieve greatest good
Theory of rights	Protects the individual, establishes sphere of freedom and privacy	Encourages selfish behaviour that can result in anarchy
	Establishes standards of social behaviour independent of outcomes	Personal prerogatives may become obstacles to productivity and efficiency
Theory of justice	Ensures fair allocation of resources	Can encourage a sense of entitlement that discourages risk and innovation
	Ensures democratic operation, independent of status or class	Some individual rights may be violated to accommodate justice for majority
	Protects the interests of the under-represented in the organization	

Source: Based on Velasquez et al. (1983)

Their approach is based on the normative ethical concepts of utilitarian-ism, individual rights and natural justice. They argue that these criteria are complementary, and that they should be combined in reaching ethical judgements of political behaviour. Table 3.1 summarizes the strengths and weaknesses of the three approaches.

Utilitarian theory

A utilitarian approach judges behaviour in terms of the 'balance sheet' of benefit and damage to the population involved. Behaviour is acceptable if it passes the test of meeting 'the greatest good of the greatest number'. Performing the necessary calculation of interests, satisfaction and other potential consequences can be problematic.

Theory of rights

This approach judges behaviour on the extent to which fundamental individual rights are respected. This includes, for example, the right of free consent, the right to privacy, the right to freedom of conscience, the right of free speech, the right to due process in the form of a fair and impartial hearing. Performing the ethical calculus here is a relatively simple matter of establishing whether an individual's entitlement has or has not been violated.

Theory of justice

This approach judges behaviour on the extent to which the benefits and burdens consequent on an action are fairly, equitably and impartially distributed. Distributive justice implies that individuals in similar circumstances should be treated equally, rules should be applied consistently, and individuals should not be held responsible for matters beyond their control. As with the utilitarian calculus, these issues can be awkward to resolve in practice. How is 'responsibility' to be established? On what criteria can differential treatment be based?

This argument becomes a decision tree (Figure 3.1) for determining whether a political act can be judged as ethical or not.

The concept of 'overwhelming factors' refers to any aspect of the circumstances under consideration that would justify setting aside one or all of the three ethical criteria. These criteria may conflict: achieving the 'greatest good' may violate an individual's rights. Some acts may have 'double effects', involving positive and negative outcomes. The negative outcomes become acceptable if the dominant purpose is to achieve the positive outcomes, and if those outweigh the negatives. The concept of 'incapacitating factors' refers to the possibility that the decision maker may be unable to apply these ethical criteria. Individual managers can be constrained by the views and actions of colleagues, and may be pressured into behaviours that they would not choose independently. Individual managers may have inadequate information on which to reach an ethical judgement in a given setting. Finally, the individual may doubt the relevance of one or more ethical criteria to a given context. The right to free speech, for instance, may not be considered to apply where such freedom would lead to the dissemination of information damaging to other members of the organization.

Beyond the apparent strait-jacket of this decision structure, there are a number of 'escape routes' or 'fudge factors' which give the change driver licence to apply reasonable judgement in the circumstances. As Velasquez et al. (1983, pp. 79–80) point out:

> The manager who is unable to use ethical criteria because of these incapacitating factors may justifiably give them a lesser weight in making decisions about what to do in a political situation. The underlying rationale for such systematic devaluation of ethical criteria is simple. A person cannot hold himself responsible for matters which he cannot control or for matters of which he is sincerely ignorant or sincerely in doubt. However, determining whether a manager's lack of freedom, lack of information, or lack of certitude is sufficient to abrogate moral responsibility requires one to make some very difficult judgements. In the end, these are hard questions that only the individuals involved can answer for themselves.

The test of such an approach to ethical decision making lies in applying this analysis to actual incidents. Does this set of guidelines serve to establish the conduct of the turf game in such a way that damage is limited and

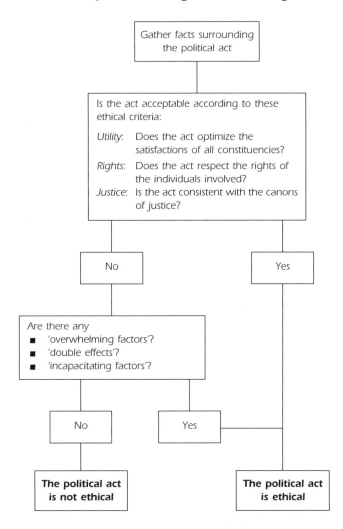

Figure 3.1   **An integrated structure for ethical decisions**

benefits are emphasized? Does this decision tree help clearly to distinguish dirty politics from responsible action? Combining this 'ethics test' with our 'warrants and reputation' framework, we need to ask four questions of each incident:

1   Is the behaviour described here *ethically acceptable?*
2   Did the change driver have a *reasonable warrant* for the behaviour described, given what we know or can presume about the context and stakeholders?
3   Can a *plausible account* be constructed to justify the behaviour described?

4   Was the change driver's *reputation* left intact, strengthened or weakened?

Incident report 1: What the chief executive wants . . .

This incident was reported by one member of an external consulting team working for a local authority in East Central Scotland. The assignment was to introduce structural and cultural change to an organization that had operated in much the same style since the early 1970s. A new chief executive had recently been appointed with this remit. The leader of the consulting team was a long-standing personal friend of the new chief executive.

The annoying thing was, we got this assignment against stiff competition, because we didn't want to sell any one particular solution. They were impressed by our flexibility. Local council, they wanted a review of their 20-year-old officer and member organization structures. In fact they wanted us to present options, maybe simple, maybe radical, from which they could choose, within the constraint of a no redundancy policy. We won the assignment in a presentation to [a policy and resources] sub-committee, mainly councillors, with a couple of senior officers present. The leader of our consulting team was an ex-colleague and friend of the council's new chief executive.

The following week, we were invited to a meeting with the chief executive, to launch the project, agree our liaison mechanisms, find a room to work in, and so on. We spent a couple of hours discussing the logistics, then he asked us if we would have some lunch, and sandwiches and stuff were trayed in. However, as we were hoovering this lot up, he produced a seven-page document, and gave the four of us copies. He worked through this, line by line, for about an hour. This set out what he wanted to see in our final report. Some of this had been in the original brief for the assignment, set out in general terms, and here it was again with some specific recommendations and markers for action, concerning parts of the organization structure and named individuals in specific posts, which were not expected to survive the review. We didn't have as much flexibility as we had thought.

The project rolled out over that year, and our recommendations got firmed up as we collected more information. Basically, this was an autocratically managed, hierarchical, rigid, bureaucratic organization, with lots of time and money wasted on unnecessary procedures and rule following, and with poor staff morale. So our recommendations were going to be about cutting hierarchy, empowering people, changing the management style, making procedures more flexible, getting decisions taken more quickly, and the chief executive was behind all this. The main client was the sub-committee, to which we reported about every quarter. But not before the chief executive had at his request seen an advance copy of the report, commented on it and suggested changes. Quite reasonable, as he would be directly affected by any recommendations about the structure, and also saw himself as a client for our services. This put us in an awkward position. We knew his thinking, and other managers would ask us about that, and we had to fudge answers like, 'That's one of the issues still under consideration.' This also meant we had to build his ideas into our reports, finding some rationale for supporting them, which was important because if questions came up in committee, we would have to explain and defend the point, although he might chip in and voice some agreement with and sympathy for our view from time to time.

Then we started getting bother from one of the councillors, saw himself as an expert in organization theory. He came up with a proposal for a matrix structure with multidisciplinary teamworking. The teamworking was our idea too, partly to address some communications problems. But the matrix wasn't going to fit their business. We got nowhere with the guy in the full committee, so two of us asked him if we could meet him the next day, maybe over lunch, to kick this around. Turned out his concern was not with a matrix at all, but with the way the new director roles would be specified, that they would be like the previous management group (which he didn't trust), just with new titles. So we built the teamworking ('great idea, thanks for that') and a revised role spec into the report, and he bought that.

The chief executive even sub-edited our final report, making changes to the recommendations which we then had to justify. What if we hadn't been able to roll with these pressures? We would have upset the chief executive, who saw our ability to incorporate his thinking as a reflection of our consulting expertise, and we would probably get no more work with this client. If we hadn't handled these individuals, and others, in this sort of way, the whole project could have been at risk, and the time and contributions of a lot of other staff would have been wasted.

Let us consider the four questions posed at the beginning of the chapter.

- First, is the initiator's behaviour *ethically acceptable*?

  From this account, the utilitarian calculus appears to be in favour of the organization as a whole. Changing the structure and culture of this traditional organization will benefit most employees, particularly in the context of a no redundancy policy. However, some senior managers are not expected to 'survive' the review, and their prospects will depend on prior judgements, not on evidence collected in the course of the consulting assignment. Some managers are excluded from key decisions; rights and justice are being violated. Relationships with the new chief executive can be regarded as 'overwhelming' and 'incapacitating' in this respect, effectively preventing the consulting team from acting otherwise.

- Second, did the initiator have a *reasonable warrant* for the behaviour described?

  The initiator has a warrant to facilitate structural and cultural changes which by the late 1990s were commonplace in British local government. The initiator is also concerned with the reputation of the consulting team in the eyes of their clients, particularly the chief executive (who is a potential source of more future consulting business). Further warrant for the initiator's actions can be seen to lie with the disruptive actions (complaints based on personal concerns) of one council member.

- Third, can a *plausible account* be constructed to justify the behaviour described?

Plausibility involves subjective judgement. Exploiting a personal relationship in this manner may attract criticism. However, the small number of 'losers' in this instance are going to be in that category despite the actions of the consulting team. The credibility and professionalism of the consulting team lie partly in achieving the assignment goals, and partly in working with the chief executive to achieve them.

- Finally, is the initiator's *reputation* left intact, strengthened or weakened?

The initiator's reputation in the eyes of the clients – the chief executive and the committee to which the team report – will be maintained and enhanced if the assignment is successful. A reputation for coping with politically sensitive issues will also be enhanced, in the eyes of the chief executive.

Incident report 2: Sidelining the successful salesman

This incident was reported by a senior manager working for a computing company in the British Midlands. As the computing industry became more competitive in the late 1990s, profit margins on hardware fell, and profitability became dependent on sales volume and efficient distribution. Profit margins on advisory or consulting services, however, remained extremely attractive. Our manager was recruited to develop 'professional services', but found himself in conflict with the company's most successful hardware salesman, Simon. Simon was recruited to deal with problems concerning a major customer. He established a good relationship with the customer, generating significant business for the company, and substantial commission payments for himself. The fact that one major account is now controlled by one salesman is recognized as a company problem.

When I came along, that was a threat to him. When I arrived, he was – is – a salesman, and he holds the largest account that we have. In fact, 75 per cent of my business comes through that one account, and 40 per cent of the company's turnover comes through that account. So he's quite an influential man, a key player.

He got off on the wrong foot. The very first day I met him . . . first of all he called me 'Mr Project Manager', which I don't take offence to. The second line he came out with was, 'You realize that when I want to get rid of you, I'll get rid of you?' Now, I'd been in the company for all of three days when this line came out. I'm not somebody that backs down. I take that as a threat, I really did. I didn't enjoy that at all. Once he had said that, he'd got trouble on his hands. So I guess that I've been a little rough – a little abrasive in my approach towards him on occasion.

But you have to look at the background. The relationship with the client is actually between himself and one other person. And that other person just happens to be in the position where he can spend a lot of money. Whether it's wisely spent or not is neither here nor there. The organization for which he works is huge, very poorly organized internally, especially in IT. So you have a very personal relationship, to the point of best man at each other's wedding, so it's not a professional relationship.

Of course, I came along and I looked at the situation and, somewhat unwisely, I probably expressed my opinion about the whole thing. I said, OK, well, we've got a lot of good business there, but it's not the way that we want to go forward, this isn't what our group of people does, it isn't going to work that way. Well, that immediately put him on the defensive.

The task of the professional services manager was to amalgamate four separate departments, to create a professional services section and to develop that aspect of the business. This meant absorbing two of Simon's staff, and also changing the way services would be provided – and charged – to Simon's main customer, as well as to other customers.

I challenged his authority. Simple as that. He wants adulation. That's the sort of personality he has. He's a very insecure man. My figures didn't convince him, but unfortunately they convinced others. So he was at that time on the management team. There was myself, the financial director and the general manager. Simon was on the management team but he didn't contribute a lot. He used to do a stand-up act on the whiteboard, show all his figures for the next month. He has this wonderful talent of changing between foreign currencies, so you're never quite sure what's on the board. You don't know whether it's a million in one currency or a million in another, which can be a huge difference. I think that's one of the things he does on purpose. And Simon feels he is able to manipulate in the background, to challenge you through the back door. He has various means of doing this.

The first one, which is the most common, is he has a way of capturing all your emails. I also think I know who it is that does it for him, which unfortunately is somebody in my team, so I have a double problem here. I know that he keeps it on the general manager, he keeps it on the finance director, he certainly keeps it on the guy who used to run field services because he's publicized it twice. I know that all of my messages are captured. Simple answer to that is, you don't put anything in there that can be incriminating – I do things like that by phone. I assume that he can't record the phone. I'm told that he holds a personal file on everybody, and I must have one so thick, and I don't know what he's got in there. A twist in the tail is that Simon refuses to use email, because he doesn't believe it's safe.

The second thing that he does, because of his very good relationship with the customer, he can keep me out of there. That has come unstuck because I got involved in something – same client, separate department – and I got involved personally, by default, not planned on my behalf. As time has gone on, I have got more involved in that, and my position, my power in that part of the organization, has become stronger. This is very worrying for my friend Simon, because he doesn't have any friends in that side. So I've sort of closed that door off too.

His next thing was, through the management team . . . you'd be stunned at how childish some of the things are that affect him. We were due to have the

Christmas party a few weeks back. Just before it, I had to stay at home for a few days, and I sent a message out advising that something was happening. In fact it was a job had started in Taiwan, and I sent out the details and I copied Simon, it's his account, let's be open about it. And I sent these details out. Unfortunately Simon didn't know anything about this at all, until I sent them. And he took that as a big offence. Why was he not involved in the sales process? Why hadn't he been informed? With that, as I would term it, the toys came out of the pram. 'I'm no longer going to the Christmas party if he's going there. And I'm resigning from the management team.' Well, he didn't go to the party. And the management team haven't missed him.

We went out to Poland, and that was my manager being devious, because I was sat in a conference call and Simon was on the call. This was before what is potentially the largest single project that the company, globally, has ever had. This is the one that I'm programme managing at the moment, which Simon can't get his fingers on, which is a huge problem for him. The first country we're working on is Poland. Simon said, we're going out there to meet some suppliers and so on, during this conference call. My director in London said, I think you should be with Simon on that one, we'll make the arrangements from here. And I sat there on the other end of the conference call thinking, do I want to go? I had no interest in going at all, but he said, just get yourself there and see what he's doing.

So he put me out there just to keep tabs on him. And while I was there, in the hotel, it turned out that Simon had made no appointments. We arrived on the Sunday night, there was nothing to do on the Monday, so I made all the arrangements and managed to see several suppliers and parts of our organization out there as well. On the Monday evening, we arranged to meet for dinner, and I had a phone call about half an hour before. 'This is Denise, from such and such escort agency, I understand that you like blondes, we can't make it for quarter past but we'll have somebody to you at quarter to seven; would you like me to send them up to your room?' And I said, terribly sorry, I think that somebody's been playing a rather unpleasant game with you here and – this is Simon trying to trap me. I don't know how he would do it, but he would have photographs or whatever.

I have a long-term strategy here. I know that in order to either get him to change, or to get rid of him, my department has to take a controlling hand in his account. That is where all of his power comes from. It's not his personality, it's not his background, he doesn't have friends in high places. It comes purely from that account. So, I have to take control of that. And I do that through selecting and motivating and encouraging my team to go in there with a certain agenda. Number one is do the job properly. I would never put that second. I think that would reflect badly on me. So it would work against me if I said, make the job go badly. The second thing is that you're in there to sell. Consultative selling; look for opportunities, look for areas where we can spread further in there, stay clear of the internal politics because they're not going to do you any favours. Their political situation is far worse than the one that I deal with. And just make yourself very important in there. Make it so that the business is coming through you. Keep Simon in copy of everything you do. But if you are developing the order yourself, if you're bringing that order out, and then you inform Simon, what's Simon's purpose in there any more? He's no longer required. His power is getting less, to the point where I think he'll know that he no longer has any influence and on he'll move from that. So the politics, my fighting against him, is working on behalf of the organization.

So, bit by bit, I squeeze him tighter and tighter. I think another six months to a year and I'll have him out. Which is nasty, I know. I consider that to be a professional approach. I consider that because I don't believe that his attitude and his motivators are for the good of the organization. Whereas I consider mine to be.

You have to have sparring partners. You have to have people you can bounce ideas off, and in some ways politics can be used as that sounding board. Fighting against people, yes, but there are good things coming out of that. The new experiences that are being learned which are good for the individual. My sparring with Simon is beneficial to the organization, because they know they cannot rely on one person, especially somebody as temperamental as that, to run with one contract which has such a large percentage of the revenue. Putting somebody like me in there who is abrasive, who will not lie down and surrender, somebody who will fight against it, is working on behalf of the organization, and the fights that I have with Simon will actually give me insight into the next move – how do I go on to the next stage, I've done this to him, kicked the pedestal away and he's now the same level as everybody else – his role is diminishing, what's the next stage in that? How do you actually learn what the next move is within that arena?

What will be the consequences of this political strategy for Simon and his career?

Yes it can be damaging and time-consuming. We've had a number of situations recently where Simon has threatened to resign. I very nearly had enough of it. Just couldn't be bothered with the fighting any more. So there are times when it becomes a very negative thing. But I believe the outcome will be positive for the organization. I've not sat and worked it out on paper, but there is a cost-benefit there.

The fact that Simon might be thrown on the streets at the end of this, the fact that he's 37 years old and possibly is going to struggle to get another job, recently married, hoping for children . . . actually doesn't come into it at all. In my perception, he is damaging to the company, and he is certainly damaging to me, so he's got to go. Or change. I'll give him the choice. He can do one or the other.

I think that Simon will probably leave. I think that the days of the cowboy box-selling salesman are limited. We're developing professional services. Simon will be in a world which I don't believe he understands. I don't think he can thrive in that world. And I think he will have a lot of difficulty in gaining credibility elsewhere. He may move into another organization, but he'll be the new boy on the block. Unless he gets results very quickly, he's not going to regain his old position. And I think that his career will go backwards. You play with fire, you get burned.

Let us again consider the four questions posed at the beginning of the chapter.

- First, is the initiator's behaviour towards the target *ethically acceptable*?

From this account, the utilitarian calculus appears to be in favour of the organization as a whole, considering the medium- to long-term development of the business. However, individual rights are clearly being damaged in the process. Justice is being seen not to be done in relation to the target, Simon, who is being systematically excluded from key business developments. The 'overwhelming factors' which could be cited here relate to the radically changing nature of the business in this sector. The initiator's actions clearly have a 'double effect' in developing the business while damaging the target's career prospects. The initiator faces 'incapacitating factors' in applying ethical rules to the extent that his own corporate responsibilities and personal reputation are being put at risk by the target's actions.

- Second, did the initiator have a *reasonable warrant* for the behaviour described?

The initiator has a corporate warrant to develop the professional services dimension of the business. The initiator is also concerned with the achievement of personal goals, the enhancement of personal reputation, with 'doing a good job', and with ensuring that colleagues act professionally and effectively. A further warrant for the initiator's actions can be seen to lie with the target's own actions (using personal friendship to enhance company and personal income; capturing confidential email; threats of withdrawal; entrapment) which are themselves ethically questionable.

- Third, can a *plausible account* be constructed to justify the behaviour described?

While acknowledging almost certain and serious damage to the target's future prospects, at a potentially critical stage in his career, the initiator develops a compelling justification for comparatively extreme actions. The warrant for those actions is extensive, strengthening the plausibility of this account.

- Finally, is the initiator's *reputation* left intact, strengthened or weakened?

Whatever the views of the outside reader in this case, the initiator's reputation in the organization seems likely to be strengthened considerably. The target is a 'known problem'. The strategy for handling this appears to be effective. The initiator is also enhancing his reputation based on his effective business development.

Incident report 3: Love letters in cyberspace

There is an affair going on in the group, and it's by the field services director and a lady from logistics. And it is so sickeningly open. In fact it has now caused his downfall. He's been removed from that position. It just doesn't work any more. They send each other letters. I've no idea what's in them. I've no interest in what's in them. But some people do. One morning, on the public drive of the server, a complete collection of these letters appeared.

Now the reason for that is the person who put them there wants to get rid of the field services manager. Doesn't like him, never has done. One of them in particular had references to the general manager. Bad move on behalf of the guy that wrote it, of course, but they were there. Now, what is ethical about that? To me, that is a private matter which, if it was so important that it needed to be brought to the attention of the general manager, it should be taken to him and not everybody else. Other people don't need to know that.

That's a personal attack in my opinion. You can look at it from different points of view. He was using his GSM phone to send the messages, by a system called SMS which is very expensive. So it was probably costing the company over £1,000 to send this collection of emails. Plus there was the time being wasted doing it, the time of the lady from logistics.

You can be far more underhand and damaging without being personal about it. And it doesn't help the company at all. I think that . . . putting it on a public drive and letting people know, there's 65 people in the office, and it went round there. I get in very early. I'm usually one of the first if not the first one there. One of my team turned up that morning at quarter to eight, which was very early for him as well, and came in and said, 'Very important news, I've got to tell you about this.' And automatically I knew where the information had come from and how it had been put there. By the time nine o'clock had arrived, everybody knows about it. Everybody knows that this man, who is married, is not happy with his life, and we all know why, because it's written down for us to read about it, and we all know precisely what he does with his girlfriend. I'm sorry, but . . .

Incident report 4: The management development programme

I think political behaviour is being able to get your own agenda through, possibly through means that wouldn't normally work, or through routes that aren't direct. For example, when we originally set up the management development programme, that was driven by a small group of senior officers who wanted it to happen. I sat on the senior officers' working group, but the interesting thing was, out of that group, if you really wanted to get something done, you knew there were only two or three of them that you needed to influence. The political game for me was making sure that what I wanted and what they wanted actually lined up, and then we knew we could get it. But it was also watching the other alliances in that group. Politics to me in the organization is about knowing who's in with who and who's out of favour now, so that you don't actually back the wrong horse.

It's about knowing the key individuals, the opinion leaders, and knowing the alliances that exist between them and others on the same level. I think, you almost need to know who's sleeping with whom. There's a wonderful tale of the leader of the Conservative group on a particular city council, having the chief executive's secretary moved from her post because she was sleeping with the leader of the Labour group, and he didn't want confidential discussions with the chief executive being reported back to the opposition. Is that a political decision? It's about who you influence and who's in and who's out. So, if you're dealing with politicians, the elected member, it's about what alliances there are in the groups, because there's no point a chief executive or a senior officer talking to X, if X is not in favour with the decision makers in that group, and you know that. Similarly if I want to get the department to do something, it's about who do I need to speak to, and who's actually in the position of influencing the chief officer that this is a good thing? Now, sometimes you can go direct to the chief officer because it's quite obvious that if you can convince them, you've solved it. Other times, you need more subtle ways in.

Well, the management development programme became political because a group of deputy chief officers were worried that we did nothing about corporate management development. We were very good at doing postgraduate and post-experience, post-qualification training for people to get higher qualifications. And departments did their own thing. So, we got people doing a myriad of stuff, and we were also using a national higher management development programme, but the cost was such we could only send two or three people a year. And they were worried that nowhere had we got a critical mass of managers whose thought processes were going in the same way, such as to be able to influence the direction of the authority in a rapidly changing environment.

They got on board the chief exec's PA, who is the current chief exec, and they engineered this being raised because Jack had briefed the chief exec. They engineered this being raised at the chief officer's management team, knowing that they'd got the support of the chief exec. So after the discussion, he was able to steer it in a way that said, yes, we ought to explore this. Then, Steve also had to . . . when they got a bit further and said, yes, we want to do this, but in order to do it we need a post, or two posts, we need money . . . he was able to move the elected members by judiciously lobbying the key members that this was a good thing.

Incident report 5: Telling tales really, uncomfortably

About six months after the organizational change, in another part of the organization, I was attacked by one of the managers. I think he used the fact that he was on his own territory to pass on information to me that he thought . . . I think he was saying, my territory, I decide what happens here, it doesn't matter what you lot say we should be doing, this is what I'm doing here. Now, in response to that, I managed to, through my network of people, pass on that message. I wasn't very comfortable about how I should deal with this information. So I brought it to the attention of someone very quickly, who would be far more comfortable in passing this up the chain to senior management. Probably within half an hour, the message that he had passed to me had moved up to the top of the organization, he was brought in, this individual manager, and put on a far tighter chain for a period of time.

It was a bit like telling tales really, but it was telling tales in a way that . . . he knew very well that it was me, but I hadn't formally done anything about it. It was a very quick response to the information he passed on to me. Purely because, I think, the person I passed the information on to was quite well placed to go to the senior manager whose ear we were seeking, to attract him into taking action about it quite quickly. I genuinely think I don't engage in that kind of thing very often, and I don't think I instigate it – more in response to what other people do.

Incident report 6: Swing the budget, vilify the opposition

When I went to work with the council, the biggest problem they faced was a major budget deficit. They had built a new organization which planned to spend £140 million because that was the cost of the services they had to provide, on the basis of disaggregation of the budgets of the three constituent authorities which the new council comprised. But their rate-capped expenditure limit was £129 million. So they had a major, fundamental error.

And so £11 million had to be taken out of the budget virtually before the organization started. There was a big lobby to protect education, and the big battles were between expenditure on education, social services and central support services. And the chair of the education programme area and committee and the director of education, in advance of any sort of rational assessment of expenditure priorities, started a campaign which was aimed at suggesting that if any reductions were made in proposed education expenditure, then a secondary school would opt out of local authority control and go for grant-maintained status. To a prospective unitary authority, the thought of losing a school in its first year as an education authority was a frightening thought.

Much more frightening than concern over expenditure on social services because the education lobby is much more able to mobilize . . . much more middle-class, more articulate. The social services lobby takes a bit of time to get out on the streets and it's not as attractive as the education lobby. The halt, the lame and the blind don't turn people on. So, that campaign was started right up front, so that any critical examination of expenditure in the education area was effectively cut off.

Now to make that stick, because reduction in expenditure has got to be found in another area, the same director and chair (elected member) began a campaign of complete vilification of the two people – political and officer management – in the social services area. So they were portrayed as incompetent, and as 'waving shrouds' to use the health service term. So that set up a platform in which social services expenditure would be very critically examined.

The surrounding politics of all of this were, you had a new local authority which was the amalgamation of two district and one county council. The county elected members just disappeared from the scene, so the new council was comprised of ex-district members. One district had always been strongly Labour-controlled, and the other council had tended to be balanced with Labour and the Tories, who were in a very small minority, combining in an unholy alliance to keep the Liberal Democrats out of power. There was not a lot of love lost between the two Labour groups when they were brought together to form the new council, although these were neighbouring authorities and to the naked eye you could hardly tell the difference between the two. None the less, they didn't particularly like each other.

So you got a battle over who was going to take control. Both politically and at officer level, the Labour people had most of the positions of influence. The chief executive of the new authority was from the Labour-dominated council, as was the guy who was heading up the area which included education. They had been rivals for the job of chief executive. There were two factions, maybe three, on the old Labour-dominated council and they carried over to the new council. The leader of the new council had been elected as much really because the other two factions couldn't unite against her so that was a positive vote for her, which is very typical in a local authority. That had led to the appointment of a new chief executive, not by a consensus of members on the employment panel but by a formal vote and a split vote, and he got the job by one vote. That meant that several powerful members on the council did not think he should be chief executive, would not have appointed him, and made that quite clear.

The guy who was now running the education area, one of the four programme area directors, was the guy who didn't get the job. And the chair of the education area was his main supporter and the main opponent of the leader of the council, and therefore a guy who was highly critical of the new chief executive.

In that context, the politics of it were that, the chief executive, rather than facing this piece of manipulation head on and saying, now hang on, we're treating education with absolutely kid gloves, and we should be looking at it more critically because there are some important issues in social services which you don't really understand and you can't afford to underfund them, decided that he didn't think his position was strong enough to do that, therefore he went with the flow and joined in the ritual mauling of the social services area.

Incident report 7: Quality tactics

As a 'traditional' university, we had never had to face any kind of systematic audit of our teaching quality. So mounting a response to this in 1994–5 meant putting in place a lot of new procedures and documentation that we never had before, and also tidying up processes that had decayed somewhat. It also meant changing staff behaviour, with regard to teaching preparation and keeping records and files, and standardizing student handout material on courses, and also with lecture theatre – and tutorial room – behaviour. But we were also facing a research assessment exercise in 1996–7. Putting so much effort and resource into teaching quality inevitably meant reducing the time and energy available for research.

Well, the senior staff in the department, mostly the professors, looked at the options. We could do nothing, concentrate on improving our research rating, we were one of the top 10 in the UK, and accept a lousy teaching rating. Or we could concentrate on research while doing just enough to get a 'satisfactory' rating on teaching, not too damaging. Or we could push the boat out and go for teaching excellence. I reached my conclusion on these options pretty quickly, and most of the rest of the top team agreed. It would reflect badly on the university as a whole if we got a lousy rating. No other department had at that time been rated excellent on teaching. It would reflect badly on the department within the university if we went down. People could use that to block and snipe at all sorts of initiatives we wanted to put in place. How would it affect staff morale, retention and recruitment if we got a poor rating? And I didn't want to be known as the department head that botched this one, on the campus or off.

However, there were a couple of voices, one in particular, in the senior group who disagreed with this, felt we should do little or nothing to change our teaching activity, and concentrate on research output instead. A reasonable view, which we did consider, but which the majority decided was unrealistic. We reasoned with these guys, at length, and they saw they were outnumbered at an early stage. I thought, naïvely, they would accept the decision and pull along with it. Not a chance. One guy in particular wouldn't let it go, kept bringing the issue to committee meetings, kept getting the junior staff agitated about this – were they doing the right thing, should they be thinking of promotion and publishing instead? At first this was just annoying and time wasting. But it soon became damaging, in terms of the arguments other staff were getting into, in terms of the credibility of the top team and the approach we had decided on collectively. The rest of the team wanted something done about this.

So I kept up a pattern of spoiling tactics to keep this voice down. We had pre-meetings without him, to decide how decisions would go so that he would have less opportunity to argue an opposing case. My secretary put any issue that he wanted added to a meeting agenda at the end of the list, so we would have no time to discuss it properly. We just made some decisions in his absence, didn't tell him about a meeting. I spent a bit of time with a small number of the 'opinion leaders' among the junior staff, making sure they knew what was happening and why, that they accepted we needed to go for this teaching quality rating at this time, and hoping they would spread the message along to the others. We also had full department briefings about the exercise, which were led mainly from the front. And I hate to admit that it wasn't difficult to spread a little innuendo here and there, with academic and secretarial staff, to damage the guy's credibility, make him look less than competent on certain issues. Colleagues helped with this without prompting from me.

I don't see how I could have acted much differently in the circumstances, without accepting damage to my own reputation, as well as that of my department and perhaps the institution. And I think he knew that a lot of this was going on anyway. I don't regard any of this as unethical. On the contrary, to have ignored the issue, or to have just walked away from it, would have been difficult for me to defend. We got the 'excellent' rating.

Incident report 8: Fraud and retribution

I had a situation, I was working as a project manager in Sheffield, and I got the impression that the team that I was working with, the two senior people in that team, were doing something dishonest. In fact I was convinced of it. They'd brought on a new contractor. I recognized the pricing that we were putting out was becoming higher and higher. I knew the sorts of margin that we were making, and I could see that something was wrong. You then match that up with Bob gets a new colour television and a holiday in Majorca with his three children, and I had a fair idea of where his salary was and I knew it wasn't that high. And Steve, whose wife has just left him, manages to sell the house, pay £12,000, get himself a new washing machine, dishwasher and microwave, new girlfriend with dresses and all the rest of it. And I'm thinking that there's something wrong with the finances here. I made that, in an implicit way, fairly clear, that I believed something was going on and I knew what it was.

Bob was a sharp man, a sharp political mover, he obviously realized what was going on as well. The next thing I saw was, I came in one day and there was a couple of cards on my desk from recruitment agencies. I'd never called a recruitment agency, and there were the cards sitting there. I then had a phone call from a recruitment agency, and then another one. I thought, headhunter, looking for senior people, you think that's good, I like the sound of that. So you go along with it. You realize that it's not a senior position at all, it's just someone who's been given your name. You don't need to be a genius to put the two together here. So what I could have done was challenge them about it, said why are you doing this, what is in it for you, if you want to get rid of me why don't you just say so, why don't you be a man about it? So I thought, OK, stick to the job, get the job done. I can't afford to fail on the job or else that will follow me along.

I contacted one of the directors of the company, and suggested to him that I may be looking for a move within the company. I met him in a hotel and gave him a brief outline of why I was not happy and why I wanted to move on. I didn't tell him that I thought something untoward was going on. I didn't tell him that I'd had cards on my desk. I just said that the relationship was not working, that we had professional differences, and that I felt it was time for me to use my skills elsewhere. I was offered a more senior position in our head office at that time, which was outside London, and I moved away from that situation. Now, the reason I'm saying this is, there are ways that you can use it to your best advantage. I felt that I could use this situation.

More importantly, I felt that if I'm . . . retribution . . . I felt that if I stayed within the company, a company I know quite well, then I would get my chance later on. This is going to sound very bad, I know it is, but if I'd have got the position that I applied for, I would actually have been their boss. And if I return in 11 months time to the position which could be open to me, I will be their boss. And you harbour these thoughts for many, many years. I still harbour it now. I know which one of them is the brighter of the two. I know which one of them leads it. I know who plays the political games, and I know that I'll keep him and sack the other because it breaks up their team.

Incident report 9: The true purpose of truth

What's the most devious thing I have done? This is not self-effacing modesty that's causing me to think for a moment, because I'm as capable or as willing to do it as the next person. Well, if I can answer in a generic way, one of the skills of playing this game is to some extent being able to present yourself to other people in a way which, while not agreeing with things with which you don't agree, somehow also not disagreeing, if disagreeing is going to cause alienation and therefore put hurdles in the way to achieving the goal that you want to achieve. I mean, my wife would say that, in that sense, I am unprincipled because I will ask what gain or disadvantage it might cause me in the circumstances.

In a social context, I would rationalize that by saying, if you're at a party then there is no particular value in upsetting somebody. Often people come to you, don't they, and in social situations people make, I think, very strong statements of personal belief which are often said without calculating the impact that they have on other people. And you have two choices. One is to take up the cudgels and say, that's the most stupid thing I've heard in my life. And establish the case why that's the fact. Or, is it the economic analogy of social interaction – if there's no particular gain in doing that, the gain might be calculated in terms of, you think they are idiots and therefore you pursue the argument because, what the hell, it doesn't matter. Or it might be the negative game of, this is a quite good party and I really like the host or hostess, and I don't want to cause a blazing row in the middle of it and upset everybody's evening.

And I would apply that in organizational terms. I am quite happy to let people think that I agree with them and I'm on their side, if that suits my purpose at the time. And I think I've got the skills of doing that, without blatantly lying.

I suppose, and what goes with that is . . . I would, if somebody is then being run down in the organization, somebody that I'm opposed to, if I thought they were unfairly being run down, and it suited my purposes that they would continue to be denigrated, then I wouldn't step in and stop it, and say, well, look in the interests of fair play and so on. I'll quite happily sit to one side and . . . I suppose I would only stand up for people if I thought there was an advantage to be gained.

I'd draw a differentiation there between managers at the same sort of level, as opposed to direct reports. In the sense that, and I don't know whether this is a moral point or a practical point, but I think direct reports, people like personal assistants, then I think you actually have a duty to fight their corner because they are relatively weak organizationally. If they're not any good then you should do something about it. But if they're OK, then I think you should protect people like that. You do have a degree of duty and loyalty.

But for the people in the competitive group, you don't have any particular duty of loyalty to, so their success or failure is an instrumental thing as far as I am concerned. Fair game. There must have been occasions where I've been prepared to lie, on the facts as I saw them, to gain a particular end. I just can't think that I wouldn't have done that. It's a bit like . . . goes back to what we said earlier about what people admit to doing and what they actually do. Nobody ever admits to fiddling their expenses; although because everybody fiddles their expenses, you'd be a very foolish person to ever admit to fiddling yours, because that would be something which people would never forget you'd said. However honest you'd been, you'd be dead in the water. The reality is, we have all fiddled our expenses to some degree, at some time, for whatever reason. Just happened to need a few quid at that time. But you just wouldn't say that in public, would you. That would be a career-threatening admission to make. What you learn as you go through your career, and get more experienced, is how to present these things, and rationalize these things, in an acceptable way.

Incident report 10: Frustrate you, frustrate me in return

When I was director of personnel and management services at [a London council], the Labour group was in a strong majority, but it was, as all Labour groups are, riven with factions. And it was under the control of what you might call 'the soft left', the leader of which was probably more by default than by positive choice. For some reason, factions don't get themselves organized as well as they could, and when all the offices – bit like the shadow cabinet – all the chairs of committee and all the group offices are elected, and while people broadly belong to a single faction, they don't always vote completely for the slate.

So you get some rather freakish results. The staff and management services committee was under the control of the London Labour Briefing Group, which was 'the hard left', in the days when [a well-known Labour politician] represented the hard left. He was a sort of populist, opportunist politician, but some of his fellow travellers were genuine hard left. His long time live-in companion was a woman – Karen – who was christened by one of my staff as Vinegar Lil. She really was a thoroughly unpleasant person. And she hadn't been on the appointment panel which appointed me, and I had several disadvantages in her eyes, which were to do with the fact that I was white, male and middle-aged. OK, I could understand that. She was involved in what was then called 'the rainbow coalition' in politics. Her primary concern was equality of opportunity. She had a sidekick, and they alternated between being chair and vice-chair of this committee. It was actually quite a powerful committee, controlling more than it really should have done in terms of where resource was spent on staffing. It was superordinate to the service committees in these areas.

Her sidekick was called Sarah, who was a genuine working-class London Labour Briefing hard-liner. Karen was more of a middle-class carpet-bagger in my view. Ironically I got on OK with Sarah, who was a sort of not-quite-out lesbian – didn't get on at all with Karen, and I don't think they really liked one another.

The leadership of the council, their group secretary, phoned me up one day in the middle of all the sort of difficulties they were having with expenditure and rate-capping . . . making 2,000 people redundant, very awkward industrial relations . . . they'd just had their group elections and Karen had been re-elected to chair the committee. I got a call from the group secretary saying, we'd like to meet you in the pub in a back street of somewhere tomorrow night. Come alone. So, I come alone, there's a group of the secretary, chief whip, deputy leader, and they said, right, Karen has been elected chair of this committee, we don't like that, your role is to frustrate everything that she does and report back to us, so that we know exactly what she's plotting and planning against us. And, by the way, if she finds out or gets any hint of this or complains, this conversation has never taken place. And if it comes to it, well, you'll have to go. But really, you haven't got much choice, have you, because if you don't do it, you'll really upset us?

So, I guess I did it, because I didn't want to get out of the organization. Eventually as the dawning realization of just how downhill the organization had gone, value for money, the need there was for behavioural change and radical surgery of cutting out large chunks of expenditure with it, getting rid of a lot of people who needed to go, that did happen. And I was fairly instrumental in getting that change of thinking in the leadership. Along with that, all of the hard left people were swept from office and replaced by people who were much more prepared to take these very difficult decisions.

So that was fairly devious on their part, and was fairly devious on my part, although I couldn't really see that I had much choice and I just had to walk the line. Even the chief executive didn't know that this conversation had taken place.

Now one of the things I did to manage this situation was, I had a vacancy for an assistant director, and I was getting a lot of grief from the women's unit, who felt that I wasn't pushing personnel policies which were to their liking. I thought, well, perhaps a smart thing to do, instead of battling with these people all the time, is to try and incorporate them. So, I suggested to the person who was my most arch-critic and thorn in my side that, while this post was being filled, why didn't she come and be the acting director for a few months? That would help us become much more communitarian, in the areas that she was concerned about, and it would be excellent experience for her, and it would build bridges. And of course my thinking was, this would reduce the criticism and endear me not only to her but to Karen, who was, I think, vice-chair of the women's committee as well as chair of the staff and management services committee.

So for a while this worked. The woman was totally incompetent. I mean, she really was absolutely incompetent. The women's unit was a collective and therefore you had five people paid the same pay; they shared all the jobs; they only worked part-time; but they were paid overtime from the end of their part-time hours whereas nobody else got overtime unless they'd had a full working week. However, she was a real pain in the arse this woman, because she wasn't particularly competent and because she was a neurotic wreck. But nonetheless, I stayed with that. It backfired on me when she of course decided to put in for the permanent post. Now, I wasn't too worried about that at the time, because I was fairly confident that a decent field of candidates would come forward, and her shortcomings would be obvious.

When it came to it so the full appointment panel, chaired by Karen, chair of the management services committee, got agreement to there just being three members on the appointment panel; herself, Sarah the vice-chair, and the chair of the women's unit committee, with the head of the women's unit and head of the race unit as the advising officers in addition to me as the chief officer. So I was absolutely stuffed. While there were two very good candidates, one a black man, the other a white woman who really knew their stuff and demonstrated it in the selection process – whereas this other woman wasn't able to answer a lot of the questions.

The five – three members and the two officers – had all previously agreed that whatever the outcome they were going to appoint this woman. And of course they all just sat there and said, well in our view she best meets the person specification, that's our judgement, we've followed a proper procedure. They exercised their judgement. Their judgement was entirely biased. As we came out of this interview panel, the head of the race unit said to me, well, sorry about this, I know she's a complete and utter incompetent and a pain in the arse, but from my point of view I'm going to go along with these people because this is another woman in a senior position, and I've got a bigger agenda that I need to coalesce with.

What did they gain? Well, I think Karen would rationalize it and say that she gained a woman in a senior management position, and even if in her heart of hearts she would admit the woman was incompetent, nonetheless I think she would be able to come up with an organizational argument which would say, increasing the number of women in top echelons as changing the style of the organization, advancing the case for women generally, and even if the odd one was incompetent – well, a lot of incompetent men have been appointed, haven't they? Which would be impossible to disagree with. And on balance there were gains for the organization. There were all sorts of subgoals; it was making life difficult for me, it was establishing with other members and officers that she could impose her will in the organization. It was a message to white males, and so on.

Interestingly, at the end of all this, I left to go to a large management consultancy organization, and by that time the hard left had been swept from office, but I had continued to get on OK with Sarah, and I had a beer with her before I left. She said, 'I know we made your – deliberately, it was nothing personal – we made your life very difficult. After wider political goals, but just for the record, as far as I am concerned, you were OK and a lot of the things that you did I was happy with, but there were other fish to fry.' And it wasn't just about equality policy. There were other issues which the hard left . . . were opposed to cuts in expenditure, they wanted illegal budgets set, no rates set, so their agenda was the disruption of the system.

Incident report 11: Your assignment, my change project

I was working for an organization, not this one, and the person I was working for was doing a management course. There was a change approach I really wanted this person to take, and I was trying to persuade them. So they had to do a piece of work, and because it was a practical management course, they had to relate to their situation. So, I wrote it for this person. Basically, a piece of work which was the change strategy I wanted this person to follow. So, I wrote it in their name. It was about why doing this change process was the best thing they could possibly do in the circumstances. And they handed it in. I would call this devious because I wanted . . . it was highly manipulative, because I wanted that person to listen and do this thing I wanted them to do. So the way I persuaded them to do it was for them to write a piece of work which set out the thing which I wanted them to do. I wrote it in their name – and they did it.

The assignment got a very, very good grade. And he did all of it. It was very successful. That worked. I had built up the case for doing this thing I wanted him to do, bit by bit, step by step. He bought into it in a way that he wouldn't have if I had just tried to persuade him in other ways. But he owned this piece of work, which is what I wanted him to do.

A framework for comparative judgements

What do these accounts reveal? The answer lies mainly in how you, the reader, judge such accounts of political behaviour. Table 3.2 provides for reference a summary overview of the main political behaviours used by the initiators in each incident.

Each account shows a central figure, an 'initiator', drawn into covert influence tactics by features of the context, by personal motives, and by the behaviours of other actors – who may become 'targets'. On their own, these tactics can be regarded as highly objectionable. We are considering the deliberate manipulation of agendas by key figures, at the transmission of damaging information to exact damage, at ignoring evidence in favour of personal desires, at presenting a false view of change for personal advantage, at mechanisms for discrediting and 'sidelining' opposition, at conscious and deliberate deceit, at blackmail, at revenge, at the wilful manipulation of appointments for personal and political ends, at academic cheating, and at manipulating critics into consent and silence.

How did you judge these incidents? Are such examples rare or typical in your experience? Are the behaviours described acceptable and common-place in your view, or disreputable and abhorrent? Table 3.3 offers a framework for judgement. For each of the 11 incident reports, how would you answer the four questions posed earlier, with respect to the 'ethics test', warrant, accounting, and reputation? It would be useful if, instead of exercising this judgement alone, you have an opportunity to exchange views on these incidents with other readers, with other managers – and with other change drivers.

What happens when we attempt to hold these incidents against the 'ethics test' set out in Figure 3.1? The first problem is that the 'facts' surrounding the political act are incomplete, difficult if not impossible to establish after the event, and are of course biased by the perspective of the narrator in each incident. In addition, many of the 'facts' are unlikely to be evident even to close observers and participants at the time, given their 'backstage' character. Without a fuller knowledge of the context, it is also difficult to hold particular behaviours against the ethical criteria of utility, rights and justice. Few, if any, of these incidents are completely 'clean' and can travel directly down the right-hand branch of the decision tree. Most, if not all, seem to fail one test or other; personal gains are being pursued at

Table 3.2 **Examples of political behaviour**

Incident report	Political behaviours of the initiators
1. What the chief executive wants . . .	Running a consulting assignment to meet the specific wishes of the chief executive and some other influential figures, despite what information collection, consultation and analysis might suggest.
2. Sidelining the successful salesman	Undermining the work of a successful individual whose style is not consistent with business development plans, and who is himself a devious political player.
3. Love letters in cyberspace	Publicizing love letters concerning an illicit affair, to discredit and remove a manager for personal reasons.
4. The management development programme	Deliberately targeting key individuals and exploiting known alliances. Lobbying one key individual in particular to bring issue to the attention of chief executive and put on agenda of management team.
5. Telling tales really, uncomfortably	Dealing with a threat by informing another senior manager, who in turn quickly engineered a reprimand for the person raising the threat in the first place.
6. Swing the budget, vilify the opposition	Exploiting a weak chief executive, and discrediting the opposition by picking on their weak spots, by showing them as incompetent, to obtain cuts in their budget and not the initiators' budgets.
7. Quality tactics	Dealing with an opponent by exclusion from meetings and decisions, by agenda manipulation, by information dissemination through public forums, and by circulating discrediting information.
8. Fraud and retribution	Using the fraudulent activities of others to secure a promoted post, from which to return in a senior position to remove at least one of the offenders from the organization.
9. The true purpose of truth	Declaring agreement and support, rather than admit disagreement and conflict, to maintain relationships for personal advantage, even if this means lying (but not if it means exploiting politically weak individuals).
10. Frustrate you, frustrate me in return	Senior managers blackmailing someone into frustrating the work of a widely disliked committee chair. 'Incorporating' critics by appointing one of their number to a key position, despite their incompetence. 'Stacking' an appointments panel to ensure that the 'right' (although incompetent) candidate gets appointed to a permanent position for political and symbolic reasons, including revenge.
11. Your assignment, my change project	Writing an academic course assignment for someone to submit in their own name, to persuade them to undertake a particular organizational change, which was the topic of the assignment.

the expense of organizations and colleagues; individuals are being sidelined in the pursuit of personal goals; due process is being ignored to advance change initiatives.

Most of these incidents founder on the branch of the decision tree that leads into overwhelming and incapacitating factors, and double effects. There are considerable grounds for claims that ethical criteria are inappropriate, or non-applicable, or have to be ignored because of special

Table 3.3 **A framework for judgement**

Incident report	Pass the ethics test?	Warrant?	Account?	Reputation?
1. What the chief executive wants . . .				
2. Sidelining the successful salesman				
3. Love letters in cyberspace				
4. The management development programme				
5. Telling tales really, uncomfortably				
6. Swing the budget, vilify the opposition				
7. Quality tactics				
8. Fraud and retribution				
9. The true purpose of truth				
10. Frustrate you, frustrate me in return				
11. Your assignment, my change project				

issues. The 'overwhelming factors' box is thus full of potential excuses, mitigating circumstances, escape clauses and 'fudge factors'. A key skill in the turf game lies in constructing plausible accounts if and when one is accused of acting in a potentially unethical manner. The fudge factors offer much scope for creativity here.

What of warrant and reputation? Viewed in context, these tactics may be seen to assume a degree of legitimacy, in the eyes of the narrator, if not in the view of the external observer. The motives of the central figure in most of these incidents can effectively be represented as combining self-interest with wider organizational concerns. Justification, if an account is necessary, involves an appeal to the context, to wider organizational as well as personal goals, and an assessment of the potentially damaging consequences of *not* acting in the manner described. Reputations seem in most cases to be largely intact or enhanced.

The fact that there are difficulties in applying clear ethical guidelines to such behaviour should not lead to a conclusion of despair. The 'ethics test' is artificial, and the penalties flowing from it are often insubstantial. But where the change driver initiating political behaviour has no warrant for such actions, where the change driver has limited creative accounting skills, where claims for personal and organizational damages can be upheld, and where a strong challenge is forthcoming, the social and organizational sanctions can be relatively powerful. The penalties for 'losing' the turf game include censure, ostracism and ridicule, curtailed future prospects, and per-haps even loss of job and career altogether. The social and organizational controls which come into play carry significantly more weight in practice than the clinical, textbook-based results of an ethical decision-tree analysis.

4 Men behaving badly

From: *Office Welfare: An Executive Survival Guide*, published by Headline Book Publishing, 1993.

Motivation, morals and legitimacy

THE CHAMPION?
'You really stooped to an all time low on this one, Bombay.'
'I am insulted by that Frank, you have no idea how low I can stoop.'
'I don't mind losing, I would just like to lose fair.'
'Fair is still losing, Frank. You've got to go for the "W" every time.'
'What about justice . . .?'

(Steven Bill as Frank, Emilio Estevez as Bombay, *The Champions*, 1993)

Jack [Nicholson] is the first to acknowledge that he is double the trouble. In response to one question about his temper (there was a nasty incident in California back in 1994, where he took a golf club to a vintage Mercedes which had carved him up), he explains politely, 'I jump from immaculately polite to violent – there's not much rudeness in between.' The audience cracks up and I can see him holding back a split-second, like an archer, before delivering the punch-line: 'Rudeness is for amateurs.'

(Pearson, 1998, p. 31)

Following the Second World War, there was considerable research interest in the 'darker' aspects of human character, such as extreme right-wing authoritarianism and Fascism, and in Machiavellian personality characteristics. The purpose of this chapter is to explore the contemporary relevance of that early work on Machiavellianism. The 'entrepreneurial hero' today is the manager who sets a vision, mobilizes others, creates jobs, generates wealth, builds an enduring organization, stimulates widespread public admiration. Surely this can all be achieved openly and honestly, working through rational argument, in accordance with established rules and procedures, exercising legitimate formal authority? Open influence processes are features of effective management, surely these are not devious and underhand politicking? We will argue that this 'sanitized' view of management behaviour is false, by demonstrating the manipulative aspects of the now popular, facilitative and empowering, 'new leadership'.

Change initiatives can be traumatic for the organization and its members. As Pinchot (1985) reminds us, Schumpeter aptly characterized periods of innovation as 'whirlwinds of creative destruction'. The more dramatic the reorganization, the more changes there are to the ways in which work is done. This involves changes in everything from the kinds of skills, attitudes and behaviours that are praised and rewarded, to the distribution of resources and the physical layout of work units and buildings. In this process, individuals and groups ask, 'What's in it for me?' (WIFM). It is rare to find change where different people do not view themselves as 'winners' and 'losers' in the process. Different groups attach long-standing issues to change initiatives, and the nature of change becomes interpreted and reinterpreted in terms of these different agendas. Small wonder that change drivers often complain about the fickleness, obstructiveness, tunnel vision and even bloody-mindedness of the people they have to deal with. While views differ over who behaves 'badly' and why, the reality of 'men behaving badly' is rarely challenged.

As outlined in the framework in Chapter 1, change drivers are forced into political diagnosis and behaviour in order to deal effectively with this world. Underlying a formal warrant to initiative change, there are typically a number of political conditions that need to be diagnosed. Change drivers have to understand the nature of the context of change, the perceived and underlying power and interests of stakeholders, the opposition and resistance they are likely to meet, and the types of ploys and accounts that will be acceptable in that context. Change drivers need to adapt their plans to these conditions, and act accordingly.

In contrast with the militaristic ethic of the bureaucratic organization ('Do your job and take your rations'), the ethic of such change agents is more complicated. It involves a substantial amount of effort, stress, risk and uncertainty. It means long hours, interpersonal conflicts, emotional highs and lows, personal criticism and vilification, stress, personal restraint and flexibility in the face of antagonism. Why do it? Why go to all this trouble? What kinds of actions are required? How will this affect your job security and career, and your relationships at work? What kind of effect will it have on you and your family life? In considering such issues, personal and organizational interests and ethics are intertwined. If you are forcing people to change, how will this benefit them? If you are also doing things differently, what are the costs and benefits to you? If people lose their jobs, perhaps even friends, how is this justified? If you have to work long, stressful hours, what does this mean for family and friends? As the pressures of change involve you in interpersonal conflict, mutual intimidation and emotional and intellectual manipulation, how does this carry over into your personal life? Do the ends (a better workplace, organizational survival, career advancement) justify the means (disruption and anxiety for employees, partners and children let down, coercion and bullying, misinformation, deceit)?

Ethical salience and legitimation

These ethical issues have a particular salience for political entrepreneurs. All managers have work pressures and are inevitably involved to some degree in organizational politics. However, the ethical dilemmas are heightened by change, for at least three main reasons:

The vision thing

Changes to the status quo challenge established practices and the ways these practices have been justified and legitimated in the past. New beliefs, symbols, ideologies and myths are required to inspire and legitimate the change to a new order. Every change process requires the 'management of meaning', and the delegitimation of opponents and opposing arrangements. As Pettigrew (1987) argues, this need for legitimation is the bridging link between organizational politics and culture. It is also means that all changes are linked to new sets of values and moral codes. This is why, for example, many socio-technical and organization development consultants emphasize what they call the 'principle of congruence'; the change process should be carried out in a manner that embodies the values which will inform the new organizational arrangements.

Trust

Change drivers are vulnerable to charges of acting 'politically'. As they cut across boundaries, they are often less trusted by those on either side of such boundaries. As they have to translate the often tacit and deep-seated ideas and interests of different sub-cultures into a conscious workable compromise, they may be seen as less sincere and as 'amoral chameleons' (Punch, 1996, p. 5). Different groups within the organization often distrust such agents as 'not one of us', and suspect them of 'working for the other side'. Where careers do not fit easily into standard career paths, the self-interested motivation and career path of change drivers is often subjected to critical scrutiny. As they are less easily controlled by established managers, and background career interests are brought to the foreground, the charge of political motivation is more often laid at their door – particularly by those concerned to delegitimate a change process and its champions.

Negative views of politics

Change depends upon the effective use of a wide range of informal influence and coercion tactics that are not officially sanctioned and, as such, often have a negative connotation attached to them. As we saw in Chapter 2, political behaviour can be regarded as both necessary and undesirable. The ethics of change drivers are thus more likely to be challenged than those of individuals operating in less uncertain and changeable circumstances. This gives an added dimension to the use of outsiders in change processes. Whether these are hired consultants, or experienced project managers, they are often perceived as less corrupted by sectional organizational interests and more expendable politically. Like the traditional Western hero, these 'hired guns' (Laver, 1997) are expected to ride out of town after the job has been done, and not stick around to become the new 'baddies'.

In such situations of heightened ethical uncertainty, and vulnerability to the challenge of indulging in negative politics, the political entrepreneur has to act politically and take a moral stand. Political entrepreneurs have to define their personal goals and codes of conduct. At an organizational level, they have to legitimate the means and ends of change to the different constituencies involved in the change drama. Insofar as we may find it difficult to lead a moral double life, there is also a challenge for political entrepreneurs to reconcile, at least to some degree, these two ethical arenas.

There is little systematic research available on political ethics in action to help inform such decisions. While interviews with managers about their views of organizational politics are useful, they are no substitute for systematic and comparative observation of how managers address ethical dilemmas in actual change processes. There are a number of legitimate reasons for this situation, not least the methodological difficulty of gaining access to and interpreting such data (Punch, 1996). The result is that texts which address the issues of how political entrepreneurs should act are often highly prescriptive in tone and speculative in character, with little referenced empirical support. (For a critique of this area, see Huczynski, 1996; Pettigrew, 1987; Punch, 1996.) This is often the stuff of 'airport texts', condemned by many critics of management fashions (Ramsey, 1996). This contrasts with empirical research that does address the politics of change, but which does not provide assistance on practical moral and ethical issues (Pettigrew, 1973).

This and the following chapter review solutions to this ethical dilemma, rejecting the simple critiques of 'negative' Machiavellian politics and naïve or manipulative praise for 'positive' organizational politics. The first set of critiques, outlined in this chapter, emphasize the negative consequences of political behaviour for individual and organization. From critiques of Machiavellianism in the 1970s to contemporary critiques of 'male politics', the costs of such behaviour are highlighted. The second tradition, addressed in Chapter 5, contrasts the 'negative' view of politics in the post-war era with an emerging positive politics of the 'integrative' and innovative organization, with its emphasis on 'entrepreneurial heroes' acting as creative innovators. Both of these traditions address the ethical issues surrounding organizational politics by looking at the structural factors underpinning Machiavellian behaviour. However, these traditions offer different solutions to the problem of 'men behaving badly'. Neither solution, it is argued, captures the complex dilemmas confronting the change driver. Chapter 5 concludes with an approach that goes beyond these traditions, proposing an alternative to guide intervention in organizational politics.

Machiavellian politics

> The difference between administrative behaviour in Machiavelli's time and today is largely one of degree. Rules of the game are more complicated and restricted (killing off or putting the opposition on the rack is replaced by discharge, and even this modern 'industrial capital punishment' has become difficult). Behaviour today is smoother, less blatant, more subtle. But feelings, needs for power, and actions to control the behaviour of others follow remarkably similar paths.

> A definition of the twentieth-century Machiavellian administrator is one who employs aggressive, manipulative, exploiting, and devious moves in order to achieve personal and organizational objectives. These moves are undertaken according to perceived feasibility with secondary consideration (what is necessary under the circumstances) to the feelings, needs, and/or 'rights' of others. Not that Machiavellianism is 'right' or even particularly 'bright', but it exists in today's leadership and needs to be recognized as such.
>
> (Calhoon, 1969, pp. 210–11)

Many managers readily admit to the use of devious political tactics in the pursuit of a range of personal and organizational goals, particularly in the context of organizational change. This view is supported by March and Olson (1983), who observe that organizational change is discussed in terms both of the rhetoric of administration and of the rhetoric of *realpolitik* – a public language and a private one. Far from being ignorant of the political dimensions of change, managers are usually well aware of 'backstage' activities.

There is a long-established tradition that brings such backstage activities to the foreground as a central political and moral issue. This is the tradition established by the Marquis de Sade, Machiavelli and Nietszche. These moral philosophers had an overriding objective – to provide an honest treatment of the realities of power plays. They criticized the double standards and hypocrisy of liberal-humanitarian and Christian philosophies that refused to acknowledge this dimension of social, organizational and political life. 'Honest dealing' for them implies open recognition of the phenomenon of politics. The term 'Machiavellian' has also been applied to élitist critiques of naïve participatory democracy (Burnham, 1943). For all such critics, any argument for open, participative, collaborative approaches to the exercise of power is either a dangerous illusion, or a blend of covert authoritarianism and deceptive manipulation – merely one power strategy among others, and a dishonest one at that. For this 'brutal' honesty, they have often been condemned by high-minded moralists.

Machiavelli's *The Prince* (*c.* 1513) is often regarded as the classic study of politics in that brutal tradition. Its inherent 'wickedness' was confirmed when the text was banned by the Catholic Church for its un-Christian morality. Machiavelli was not, however, the first to document political survival tactics. Around 300 BC in China, *The Book of Lord Chang* was written with much the same themes, and was also banned, this time for centuries by the Chinese authorities because its pragmatism was alien to traditional Chinese culture. Also around 300 BC, *Arthasastra of Jautilya* was published in India on the same topic, providing detailed instructions for setting up internal and external spies, testing the loyalty of ministers by offering temptations, and even suggesting precautions that should be taken by kings to prevent being stabbed in the back while in their harems. Anyone doubting the contemporary relevance of this last source would be

---

Morality at work: the movies move in on Machiavellian images

In the 1997 Hollywood movie *Contact*, an enthusiastic scientist played by Jodie Foster is committed to research that seeks to establish contact with extra-terrestrial life. She successfully lobbies foundations, using all the persistence and persuasive powers she has, to secure funding for her cherished research. When she finally establishes contact with aliens, the Head of the National Science Foundation (NSF), who had actually discontinued funding for the project, works to take credit for the project's achievements, and presents himself to government and the media as the inspirational leader behind the research. He also succeeds in being selected to join the mission to meet the aliens, by cynically 'selling' himself as just the kind of person the selection committee wanted. In his approach, he stands in contrast with Jodie Foster, who is unable to tell the committee what they wanted to hear, which for her would be a lie: that she believed in God. Before the mission, the NSF Head tells her that he admires her honesty and courage, and wishes that the world was a place where her kind of honesty would triumph. However, he observes, the world is not like that. He had to act within that world knowing how it worked – and he was successful.

In the film *The Mission* (1986), Robert De Niro (a new Jesuit convert) tries to convince Jeremy Irons (a Jesuit priest) that he must fight the armed forces that are seeking to take over his mission. When Irons decides not to fight, De Niro argues, 'This is the way of the world. You have to fight to save what you believe in.' Irons replies, 'I fear you may be right. But if that is the case, it is not a world I want to live in.'

---

advised to study the fate of one American President, and of a number of British Conservative Members of Parliament, during the 1990s.

Applying this tradition of political thought to organizational life highlights the existence of self-interested power motives and devious and coercive methods. The 'dark side' of politics becomes an inevitable feature and one that needs to be understood and addressed. While for many critics and practitioners, this feature is a 'backstage', informal and illegitimate activity, this argument is not the crucial one. The most important point is that self-interest, pursuit of power, manipulation and ruthlessness are seen as a part of 'normal' organizational politics. These features may infuse both the formal and informal aspects of organizational life – even though the rational character and social legitimation of modern organizations often makes public recognition of this fact difficult if not impossible.

The term 'Machiavellian politics', addressed by this tradition and brought to the centre of political analysis, is used here to refer to such organizational conditions as:

- self-serving manipulation and ruthlessness as widespread features of organizational life;
- the acknowledgement, however grudging, that the concern of organization members with their own job security and careers inevitably involves some use of these tactics;

- public condemnation and a refusal to acknowledge such activities, at the same time as most people recognize its widespread influence;
- the view that this type of behaviour is a necessary, if undesirable, evil, feeding on and encouraging 'lower' human instincts and passions;
- the continuing fascination of 'backstage gossip' (Burns, 1961), the enjoyment that some people get from playing 'power games', and the celebration of 'macho management' power;
- the typically male domination of both the conduct of these activities and their analysis;
- the need for even the most high-minded moralist to indulge in some form of self-interested manipulation of impressions, ruthlessness or coercion in defence of their conduct and in order to achieve valued personal goals;
- the realization that any mature organizational politician or change driver has to take this world of politics into account if anything is to be achieved.

In contrast to the sanitization of politics, and the autobiographical celebrations of success by many senior managers, the recognition of Machiavellian politics addresses the reality that 'men behave badly'. It raises the spectre of the personal and organizational costs of careerism, manipulation and intimidation. The entrepreneurial leadership of Iacocca (Chrysler), Semler (Semco), Welsch (General Electric), Branson (Virgin) and Roddick (Body Shop) is matched by the apparent corruption and ruthlessness of Ford, Rockefeller, Getty, Disney, Geneen, Hughes, Maxwell, Saunders (Guiness) and Rowland. Entrepreneurs such as Gates (Microsoft), Packer and Bond illustrate more clearly in the popular mind a more complex picture of entrepreneurial drive, ruthlessness and corruption.

Almost as controversial as the existence of Machiavellian politics are the views about what to do about it. Three broad responses are common.

First, some commentators have focused on producing what might be called *macho-Machiavellian managerial handbooks*. Here, the best strategy is to accept the inevitability and centrality of politics, and offer practical advice on how to operate within the 'corporate jungle'. The 1960s and 1970s saw Burger's (1964) *Survival in the Executive Jungle*, Jennings' (1971) *Routes to the Executive Suite* and Korda's (1976) *Power*. More recently, we have seen *The Mafia Manager: A Guide to the Corporate Machiavelli* ('V', 1991), *Leadership Secrets of Attila the Hun* (Roberts, 1995) and von Zugbach's (1995) *The Winning Manager: Coming Out on Top in the Organization Game*. One problem here is that the fine line between documenting political behaviour on the one hand, and positively advocating it, on the other, is easily crossed. Descriptions of mistrust, manipulation and ruthlessness can appear to celebrate these acts.

For these analysts, survival requires an understanding of the corporate war of all against all, and the development of the skills and abilities necessary to deal with this. Jennings (1971) documented the survival strategies adopted by managers faced with infighting and intrigue. In an era of mobility, he argues, style and panache are as important as job performance. Managers need to know how to handle colleagues as well as superiors, and how to achieve high visibility with the main power players in the organization. This for Jennings is an executive success game much like an athletic contest, or a game of chess, in which the substance of executive life and work is irrelevant to success. The goal is to maintain momentum, to sustain the winning image, to establish a reputation as a winner. This parallels the cult of the celebrity in the worlds of politics and entertainment. To perform is to arrive.

The rules of success chess

Rule 1:   Maintain the widest set of options possible.
Rule 2:   Avoid the penalty of loss of career time.
Rule 3:   Become a crucial subordinate to a mobile superior.
Rule 4:   Always favour increased exposure and visibility.
Rule 5:   Be prepared to practise self-nomination.
Rule 6:   Leave the company at your convenience, not that of others.
Rule 7:   Quitting requires the benefit of a rehearsal.
Rule 8:   Define the corporation as a market.
Rule 9:   Never allow success to pre-empt your future. (Jennings, 1971, p. 103)

Some commentators strongly emphasize the devious, underhand nature of tactics in the turf game. Burger's (1964) anecdotes of 'jungle warfare', for example, include simulation of friendship, deliberate provision of misleading information, spreading destructive rumours, and withholding critical information. Yet, while self-interest, ruthlessness and deceit are not only acknowledged but prescribed, this does not mean that political entrepreneurs should admit their existence. In a world in which organizational decisions are legitimated by appeals to rationality, profit, efficiency and humanitarian concerns, political behaviour is still generally regarded as illegitimate. Discovery involves condemnation, unless a suitable account can be fabricated. Revelation can undermine the power and influence of the key actors, whose tactics become transparent and open to challenge. Discovery can also lead to a collapse in personal credibility and to a downward spiral of organizational trust. As Machiavelli observed, in the face of such a situation, not only may it be better to act with honesty and integrity whenever possible, but when it is not, an appearance should always be given of such virtues. This risk of discovery is one to be considered in the use of any impression management tactic (Liden and Mitchell, 1988).

The second response is what might be called the *tradition of denial*. Commentators in this camp affirm the significance of politics, condemning its insidious and debilitating character. In many prescriptive management texts, in organization development to ethical leadership, any association with self-interested, manipulative or ruthless tactics is condemned as underhand and illegitimate. Even the term 'politics' is often relegated to an avoidable and morally retrograde underworld of conspiracy, manipulation and deceit, to the turf game arena of wheeling and dealing, gamesmanship and careerism. In this case it is argued that any recognition of the inevitability of this world, and participation in its practices, becomes a self-fulfilling prophecy. In the tradition of the sixties slogan, 'Don't vote – it only encourages them', politics is to be avoided. Participation in politics creates a cycle of distrust, a war of all against all, where 'everyone is trying to outwit and outmaneuver everyone else' and all knowledge and events are merely 'tools to be used to advance our own personal interests' (Morgan, 1989, p. 197). This negative and dark world of politics is a threat that must be at worst contained, and at best eliminated.

In their crude forms, both of these approaches are inadequate as a basis for understanding or intervening in organizational politics. The macho-Machiavellian handbook approach may provide useful advice, but tends to over-estimate the degree to which the ruthless cut and thrust of self-interested politics dominates (Morgan, 1989). Moreover, it provides no guidelines for understanding why such conditions are more predominant in some settings than others, and no adequate advice on when it is suitable to enter this game and when to avoid it. In so doing, paradoxically, it may be betraying the spirit of Machiavelli himself. Interpreting Machiavelli is, of course, a contentious task. In reading into his work what one wants, and claiming this to be the 'real' Machiavelli, one is reminded of Harold Laski's quote about Marx: 'You interpret him in your way, and I will interpret him in his.' While there is a popular understanding of Machiavellian politics, many commentators also recognize that Machiavelli recommended operating fairly, maximizing the interests of citizens, and generating trust and respect whenever possible. In the face of threats and challenges, Machiavelli admitted (and even admired) the ruthlessness that is sometimes required and the potential value of a reputation for ruthlessness. Deception is necessary because of the inevitable need to lead this 'double life'. Neither ruthlessness nor deception was, however, seen by Machiavelli as appropriate in all circumstances. An important task of *The Prince* was to diagnose when such actions were required and to act effectively in those circumstances:

A prince can easily secure himself by avoiding being hated and despised, and by keeping the people satisfied with him, which it is most necessary for him to accomplish. It is unnecessary for a prince to have all the good qualities I have enumerated, but it is very necessary to appear to have them. And I shall dare to say this also, that to have them and always to observe them is injurious, and that to appear to have them is useful; to appear merciful, faithful, humane, religious, upright, and to be so, but with a mind so framed that should you require not to be so, you may be able and know how to change to the opposite. (Machiavelli, 1988)

Our main concern in this chapter is with a different approach to Machiavellian politics. This approach neither unquestioningly accepts this feature of politics, and the need to play solely by these rules, nor denies its reality. This third approach is more contingent and historical. It recognizes that particular circumstances create manipulative and coercive forms of political behaviour, details the individual and organizational costs that this incurs, and considers how to deal with or transform such politics. During the 1970s, this approach took the form of a critique of the emerging character of the modern manager playing politics in large corporations. This was apparent in analyses of the corporate 'gamesman', the 'Machiavellian manager', and the 'narcissist', by Maccoby (1976), Christie and Geiss (1970) and Lasch (1979) respectively. Circumstances in the closing decades of the twentieth century have enhanced rather than diminished the relevance of such analyses. More significantly, they have been developed in critiques of the male politics and work orientations dominant in the 1970s (McKenna, 1997), and in Jackall's celebrated analysis of corporate 'moral mazes' (Jackall, 1988).

From organization man to gamesman

> *Member of the audience*: How do you spend your time?
> *Manager's answer*: We worry about our careers a lot. Don't we guys?

> (Kanter, 1977, p. 129)

> If the morality of 'thou shalt not lie' is rejected, the 'sense of truth' will have to legitimize itself before another tribunal: – as a means of the preservation of man, as *will to power*.

> (Nietzsche, 1968, p. 272)

The traditional image of bureaucracy is of rule-governed employees steeped in the logic of formal rationality, immune to appeals to principles and objectives not enshrined within the bureaucratic system. This image combines what Mills (1951) called 'the bureaucratic type' (glum, rule-dependent, lacking in self-confidence, rejecting change), and the 'old veterans' (pedantic, deferential, followers of instructions, insecure in operating outside orders, abilities lagging behind experience, and sentimental about office structures). These are the characters Balzac recalled when describing bureaucracy as 'the great power wielded by pygmies'. Such character types are the traditional opponents of innovation, and stand condemned by enthusiasts for the contemporary, dynamic, visionary management.

In the decade following the Second World War, the character of the modern manager was subjected to a different challenge. This was popularized in the work of Riesman (*The Lonely Crowd*, 1950), Mills (*White*

Collar, 1951) and Whyte (*The Organization Man*, 1956). The traditional manager was seen as task-oriented and inner-directed, motivated by inner drives and technical competence. The 'new manager' was people-oriented and other-directed, motivated by corporate goals and dependent on human relations techniques to satisfy others and manage the organization. Sound familiar?

Riesman (1950) explored the implications of 'other directedness' on social character. Riesman noted that the manipulation of others had become more significant, as basic material and technical challenges had been met, and as large bureaucracies created conditions in which the appearance of success was more important than the performance of the individual. Riesman argued that modern character was moving away from 'tradition direction' and 'inner direction' (in which character is set early in life, and guilt and shame are driving motives), to 'other direction' (in which character is shaped by social experience and approval, and anxiety is a driving motivation). The increasing importance of influencing others rather than overcoming technical problems had encouraged the rise of an 'other-directed' managerial stance that emphasizes 'manipulative skill' above traditional 'craft skill'. The inner compulsion or 'psychological gyroscope' of those driven by the Protestant Work Ethic is replaced by an outer compulsion of attending to the opinions and desires of others. The 'inner-directed cowboy' is replaced by an 'other-directed advertising man'. Concern with morality is replaced by attention to 'morale'; 'authority' is replaced by 'manipulation'. The stage was thus set for the introduction of a particularly manipulative, and personally insecure, form of Machiavellian politics, led by those concerned with survival in the corporate jungle.

This theme was developed by Mills (1951) in his analysis of the 'new entrepreneur'. The social engineering of 'cheerful robots', as 'the Protestant ethic, a work compulsion, is replaced by the conscious efforts of the Personnel Department to create morale' (Mills, 1951, pp. 233–4). Whyte (1956) documented and condemned the rise of the 'organization man', who does not just work in the organization, but belongs to it. He describes the rise of a social ethic that believes in the group as the main source of creativity, belongingness as the ultimate individual need, the application of science to achieve belongingness, and the identification of individual morality and social ideals with the goals of the unit and the organization. This is the personality with a 'commercialized friendliness', a 'bland surface of [American] sociability'. Character now means little more than 'white teeth and an absence of bodily odour' (Horkheimer and Adorno, 1947). The apparent inner emptiness and conformism of such managers was widely caricatured and condemned in the 1950s and 1960s.

During the 1970s, the image of the other-directed, manipulated and manipulative manager was given added bite as attention was focused on the competitive individualism and careerism of the organization man. Continuing earlier views of the 'new managers', Lasch characterized such men (they were typically men) as:

Live wires and fixers

The 'live wire' is characterized by Mills (1951) as coming from the 'flashier' areas such as sales and marketing, and can be seen as a threat to those above. After a while, such individuals become 'someone's boy' or a 'new entrepreneur', bringing the 'old go-getting competition into the new setting'. Such 'fixers' work best in uncertain and non-routine areas, and operate well in public relations, in new industries, in the 'boundary spanning' areas and, in general, on the 'guileful edges' of established bureaucracies. Such individuals specialize in fixing things for the 'powers that be' and, as a result, getting their 'cut'. They live on the fears, anxieties and stupidities of those above. As an agent of the bureaucracy, they compete for the praise of those they serve, but the picture is complicated by the existence of conflicting bureaucracies and loyalties. Power often rests on personality and ability to exploit the anxieties of the chiefs, and knowledge of hidden secrets at higher levels. Like other bureaucratic office holders, however, such individuals are also prone to 'status panic'. This takes the form of concern with white-collar hierarchies and minute gradations of rank, personal career and maintaining the 'right' image. Under modern conditions, said Thorstein Veblen (1958), the struggle for existence has been transformed into a struggle to keep up an appearance. This spills over into private life as even vacations become 'image' elements, with officials buying images of high status for a short time. Often an individual's reputation for excellence has to be restricted to a very few people, and managers are dependent on these people. Thus, when your patron goes, so do you.

- anxious to get on with others;
- organizers of their private lives to meet the demands of the corporation;
- sellers of themselves as if their own personalities were a commodity with a market value;
- possessors of a neurotic need for affection and reassurance;
- corruptible in their values.

However, the apparent 'cult of friendliness' should not be exaggerated. As Lasch (1979) argued, organizations do not perfectly socialize new recruits into bland corporate citizens. Beneath the surface lies a continuing competition for status and rewards. Lasch argued that modern narcissists are exploiters of the pleasures and quirks of others for their own interests. The competitive status-seeker has to assume commanding positions in cocktail parties, recruit loyal retainers, avoid turning their back on enemies and, in the struggle for interpersonal advantage, use all the impression management and counter-manipulation tactics they can deploy. The result is 'a way of life that is dying – the culture of competitive individualism, which in its decadence has carried the logic of individualism to the extreme of a war of all against all, the pursuit of happiness to the dead end of a narcissistic preoccupation with the self' (Lasch, 1979, p. xv).

Instability and change in bureaucratic life, combined with the dynamics of self-seeking careerism, create the 'gamesman'. In an attempt to document systematically the character of the modern manager, Maccoby (1976) interviewed over 250 senior managers in sessions lasting from 3 to 20 hours each. Maccoby used these data to identify a range of personality types, each representing an archetype for a stage of industrial development. The independent 'craftsman' is oriented towards the execution of an excellent task. The entrepreneurial 'jungle fighter' is reminiscent of the industrial barons of the turn of the century. The conformist 'company man' is the bureaucratic conformist of the 1950s corporation. Finally, Maccoby saw the 'gamesman' as a character produced by the faster-moving, flexible, innovative and competitive late 1970s. All of Maccoby's types have careerist aspirations. The craftsman wants to achieve concrete results. The jungle fighter wants to gain power over others. The company man wants the esteem of colleagues. But the gamesman wants to make an impact, to win, and to receive the attendant rewards.

> *Industrial Supply* is a 'Puritan Ethic' company. If you don't make it, you don't deserve it. (Executive from minority group; Kanter, 1977, p. 29)

Maccoby saw the future of management being conditioned by the careerist approach of the gamesman, who is in many respects an attractive figure with several desirable features:

- loves change and wants to influence its course;
- likes calculated risks and is fascinated by technique and new methods;
- sees developing projects, human relations and his own career as a set of options and possibilities, as if they were optional moves in a game;
- combines a complex set of tensions; co-operative, but competitive; detached and playful, but compulsively driven to succeed; a team player, but an aspiring superstar; fair and unprejudiced, but contemptuous of weakness;
- main goal is to be known as a winner, and deepest fear is to be labelled a loser;
- not energized to compete to build empires and riches, but for fame, glory, the exhilaration of running the team, and for gaining victories;
- has an ability to dramatize ideas and to stimulate and activate others;
- tends to be unbigoted, non-ideological and liberal;
- is not hostile, as nastiness and vindictiveness are indications of a loser;
- is not a jungle fighter, is not driven by a desire to conquer, and takes no pleasure in the defeat of others;
- is fair, if not compassionate, open to new ideas, but lacking conviction.

As the gamesman is concerned with winning, colleagues are evaluated in terms of what they can do for the team. The gamesman will replace people who weaken the team, and will give others 'a fair chance', dividing them

Table 4.1   **Craftsmen, jungle fighters, company men and gamesmen**

	Roots of competition			
	Craftsman	Jungle fighter	Company man	Gamesman
Meaning of competition	Drive to build the best; competition against self and materials	Kill or be killed; dominate or be dominated	Climb or fall; competition is the price for secure position	Win or lose; triumph or humiliation
Source of energy	Interest in work; goal of perfection; pleasure in building something better	Lust for power; pleasure in crushing opponents; fear of annihilation; wish to be the only one at the top	Fear of failure; desire for approval by those in authority	The contest, new options, pleasure in controlling the play

Source: Maccoby (1976, p. 105)

into 'winners and losers' and removing 'deadwood'. Maccoby's four character types can be summarized in Table 4.1.

The gamesman has a number of strengths, particularly in a world that puts a premium on flexibility and dynamism, and on the integration of innovative teams. The gamesman's main strengths are what Maccoby defined as being those of 'adolescence': playful, industrious, fair, enthusiastic, open to new ideas, yearning for independence but aware of limitations. Yet, while Maccoby's gamesman is dependent on others, he fears becoming trapped in an organizational web. A limited capacity for social commitment and personal intimacy is further handicapped by the desire to maintain the illusion of limitless options. The gamesman does not, therefore, develop deep or intimate friendships.

At their worst, Maccoby's gamesmen are unrealistic, manipulative and compulsive workaholics. Their hyper-activity obscures doubts over personal identity and purpose. The most compulsive players require competitive pressure to 'turn them on' and energize them. Deprived of a challenge, they become bored and depressed. Life outside the game is meaningless. Retirement from the game also means depression and a loss of purpose and goals. The desire for autonomy and the fear of being controlled can combine, Maccoby argues, to create a mid-career uneasiness. Even the most successful gamesmen, he claims, experience self-contempt at performing for others rather than developing their own goals, often unable to resolve the conflict between their desire for total independence and their ambition to run the organization team.

Maccoby is ambiguous about the leadership qualities of the gamesman. He argues that the gamesman may create a successful project and energize the whole organization for a time. But, in the long term, the gamesman seems to lack the patience and commitment, to people and principles, necessary to sustain a dynamic organization. The fatal danger for the gamesman is, 'to be trapped in perpetual adolescence, never outgrowing the self-centred compulsion to score, never confronting their deep boredom with life when it is not a game, never developing a sense of meaning that requires more of them and allows other to trust them' (Maccoby, 1976, p. 109). Younger gamesmen apparently fantasize about power and glory, and their passion may be enough to motivate a project team, but not to direct a large corporation, lacking the endurance and corporate belief of the company man. Maccoby (1976) and Lasch (1979, 1995) offer a characterization of the narcissistic gamesman, and also a systematic critique of this character type. As Maccoby's portrayal of the gamesman is, at times, sympathetic, his critique is typically neglected.

The gamesman may not wish to destroy the competition and fire people, is prepared to play by the rules, and he is not exceptionally hungry for power. It is true that the gamesman lacks passion and compassion, and carries emotional self-protection against intense experiences. To blend their will to corporate goals, and to progress up the hierarchy, gamesmen require a degree of meanness and emotional stinginess, and are concerned with adapting themselves and with 'marketing' their personalities and achievements. This also means ignoring the idealistic, compassionate and courageous impulses that might jeopardize their careers. They do not develop a strong independent sense of self. They are inevitably detached from empathy and compassion where colleagues are concerned. Enthusiasm, rapid decisions, risk taking – all take place within the confines of the corporate game, detached from broader and deeper personal emotions and social contexts. The gamesman experiences guilt from a loss of self-respect, and a nagging sense of self-betrayal at the choice of career above self, family and society. Dominant motives are fear, anxiety and restlessness, a concern that performance will not continue, that a lack of broader knowledge will be discovered, with a general careerist concern that, 'external events beyond his control or his inability to control himself will damage or destroy his career' (Maccoby, 1976, p. 191). Maccoby in this diagnosis holds up a mirror for the contemporary political entrepreneur – but this is a critical mirror, one that warns of the unrecognized personal costs of 'men behaving badly'.

Lasch (1979) observes that the upwardly mobile executive is no longer an 'organization man'. The 'self-sacrificing company man' has become 'an obvious anachronism'. While the pursuit of organizational goals is essential, there is an increasingly greater loyalty to personal career than to the needs of a particular organization. Lasch (1979, pp. 43–4) thus argues:

> For all his inner suffering, the narcissist has many traits that make for success in bureaucratic institutions, which put a premium on the manipulation of interpersonal relations, discourage the formation of deep personal attachments, and at the same time provide the narcissist with the approval he needs in order to validate his self-esteem. Although he may resort to therapies that promise to give meaning to life and to overcome his sense of emptiness, in his professional career the narcissist often enjoys considerable success. The management of personal impressions

comes naturally to him, and his mastery of its intricacies serves him well in political and business organizations where performance now counts for less than 'visibility', 'momentum' and a 'winning record'. As the 'organization man' gives way to the bureaucratic 'gamesman' – the 'loyalty era' of American business to the age of the 'executive success game' – the narcissist comes into his own.

Lasch (1984) noted the increasing number of management handbooks offering advice on how to survive in the social and corporate world, and noted also the manipulative and self-centred emptiness of the competitive life and its ever-present anxieties. So, 'competitive advantage through emotional manipulation increasingly shapes not only personal relations but relations at work as well' (Lasch, 1979, p. 65).

In a parallel set of studies, Christie and Geiss (1970) sought to provide a more in-depth empirical analysis of the character of the contemporary manager. Like Riesman, Maccoby and Lasch, they speculated that contemporary conditions encouraged the predominance of a particular character type. Increasing rates of organizational change, higher levels of uncertainty, and the spread of cosmopolitan urbanism were all seen as creating conditions in which 'Machiavellian' managers were more prevalent and successful. Continuing the earlier work of Adorno et al. (1950) on the 'authoritarian personality' of political followers, they sought to document the attitudes, ethics and tactics of leaders. Drawing on Machiavelli's *The Prince*, Christie and Geiss developed and refined questionnaires and laboratory experiments designed to elicit the main features of the Machiavellian personality and determine the likelihood of success of such a personality type. The main features of a Machiavellian personality, they argue, are as follows:

- *Lack of emotional involvement in interpersonal relationships*: Machiavellians view others as objects to be manipulated, rather than as individuals with whom one empathizes. Attention to the character and opinions of others is thus pragmatic. Emotional involvement may lead to identifying with the opinions of others, and thus make it more difficult to use leverage to persuade others to do what they may not want to do.
- *Lack of concern with conventional morality*: Machiavellians are less committed to the view that lying, cheating and deceit are reprehensible. They adopt a utilitarian view of others, and are less concerned with the amoral or immoral nature of their own actions.
- *Lack of gross psychopathology*: The Machiavellian's instrumental view of others is typically accompanied by an accurate evaluation of them, reflecting reality and not their own psychological needs.
- *Low ideological commitment*: Machiavellians focus on 'getting things done' rather than on long-range ideological goals, and make flexible use of tactics to achieve their ends, avoiding an inflexible striving for ultimate and unrealistic goals.

Christie and Geiss (1970) developed the Mach IV questionnaire (Appendix II) to measure the degree of Machiavellianism in an individual's personality. The typical 'High Mach' resists social influence, concentrates on winning, and likes to initiate and control the structure of social situations. High Machs manipulate more, win more often, are persuaded less, and persuade others more. High Machs tend to win in negotiations involving face-to-face interaction and scope for improvisation, and where emotional involvement is irrelevant. Their 'cool, cognitive, situation-specific' strategy makes them less amenable to manipulation by others, more focused on outcomes, and less distracted by personalities and feelings. These results have not been unambiguously confirmed in empirical studies using the Mach IV scale. Some studies have found career success correlated with Machiavellianism, others have failed to identify such a correlation.

Medical Machiavellis

Christie and Merton (1970) discovered the controversial nature of their Machiavellian research when they presented a paper on medical students to a medical audience. One of their 21 slides addressed Machiavellianism – the belief that one should not trust others completely, that it is wise to flatter important people, that there is a need to cut corners to get ahead, that one should only reveal the real reason for doing something if it is useful to do so. They had found that medical students were more likely to have such beliefs than Washington lobbyists or business executives. The ensuing debate focused on this finding, with an emotive disagreement between the young urban medical dean – who praised students for their realistic attitudes – and an older rural medical dean – who condemned this situation as indicative of a general failure to give adequate professional training to medical students.

Christie and Geiss found no correlation between Machiavellianism and sex, intelligence, class, social mobility or nationality. Similar results were obtained, for example, from groups in America, Hong Kong and Germany. They did find, however, that the young, the inexperienced and students tended to be more Machiavellian than the older, more experienced and gainfully employed.

One other interesting outcome was that Christie and Geiss changed their attitude towards the High Mach personality during their research. They began with critical contempt for this scheming and self-centred character, but gradually developed a more ambiguous attitude. What they saw as the more attractive dimensions of the Machiavellian include:

- High Machs do not use ingratiation to make friends. They are less socially pressured to change their opinions to fit the arguments of others.
- High Machs are more resistant to unjustified attempts to get them to lie or cheat. They adjust the amount of manipulation and deceit used to fit

the situation. They try to avoid being obviously manipulative, when discovery would be disadvantageous.

- High Machs have less investment in their own self-image and beliefs. Consequently, they are more likely to be open and honest about their character and motives, and to admit their own less desirable features.
- High Machs perform better in situations where power is balanced, as well as in situations of authority, so they can operate as effectively with uncertain and flexible democratic processes as they do under authoritarian conditions, possibly more so.
- High Machs pay attention to the personalities and wishes of others, and perceive these accurately, even though they use this knowledge in an instrumental way.
- High Machs are exploitative, but they are not vindictive or vicious.
- The High Machs' sense of emotional distance and games-playing mean that they can inspire admiration among observers. Others thus tend to want them as partners. High Machs are easier to schedule, because they are more likely to turn up.
- High Machs tend not to have authoritarian traits or have extreme right-wing political views.

In the light of these findings, can we so readily equate Machiavellian manipulation with low ethical or moral standards? Not necessarily. Leary (1986) argues that High Machs are neither immoral nor amoral, but that they adhere to a code of ethics different from the orientation of Low Machs. Machiavellians are more likely to subscribe to a system of situationally based ethics. This implies that moral decisions are based on personal and relativistic ethical guidelines rather than on moral absolutes.

The empowered manager and male politics

Many of the insights into the 'gamesman' and the 'Machiavellian manager' developed in the 1970s may appear somewhat old-fashioned today, particularly given the sexist language in which the research work and debate were conducted. This is, however, to mistake form for substance. There may be less concern today among social psychologists with 'social character' and the identification of universal types. However, the proliferation of 'Myers–Briggs', 'Belbin' and 'Team-Wheel' personality assessments testifies to a continuing interest in such typologies. The popular and commercially successful work of the Covey Leadership Center is explicitly based on a return to the 'character ethic' focusing on the 'effective person' (Covey, 1989). As explored further in Chapter 5, there has been a growth in the popularity of 'coaching' and 'facilitative' management styles rather than a reduction.

What has changed, however, is the degree of commitment to critical analysis of these new conditions. This has been noted in a number of overviews of the state of management research, the rise of prescriptive management texts, and the proliferation of consultancy fads and fashions (Adams, 1996; Clegg and Palmer, 1996; Micklethwait and Wooldridge, 1996; Shapiro, 1996). While coaching, facilitation and participative management have flourished, criticism of the politics of manipulation and authoritarianism underlying such practices has declined. Where there has been criticism, it is as if the critical 'sociological imagination' (Mills, 1959) exercised by writers such as Lasch (1979) and Whyte (1956) has been exchanged for obscure academic élitist critiques, developed and consumed by a narrowly focused research community, isolated from managerial practice. As Chapter 8 suggests, the contributions of Michel Foucault and his acolytes have been significant, but in many respects they simply repeat the views of Lasch and others, while adopting an increasingly obscure and élitist attitude and language.

The criticisms made during the seventies have an enduring relevance. This is particularly so given that the conditions that led to the initial concern with the other-directed and self-serving Machiavellian personality type have arguably increased and been extended rather than declined. In particular, the rate of organizational restructuring and the delayering of middle management have increased insecurity and fuelled an even greater concern with job security and the future of careers. Kanter (1997), for example, points to the competitive threat posed by new young and female entrants into the workforce. She observes how the traditional concern with individual careers and success among one's peers, and professional protection of autonomy and control over work and standards, has been intensified by the linkage between careers and the struggle for departmental survival in the new 'lean' environment. Moreover, with the introduction of radically new 'network', 'process-based', 'cross-functional' and 'virtual' structures, the question of who plans, staffs and benefits from these new arrangements raises another level of complexity and uncertainty – the breeding grounds for gamesmen and gameswomen, and for Machiavellian activities and cultures (Chapter 9).

We can illustrate the continuing relevance of Machiavellian politics in two ways. First, by analysing the continuation and expansion of personnel manipulation through participative leadership and employee involvement strategies. Second, by illustrating how contemporary critiques of 'male' politics have continued this tradition.

The empowered manager

Management and leadership training today emphasize participative, empowering, coaching and facilitative styles. It is widely accepted that the key to successful management lies with management style. The 'new leader' (typically not 'new manager') relies less on traditional formal authority and coercion and more on informal influencing strategies to motivate and inspire 'followers'. However, informal influence-based tactics can be

regarded either as humane and enlightened approaches to people management, or as more sophisticated weapons in the arsenal of the gamesman
and the Machiavellian manager. The aim, as Huczynski (1996, p. 6)
explicitly asserts is, 'to gain the commitment of employees by harnessing
the achievement of an employee's personal goals to the company's objectives'. The tactics of empowering, coaching and facilitating can then be
presented as wholly appropriate, and politically neutral, means to achieve
these ends in rapidly changing environments that require greater flexibility
and internal motivation from employees. This is what Huczynski (1996,
p. 6) defines as the general skill of influence:

> [A]bility to affect another's attitudes, beliefs or behaviours – seen only in its
> effect – without using coercion or formal position, and in such a way that
> influencees believe that they are acting in their own best interests.

There are problems with attempts to control others through coercion
and formal authority. These techniques are badly out of fashion and are
more likely to stimulate media reports and condemnation than cowed
submission and heightened performance. This suggests that management
must abandon such brutal tactics, and rely on more subtle forms of
manipulation, often disguised as coaching, empowering and facilitative
leadership styles of management. Influence-based tactics are manipulative
where the targets are not given explicit instructions, but are nevertheless
subject to the will of another. If you can swing someone's mood, emotions
or opinions through covert and symbolic means, willing compliance may
be forthcoming without the long-run social costs involved in the use of
coercion or autocratic diktat. If others are willing to accept an
organization's culture, procedures, norms and goals as 'taken for granted',
then management commands and controls may not even be recognized as
such.

The rhetorics of coaching and facilitating can be regarded as techniques
or skills of the Machiavellian manager, rather than as 'good human
relations practice'. These methods are a direct continuation of the practices
criticized by Riesman, Mills, Whyte, Maccoby and Lasch. Friedmann
(1977) describes managerial strategies for enriching and empowering the
work of employees as control by 'responsible autonomy' in contrast with
less subtle 'direct control'. Traditional managerial manipulation has simply
acquired a new set of new labels.

For those who portray such practices as a democratic partnership
between followers and leaders, there are two problems. First, the use of
such methods is always contingent. There is a continuing background
threat of force, and a switch to more coercive tactics when conditions
change – such as when radical restructuring or rapid change is required.
As Machiavelli himself warned, there are limits beyond which this 'facilitative' style cannot go, and where direct coercion and formal authority are
necessary:

Voss (1992, p. 46) reports the following exchange between himself and Walter Keichel, Assistant Managing Editor of *Fortune* magazine, and the author of a book on office politics:

Interviewer: What are some of the key issues in office politics today?

Keichel: There's a shifting away from hierarchy. People in their thirties or forties – the very smartest of them – are pretty uncomfortable with the old command-and-control models. What's more important now is how people do on teams. Being a member of a collective or co-operative effort requires different skills than being a good subordinate or being a good boss.

Interviewer: Different in what way?

Keichel: The organizing principles are very different. You'll be picked to work on a particular team or a special task force based on your talent and skills, not on who you backed or who you know. It's interesting that the gradual move away from hierarchy means a really subtle shift in what people have traditionally thought of as politics, which was: Some people will get ahead; I'm going to bet on them rising to the top; what can we do to foil the other contenders for that position?

A controversy has arisen about this: whether it is better to be loved than feared, or vice versa. My view is that it is desirable to be both loved and feared; but it is difficult to achieve both and, if one of them has to be lacking, it is much safer to be feared than loved.

For this may be said of men generally: they are ungrateful, fickle, feigners and dissemblers, avoiders of danger, eager for gain. While you benefit them they are all devoted to you: they would shed their blood for you; they offer their possessions, their lives, and their sons, when the need to do so is far off. But when you are hard pressed, they turn away.

Men are less hesitant about offending or harming a ruler who makes himself loved than one who inspires fear. For love is sustained by a bond of gratitude which, because men are excessively self-interested, is broken whenever they see a chance to benefit themselves, but fear is sustained by dread of punishment that is always effective. (Machiavelli, 1988, p. 59)

I know that everyone will acknowledge that it would be most praiseworthy for a ruler to have all the above-mentioned qualities that are held to be good. But because it is not possible to have all of them, and because circumstances do not permit living a completely virtuous life, one must be sufficiently prudent to know how to avoid becoming notorious for those vices that would destroy one's power. . . . Yet one should not be troubled about becoming notorious for those vices without which it is difficult to preserve one's power, because if one considers everything carefully, doing some things that seem virtuous may result in one's ruin, whereas doing other things that seem vicious may strengthen one's position and cause one to flourish (1988, p. 55).

Second, the background authoritarianism is often hidden and denied. The presentation and illusion of this managerial style can be illustrated by the 'new leadership' promoted by DDI (Development Dimensions International) consultants. DDI consultants advocate a model of the modern manager as coach in establishing self-managing work teams (Wellins et al., 1991). The ambiguities, tensions and elisions in this work illustrate the lack of transparency and, arguably, deliberate manipulation embedded in such an approach.

The DDI consultants are well known for having developed a method for creating empowered, autonomous, self-managing work teams. Anything short of outright control by teams over the goals and means of their work is condemned as an inadequate and restricted version of empowerment. However, the creation of these self-managing teams is accompanied by a 'new leadership' style that imposes a sophisticated system of monitoring and control over individual team members, as well as the goals and operations of the teams. The talk of teams selecting their own goals, and managing their own operations, moves easily to a discussion of a system where decisions are 'shared' with management, to outlining detailed measures for continuously monitoring and disciplining team members in their choice of performance objectives, their achievements and the methods that they use. The rhetoric of participation and empowerment is thus accompanied by a continuing, yet often hidden, system of control. As one manager commented (Badham et al., 1997b, p. 85) when he removed the need for team members to use the time clock ('Bundy clock') to clock in and out of work: 'I still kept my eye on them. I knew who some of the offenders were and I pulled them aside and had a few words with them. A manager still has to manage.'

Rather than removing manipulation, deceit and a cycle of distrust from workplace relations, such rhetoric may only re-create it in a new form, as both perpetrators and victims of human relations practices recognize the 'unspoken' manipulation that is underway. As Lasch (1979) observed, advocates of participative leadership styles, such as McGregor ('Theory Y'), have urged managers to accept limits to authoritarian command. 'Theory X' styles are inappropriate in an era of 'interdependence'. In contrast to some earlier human relations research, however, such advocates of 'self-actualization', from Maslow onwards, have not advocated the abdication of managerial responsibility. Employees still need direction, but as partners in an enterprise, not as submissive subordinates. Participation, encouragement to communicate needs and suggestions, the elicitation of constructive criticisms, support for 'group' identification where individuals are encouraged to speak their mind – all these are part of the arsenal of subtle managerial influence and control.

To Lasch (1979), this represented what he called a 'therapeutic view of authority'. This involves the preservation of hierarchy while encouraging participation. Therapeutic mechanisms are applied to soften or eliminate adversary relations between subordinates and superiors. These do not depend on clear enforcement of legal and moral codes, nor on the internalization of moral standards of the community. It is, rather, 'conformity to the conventions of everyday intercourse, sanctioned by psychiatric definitions of normal behaviour' (in this respect, Lasch's view of therapeutic authority is strikingly similar to aspects of the perspective on power developed by Michel Foucault, examined briefly in Chapter 8). People become increasingly dependent on the 'indulgence' of those above them.

Empowerment or a velvet glove?

A new factory is being built by Echidna Chemicals under the supervision of Bruce, the new factory manager. With the new technology, new forms of work organization are being introduced. Self-managing work teams are being used to run different product-based 'cells'. Bruce decides to invite self-nominations for the roles of team leaders. More people apply than there are positions available. Bruce asks them to get together in a room and sort out for themselves who will be the team leaders. The employees self-select the required number. Participation has not only occurred, but has also been seen to be done. Bruce remarks, 'It's incredible. They picked exactly the people that I would have wanted for the job.' Sheila, an external consultant, asked, 'What if it had turned out the other way around?' Bruce smiled and said, 'I don't know. We would have had to deal with that problem if it had arisen.' (Personal interview with a factory manager, February 1996, Sydney)

In earlier critiques, Maccoby (1976) similarly argued that the 'new-style bureaucrats' possessed an ideology and character that supported hierarchy even though they were no longer directly paternalistic or authoritarian. The new manager, he argued, does not order inferiors around, but uses subtler means. Subordinates may realize they are 'conned, pushed around, and manipulated', but find it more difficult to resist less overt methods. Bureaucratic diffusion of responsibility makes it possible for managers to delegate discipline, to blame unpopular decisions on the company, and to sustain their image as 'friendly adviser'. As their positions are allegedly open to all, a meritocratic ideology (Young, 1958) makes it even more difficult to resist this process of control. Lasch and others identified similar uses of expert knowledge as a basis for control, expert definitions of 'normal behaviour', and the use of detailed observation and analysis to enforce conformity to these definitions. Contemporary empowerment and coaching styles of management may not, therefore, mark the end of the gamesman or of the Machiavellian manager but, rather, the extension of this set of tactics. The Machiavellian manager has to master and to work within this game of masks and charades, using more subtle, manipulative methods of control – even if, for many, the result may be more desirable forms of work.

Male politics

The books on power and politics in the 1970s were male-oriented. They were predominantly written by men, about men, for men. During the 1980s and

1990s, however, there have been an increasing number of critiques of this gendered view of politics (Helgesen, 1990; Naisbett and Aburdene, 1986). In *When Work Doesn't Work Anymore: Women, Work and Identity*, for example, McKenna (1997) describes the world of male politics in terms similar to the earlier critiques of Machiavellian politics. It is a world in which loyalty, dedication, excellence and hard work do not result in success. Sitting back and hoping for recognition is seen as passivity, a lack of fire, guts and ambition. Essential for success is self-promotion, and conformity to the 'unwritten rules of success'. This world determines who will be leaders and who will be followers by a 'Darwinian system that weeds out those with no stomach for politics, competition, or monofocused ambition' (McKenna, 1997, p. 51). Success is about 'maintaining silence in the face of politics and backstabbing, by living in a crisis and pressure mentality all the time. It has little to do with performing good work or being productive and everything to do with pecking orders and egos' (McKenna, 1997, p. 71). Any questioning of this world is an indication of a lack of ambition, and that one cannot 'cut it' in a 'man's world'. Total self-sacrifice is equated with success.

The unwritten rules of success

Rule 1: Work comes first, above any personal or family concern.

Rule 1a: If you are a man and a father, you can break Rule 1 and be a great guy; if you're a woman and you break Rule 1, you're not serious about your future.

Rule 2: Long hours are a requirement. If your boss wants you and you're not there, he or she will learn quickly to want someone else who is.

Rule 3: Take credit for what works (no matter how tangential your role) and run from what doesn't.

Rule 3a: If you're a man and you break Rule 3 because you gave credit to a woman, you immediately get more credit for yourself because of your fairness and magnanimity. If you're a woman and you think that Rule 3a behaviour is disgusting, the resulting failure to follow Rule 3 results in perpetual middle management and the possibility that the words *good old* might eventually precede your name. On the other hand, too much exercise of this rule gets you the hard-to-lose epithet 'aggressive' – and it's not a compliment.

Rule 4: There is only one career in your life and only one path. If you step off it, you're out of luck.

Rule 4a: If you are a man and you break Rule 4, you were probably down-sized; tough luck, it won't hurt you. If you broke Rule 4 because you are a woman who stayed home with your children for a while, you are a swell person, but a bad bet for future employment, to say nothing of advancement.

Rule 5: This is about hierarchy. Your job is to make your boss look good and your boss's job is to make his or her boss look good.

Rule 6: The goal is to get as close to the top as possible. There is no end to what you are supposed to achieve or want. (McKenna, 1997, pp. 189–213)

Riesman in the 1950s condemned the subtle forms of manipulation embedded in childrearing practices, and the manner in which these permeate the workplace. Contemporary critiques of the male world of work regard domestic life and family values in a different way. They are seen as a preserve of 'female' values of co-operation and community, and represent and develop the managerial skills of motherhood. Helgesen (1990) found that women tend to look more towards the long term, see their work as only one element of their identity, schedule regular times and places to share information, and to value being at the centre of things, facilitating communication. In contrast, men more often focus on the short term, define themselves by their work, hoard information to increase power, and pursue being at the top of things, where the control is clear and lines of communication flow down. In her studies of women-owned businesses, Godfrey (1996, p. 21) noted:

> The very basic notions of what women defined as success seemed to make their businesses different. What female business owners called 'normal' was now being tagged the 'new paradigm' by business gurus worldwide. And the national effort to 're-engineer' everything was an attempt to get to where women already were. The new psychology on women revealed that relationships are a source of power that women are comfortable nurturing. Success among women is less a matter of conquest than of collaboration, and priorities may be determined as much by family and community imperatives as by a desire to amass wealth of things.
>
> As the '80s came to a close we could see that women relied less on authority and traditional power relationships with other employees than men did. The very qualities that had been devalued because they were female were now claimed by many male writers as integral to a new and radical approach to the business of management.

The problems and challenges facing women, at the managerial level, are due to the fact that the male world of work politics does not allow the expression of female qualities – with a claimed result that there has been a moral and physical desertion of women from the world of work. McKenna cites the fact that in February 1996, the *New York Times* devoted six pages to the loss of faith of American corporate workers in their corporations. A 1993 Roper Starch World Wide poll found that the view of success held by two-thirds of professional women had changed, and two-thirds agreed that making money wasn't as important to them as it had been five years ago. In 1995, a Deloitte-Touche survey showed that only 2 per cent of professional and executive women were very satisfied with their work. Only 7 per cent said they were in it for the money. The world of work, McKenna argues, was built for men with full-time wives at home to take care of the rest of life. Men thus became defined and valued by what they did, not who they were. Women, on the other hand, were forced to operate with a double standard of success: personal and domestic contribution and business achievements. In a male world of work, however, it is impossible to attain these two goals, and women become subject to a 'slow release schizophrenia' as they feel that their inability to resolve this tension is due to their own lack of will or smartness.

McKenna (1997, p. 49) recommends that women seek to 'feminize the way things work': reward collaboration, not competition among co-workers; share information; and define success more in terms of what was produced than on the system that produced it. While recognizing the difficulties involved, she recommends a number of ways to challenge this situation and remove the condition that Kanter (1977) describes as 'a public persona that hides inner feelings'. McKenna's (1997, pp. 189–213) advice includes:

- Say goodbye to the good girl.
- Break the vows of silence.
- Learn to fail.
- Stop trying to be so successful.
- Take your personal life to the office with you.
- Don't do it alone, the importance of community.
- Live by what you treasure.
- There is no such thing as women's work.
- Work outside the box – stopping out, alternative work arrangements, work for yourself.

The approaches reviewed in this chapter overview the costs of organizational politics, critiques of the 'gamesman', the 'Machiavellian' manager, the manipulative 'empowered manager' and the 'male politician'. This review holds a critical mirror to organizational politicians, to assess the value and costs of what they are doing. Where such critiques are at their weakest, however, is in offering an alternative to this world of 'men behaving badly'. The question is: 'so what?' How should we behave differently? Riesman presents a case for an autonomous individual, able to stand back and evaluate the character or personality of the age. But the substance of the autonomous individual in organizational politics is less clear. Empowered managers may be manipulative, but where are the boundaries between justifiable and unjustifiable manipulation? Male politics may be morally reprehensible, but what types of 'female' politics are to be drawn upon as an alternative? Women may be equally manipulative and self-serving.

The behaviour of the Machiavellian gamesman is embedded in contemporary organizational structures, and in male power relations, and it is perhaps misguided to view such behaviour as solely rooted in distorted individual personalities. Chapter 5 addresses one of the most developed and influential attempts to portray an alternative 'positive' world of politics, represented by champions of 'the new leadership'. However, Chapter 5 explores the morally ambiguous nature of that perspective.

5 The entrepreneurial hero

From: *Office Warfare: An Executive Survival Guide*, published by Headline Book Publishing, 1993.

The Rising Sun

Innovation for most organizations is a competitive requirement and, consequently, has a built-in legitimacy. This imperative now seems to apply across public and private sectors. Individuals and groups able to capture the mantle of 'innovators', portraying opponents as 'resistors', are able more effectively to legitimate their own positions. During this century, a number of broad managerial groupings have either adopted or been attributed with this 'innovator' status. For Thorstein Veblen (1958), the drivers of innovation were *engineers*, systematically held back by the narrow, short-term and self-interested profit motives of 'capitalist toads'. For Joseph Schumpeter (1968), the *owner-capitalist* was the innovator *par excellence*, the 'creator of new combinations' in 'whirlwinds of creative destruction'.

Earlier in the century (Berle and Means, 1935), the '*new managerial class*', with expertise in controlling large complex organizations, appeared to be laying the foundations of corporate growth and social responsibility. Subsequently, it was the infrastructure of teams of experts, professionals and knowledge workers – the '*technostructure*' – that was identified as the 'real' source of growth and innovation (Galbraith, 1974). During the 1980s, the mantle of innovation was passed to other groups. Drawing on earlier work on '*champions of innovation*' (Schon, 1963) and '*transformational leaders*' (Burns, 1978), a new focus emerged on *entrepreneurialism* in the ranks of middle and senior management (Badham, 1995). These were the '*intrapreneurs*' (Pinchot, 1985), the '*change masters*' (Kanter, 1983), the '*post-entrepreneurial heroes*' (Kanter, 1989) and '*new leaders*' (Bryman, 1996). Managers seem to enjoy catchy titles which describe their activities; academic and other commentators seem consistently willing to oblige in this regard.

How did the contemporary rhetoric of the 'entrepreneurial hero' develop? American economic success in the 1970s led to global acceptance that American technology, management expertise and business acumen was the pinnacle of corporate competitiveness. The male-dominated, specialized, careerist, competitive-business-fighter, opportunistically mobile, company functionary and corporate executive was a managerial caricature – the ultimate vision of corporate efficiency. In *The American Challenge*, the French politician Jacques Servan-Schreiber (1969) preached this gospel of American innovativeness to a traditionally sceptical European audience. His lesson was clear: adapt or go under.

Criticism from the 1970s of the 'post-industrial' economy, 'limits to growth', 'private affluence and public squalor', and the monotony of 'mass culture', only challenged the model from the outside. On traditional measures of productivity and market growth, American corporations appeared to be efficiently run. This success was reflected in 'neo-human relations' perspectives, but 'work humanization' initiatives were used to improve quality of working life, and did not question issues of technology and efficiency. Managers may have been criticized for their lack of concern with the environment, for consumerism and for conformity, but their core legitimation – their efficiency – went unchallenged.

This optimism and confidence collapsed in the 1980s, as American productivity and international competitiveness declined. This was dramatically symbolized by the success of Japanese companies in the electronics, computers, automobile and machine tool sectors. By the 1990s, this panic over 'Japanization' was seen in best-selling books such as *The Machine that Changed the World* (Womack et al., 1990), and Hollywood films like *Rising Sun* (Crichton, 1992), both reflecting and contributing to a crisis in economic and cultural confidence. It did not go unnoticed in Europe that, when the Berlin Wall came down in 1989, the departure of United Airlines from their offices on the Kurfürstendamm was rapidly followed by the erection of the new owners' sign: Japanese Air Lines.

Attention turned to how American and European managers should respond. The answers seemed simple: with a new type of business organization, and a new type of manager. This view was expressed in the 1980s in advocacy of the 'flexible firm', and 'flexible specialization', as well as in the mimicking of Japanese methods with 'total quality management', and 'lean production'. This period was marked by a recognition that Western manufacturing strategy was misdirected (Bessant, 1991). American short-term profit orientation, in particular, had undermined long-term technological capability and success. Corporate control by financial managers, narrow investment criteria, mobile and career-hungry executives, and extended organization hierarchies were challenged by a new conventional wisdom.

This new vision directed attention back to the robustness, innovativeness and competitiveness of small business. More importantly, there was a move to reintroduce those features into large organizations – and into the training and careers of managers. This occurred in a number of ways. In *In Search of Excellence* (Peters and Waterman, 1982), leading American companies were praised for breaking down traditional hierarchies and forming new 'loose–tight' structures. 'High-performance' organizations were relaxing traditional forms of control through teamworking, multiskilling and empowerment. 'Organic' organizational designs were developed as a competitive requirement in the interests of responsiveness, product variety and rapid innovation (Buchanan and McCalman, 1989).

This entailed a new strategic role for human resource management as a source of competitive advantage. In the view of Pfeffer (1994), the 'new organization' had to change vertically and horizontally. Vertically, there should be fewer hierarchical levels, more devolution of responsibilities, and more autonomous employees. The people strategies and skills of line managers were to be those of coaching and motivating flexible and self-directed teams. Horizontally, there should be a greater use of task forces, cross-functional teams, integration of production into marketing, and a collapse of the traditional hierarchical career. Accompanying this loosening of internal hierarchical ties, however, was a 'tightening' of other ties. Some 'non-core' activities became candidates for sub-contracting, creating the problem of how to integrate sub-contractors into a flexible production network. Long-term, trust-based relations were necessary to establish tighter control over sub-contractors (Kanter, 1997). Declining loyalty to the organization, combined with increased mobility and insecurity, required the creation of other approaches for generating commitment.

The celebration of new high-performing companies took an ambivalent stance towards the 'Japanese model'. This celebration drew from Japanese 'best practice', but attempted to create new structures that would 'out-innovate' the Japanese. The theme of radical innovation was most prominently taken up in the 1990s fashion for business process re-engineering, but it has informed the whole 'high-performance company' perspective.

The new 'post-entrepreneurial hero' was to be both change driver and managerial type, characteristic of the new era. But significantly for our purpose here, embodied in this notion was a particular view of the 'positive' organizational politics played by such heroes. Earlier research on champions of innovation had also argued for the importance of committed individuals and coalitions using whatever resources they could obtain to 'get things done' (Beatty and Lee, 1992). Our concern in this chapter lies with the ethics of the political behaviour embedded in this tradition. We will explore the assumptions underlying key representatives of the 'entrepreneurial hero' and 'transformative leadership' approaches.

Intrapreneurs and change masters

Following *In Search of Excellence* (Peters and Waterman, 1982), attention focused on a new type of organizational innovator. The 'hero entrepreneur' (Pettigrew, 1987) who works in 'adhocracies' comprising project groups, 'skunk works' and cross-functional teams (Waterman, 1990). The characteristics of hero entrepreneurs include their separation from and antagonism towards corporate hierarchies. Another feature is their ability to mobilize the collective intelligence of the workforce, in opposition to traditional scientific management (Nonaka and Takeuchi, 1995). While, as Kanter (1979, p. 65) noted, 'Power is one of the last dirty words. It is easier to talk about money – and much easier to talk about sex – than it is to talk about power', the hero entrepreneur challenged this negative view. As Peters (1994) asserts, a common theme is that, 'anyone who loves accomplishing things must learn to love (yes, love) politics'.

This positive vision of entrepreneurial politics is based on four assumptions:

(1) Working the bureaucracy

Modern organizations trigger politics through a number of characteristics (see Chapter 8). Their internal specialization and diversity create occupational groups and departments with different skills, goals, values, beliefs and interests. A high level of internal interdependence means that co-operation is required from many different sources in order to get things done. In a rapidly changing external environment, the ability to obtain the active contribution of those diverse groups is essential for innovation. The entrepreneurial hero has to be able to mobilize and focus these groups. In the traditional mechanistic bureaucracies, innovators face considerable resistance.

(2) The power gap

Whatever the context, however, innovation is always difficult. Good ideas are one thing, getting them implemented is another. Kotter (1985) traces the problem to the managerial 'power gap' – a discrepancy between the resources and authority attached to formal positions, and the power needed to obtain co-operation and support from the different groups on which a successful innovation depends. This gap leads to frustration from managers who see superiors, colleagues and subordinates obstructing change. The consequence is that entrepreneurial heroes have to increase and deploy their power. This becomes particularly important in cross-functional and matrix structures, where managers have to use influence rather than direct authority to obtain collaboration. 'Organizational genius', Kanter (1983, p. 216) notes, 'is 10 percent inspiration and 90 percent acquisition – acquisition of power to move beyond a formal job charter and to influence others.'

(3) Pathological versus positive politics

The acquisition of power by the entrepreneurial hero takes a particular form. For Kotter (1985), this involves:

- creating visionary agendas and resource networks;
- collecting and using information – political diagnosis, monitoring relationships, identifying directions of mutual interest;
- developing good working relationships – different types of relationships with various groups, and in the face of difficulties such as separation and time pressures;
- establishing credibility – a reputation that saves time in dealings with colleagues and subordinates.

Kanter (1983, p. 179) paints a similar picture of politics in the 'integrative' organization:

> Even though the system in innovating companies is more 'politicized' in one sense – with managers having to capture power that they are not directly given in order to get anything done – it is also more 'civil' at least on the surface.

'Opponents' are won over by persistent, persuasive arguments; open communication is used to resolve debates, not back-stabbing. Perhaps the very publicness and openness of the battlegrounds – if that word even seems appropriate – makes 'reason' prevail. It is hard for back-room bargaining or displays of unilateral power to occur when issues are debated in group settings. Public meetings require that concerns be translated into specific criticisms, each of which can then be countered by data or well-mounted arguments. And the heavy reliance on informal communication networks as a source of reputation places a check on dirty dealing. 'Bad press' would ensure that such a person gets frozen out. An innovating company, then, begins to substitute a control system based on debate among peers for one based on top-down authority.

'Positive' politics implies 'campaigning, lobbying, bargaining, negotiating, caucusing, collaborating, and winning votes. That is, an idea must be sold, resources must be acquired or managed, and some variable numbers of other people must agree to changes in their own areas' (Kanter, 1983, p. 216). One company described it as a process to obtain 'buy in', 'preselling', 'sanity checks', and a log-rolling process of 'tin cupping' (Kanter, 1983, p. 157). This does not directly imply domination, winning, cutting others out or monopolizing resources.

Kotter (1985, p. 3) argues that this defeats the 'pathological aspects of modern organizations: the bureaucratic infighting, parochial politics, destructive power struggles and the like, which regularly reduce initiative, innovation, morale, and excellence in all kinds of organizations'. Backstage politics involves backstabbing to resolve debates, covert bargaining and displays of unilateral power, dirty dealing, and spreading rumours to destroy reputations (Kanter, 1983). Our entrepreneurial hero does not engage in such tactics.

Kotter (1985, p. 36) also argues that there is a clear choice in determining how to plan and support change (Figure 5.1). One suggested dynamic – favoured in the entrepreneurial hero tradition – involves exploiting the originality, creativity and exciting dimensions of conflict. The other – the province of entrenched bureaucratic opponents of that tradition – emphasizes infighting, alienation, frustration and reduced efficiency. Is this such a clear choice in practice?

(4) The heroic drama

The role of entrepreneurial hero is defined in relation to a complex cast of other characters. In her book *When Giants Learn to Dance*, Kanter (1989) contrasts the entrepreneurial hero with the managerial 'cowboy' and 'corpocrat' (Table 5.1). Kanter's entrepreneurial hero represents a different organizational philosophy. She argues that this new-style change driver combines the entrepreneurial creativity of the 'cowboy' with the discipline, co-operation and teamwork of the 'corpocrat', blending these features into a new type.

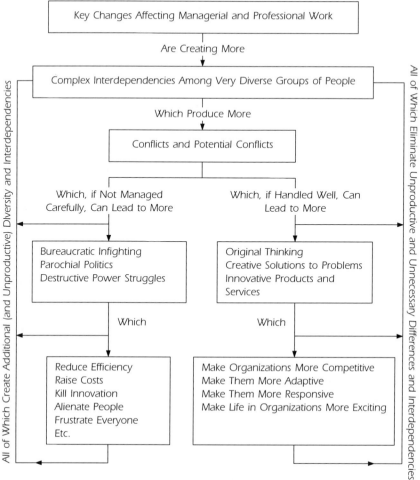

Figure 5.1 **The challenge we now face (Kotter, 1985, p. 36)**
Reprinted with the permission of The Free Press, a Division of Simon & Schuster from *Power and Influence: Beyond Formal Authority* by John P. Kotter. Copyright © 1985 by John P. Kotter.

Table 5.1 **Cowboys and corpocrats**

Cowboy	Corpocrat
High risk	Recognizes and makes complex decisions
Speculative	Balances investments and opportunities
Rule breaking	Establishes rules to guide others
Hires and inspires loyalty from cronies	Impersonal organizational commitments
Shoots from the hip	Creates complex, long-term agreements
Rejects trappings of power and success	Adheres to symbols of wealth and status
Focus on revitalization and growth	Low risk, planned growth
Entrepreneur	Organization man

Source: Based on Kanter (1989)

This entrepreneurial hero, this winner of the new 'corporate Olympics', is a focused, fast, friendly, flexible (4Fs) 'business athlete' with the following characteristics:

- operates without the might of the hierarchy behind them; develops personal relationships rather than relying on organizational status;
- competes in a way that enhances rather than undercuts co-operation; good negotiator for the unit, but also concerned with long-run corporate performance;
- operates with the highest ethical standards, because trust is crucial in establishing good working relationships and mobilizing people for change;
- has a dose of humility as well as self-confidence;
- develops a process focus, concerned with implementation as well as design, with how change is achieved as well as what is achieved;
- is multifaceted and ambidextrous;
- gains satisfaction from results.

Kotter's (1985) new leader steers a course between the 'naïve' and 'cynical' approaches to politics. 'Naïve' managers assume that people want to co-operate, that unselfish motives are dominant, that people have warm and supportive relationships, and that differences are minimal, and relatively easy to overcome. 'Cynics' assume the inevitability of conflict, that selfish motives are dominant, and that relationships are predominantly adversarial. The problem with both approaches lies in their inability to diagnose different situations. Neither can explain where and when co-operation or conflict will be found because they always expect either co-operation and harmony, or bureaucratic infighting respectively. Both positions fail to recognize the array of issues and legitimate constituencies involved in organizational change. By adopting such a simplistic interpretation, these extreme views cannot tailor political solutions to the legitimate claims of a variety of stakeholders.

Beyond naïveté and cynicism: the new leader

Beyond the yellow brick road of naïveté and the muggers' lane of cynicism, there is a narrow path, poorly lit, hard to find, and even harder to stay on once found. People who have the skill and the perseverance to take that path serve us in countless ways. We need more of these people. Many more. (Kotter, 1985: preamble)

Attention to superiors, tact and consideration towards colleagues, and understanding of subordinates are all key features of the new politics. The new entrepreneur has to cut across divisions, operate without sanction, operate with the motives and skills of others in networked organizations, and address a complex and changing environment.

The problem for the change driver is not so much the presence of resistance, but the 'powerlessness' of other players. In other words, it is 'organizational powerlessness' that corrupts (Kanter, 1997, p. 136). Why? Because powerful leaders are more likely to delegate, to reward talent, to support their subordinates. Powerlessness 'breeds bossiness', and creates 'ineffective, desultory management and petty, dictatorial rules-minded managerial styles' (Kanter, 1997, p. 135). The powerless manager uses 'oppressive' tactics, holds back others and punishes with whatever threats they can. Kanter (1997, p. 153) (Table 5.2) points to the effects of powerlessness among first-line supervisors, staff professionals and top executives.

Kanter (1977) notes that discrimination against women sustains the conditions that foster their powerlessness and, consequently, can generate in women the 'bossiness' that derives from powerlessness (Kanter, 1997, pp. 140–3). Action thus should be directed at powerlessness, not against the presumed power of particular occupational groups.

Table 5.2 **Symptoms and sources of powerlessness**

Position	Symptoms	Sources
First-line supervisors	Close, rules-minded supervision Tendency to do things oneself, blocking subordinate development and information Resistant, underproductive subordinates	Routine, rules-minded jobs with little control over lines of supply Limited lines of information Limited advancement or involvement prospects for oneself or for subordinates
Staff professionals	Turf protection, information control Retreat into professionalism Conservative resistance to change	Routine tasks seen by others as peripheral to 'real tasks' of line organization Blocked careers Easy replacement by outside experts
Top executives	Focus on internal cutting, short-term results, punishing Dictatorial top-down communications Retreat to comfort of like-minded lieutenants	Uncontrollable lines of supply because of environmental change Limited or blocked lines of information from lower levels Diminished lines of support because of challenges to legitimacy from public and special interest groups

Source: Kanter, 1997, p. 153

The new leadership

The term 'entrepreneurial hero' is a contemporary label of convenience. Various titles and qualities have been given to this character: *'leadership'*

(Bennis and Nanus, 1985; Kotter, 1990); *'transformational leadership'* (Bass, 1985; Tichy and Devanna, 1986), *'charismatic leadership'* (Conger, 1989), *'visionary leadership'* (Westley and Mintzberg, 1989) and *'new leadership'* (Bryman, 1996). This 'new leader' is someone who articulates and communicates an inspiring vision. As Bennis and Nanus (1985, p. 21) observe, in their celebrated phrase, 'Managers are people who do things right and leaders are people who do the right things.' Rather than leading by coercion and reciprocal exchange, the new leader pays attention to the motives and purposes of followers and obtains commitment from them to higher-order goals. This approach became prominent as a prescriptive model during the 1980s as organizations sought to address accelerated rates of change, the effects of world-wide recession, and the Iranian oil shock (Pettigrew, 1987).

In the 1990s, this management model was extended to include *'team leaders'* (Zenger et al., 1994), *'superleaders'* (Sims and Lorenzi, 1992), *'project leaders'* (Geddes et al., 1990) and *'real change leaders'* (Katzenbach and the Real Change Team, 1996). Organizational change and innovation was no longer the preserve of 'visionary heroes' but fell into the hands of a dispersed cast of organizational characters (Bryman, 1996). The focus shifted from the 'charismatic' leader to ongoing 'participative' leadership, as higher level managers 'lead others to lead themselves' (Sims and Lorenzi, 1992).

This new leadership approach also entailed a distinctive perspective on organizational politics. From the leadership work of McClelland (1975) to Lee (1997), there is a particular treatment of power and politics. Because of their extensive and explicit treatment of the subject, we shall explore in more depth the classic work of McClelland and the recent influential treatment of the subject by the Covey Leadership Center.

Two faces of power

McClelland was critical of what he called the American 'anti-leadership vaccine'. Through fear of the negative aspects of power, he argued, American managers were in danger of losing their leadership capacity. McClelland (1970, 1975) sought to restore an understanding of the importance of power and to distinguish between its positive and negative forms. He sees modern leaders as 'getting things done' by influencing people to support innovation and change. He also observed that, in contrast to traditional entrepreneurs, successful leaders of large corporations had a higher need for power. He called this need 'N Pow', defined as a concern for influencing people, contrasted with 'N Ach', the need for achievement (McClelland and Burnham, 1995, p. 100). Leaders in large, complex organizations have to be able to mobilize others to carry out their wishes, rather than do everything themselves, so managers with high N Pow tend to be more successful. However, McClelland saw N Pow as having two faces: one based on domination and the instrumental use of others; and one grounded in influencing people to work together towards inspiring goals and a treatment of people as ends in themselves.

A 'personal' view of power involves seeking to win over one's adversaries. The world is seen in terms of dominance and submission, a zero sum game where 'if I win, you lose'. The imagery is that of the 'law of the jungle' in which the strongest survive by destroying their opponents. It involves treating others as pawns in a world of conquest. It is a 'primitive' psychological mode, in that it is commonly employed by children before they have been socialized into using more subtle forms of influence (see Chapter 2).

The 'socialized' face of power is characterized by a concern for group goals, for finding goals that will inspire, for helping the group to formulate them, for providing members of the group with the means of achieving goals, and for giving group members the feeling of strength and competence they need to work toward such goals. Group members are not pawns, but feel that they belong. Power is here exercised for the benefit of others. Holding power is regarded with ambivalence, accompanied by doubts of personal strength, the realization that victories must be carefully planned in advance, and that every victory means a loss for someone. This is a concern with exercising influence *for* others.

Principled leadership

This concern to avoid the negative face of power has been taken up by a number of advocates of new leadership. For some, commitment to 'ethical leadership' (Johns, 1995) involves avoiding the coercive and manipulative dimensions of politics. The front cover of *The Power of Ethical Management* (Blanchard and Peale, 1988) exclaims, 'Integrity Pays! You Don't Have to Cheat to Win'. Blanchard and Peale emphasize the '5 Ps' of leadership: Purpose, Pride, Patience, Persistence and Perspective. The other '2 Ps' – Politics and Power – are notable by their absence. The Covey Leadership Center, building its reputation and influence on *The 7 Habits of Highly Effective People* (Covey, 1989, p. 53), has integrated and formalized thinking in this area in *The Power Principle* (1997) by Blaine Lee.

Covey (1989, p. 53) claims that 'effective people' share seven key habits:

1   Be proactive
2   Begin with the end in mind
3   Put first things first
4   Think win-win
5   Seek first to understand, then to be understood
6   Synergize
7   Sharpen the saw
    (© 1989 Stephen R. Covey. The 7 Habits are registered trademarks of Franklin
    Covey Co. Used with permission. All rights reserved.)

Managing with power

In a study of 50 managers in high and low morale units, McClelland and Burnham (1995) found a higher than average need for power among managers in general, and a particularly high need among managers in the high morale units. Most importantly, however, they found in the high morale units that managers had a greater need for power than desire to be liked (N Aff, or need for affiliation). Comparing 'affiliative' with 'personal power' and 'socialized power' managers, it was the affiliative managers who were least successful in generating high morale. Affiliative managers tended to make exceptions to rules to please people, which often antagonized others, and people did not have a clear sense of purpose or workplace rules. The 'socialized' or 'institutional' managers were the most successful, combining a high need for power with greater self-control and inhibition.

The 'institutional managers' play the influence game in a controlled way. They are empire builders and tend to create high morale as well as expand the organizations they head. They are more organization-minded than other managers, they report that they like to work, they are willing to sacrifice some of their own self-interest for the welfare of the organization, and they have a keen sense of justice. It was as if they believed that everyone had to work hard, sacrifice for the organization, and get a just reward for the effort. This motivation cuts across the traditional 'authoritarian–democratic' leadership-style framework. However, McClelland's research (1970) revealed that institutional managers made their subordinates feel strong and powerful rather than weak and powerless – the opposite of a traditional authoritarian leader. McClelland and Burnham (1995) also found that a large majority of the better managers scored higher on democratic or coaching styles of management in comparison with the poorer performers adopting authoritarian and coercive styles.

Covey contrasts his approach to the manipulative and Machiavellian dimension of the 'Personality Ethic' promoted in the 1970s, and advocates a return to the principled 'Character Ethic'. However, looking at these seven habits as techniques, they can readily be used by individuals or groups effectively to dominate and to control others, rather than for Covey's stated purpose of uplifting and encouraging an alignment between individual and organizational principles. This is not Covey's purpose and his introduction to 'principle-based power' in *Principle Centered Leadership* (1990) is further developed in *The Power Principle*, where Lee (1997) defines the distinction between negative and positive politics more clearly.

Lee criticizes the 'spiral of powerlessness' (Table 5.3) and recommends the use of power in organizations. Lee defines and contrasts three 'paths to power' through *coercive* power, *utility* power and *principle-centred* power. In other words, once the choice has been reached to use power and to shun powerlessness, three paths are available. Following a coercive path, leaders are obeyed because they can deploy unpleasant sanctions ('hard' or 'soft') for non-compliance. With utility power, compliance is based on exchange,

Table 5.3 **Powerlessness**

What we do when we choose to be powerless	What we get when we feel powerless
ignore	status quo
disregard	lose/win relationships
wait	helplessness
delay	unpredictable, unknown results
take no action	uncertainty
despair	wishes and fantasies
become indifferent	diminished capacity
neglect	
become apathetic	

Source: Lee, 1997, p. 37. © 1997 Franklin Covey Co. Used with permission. All rights reserved.

on a trade, on negotiation. With principle-centred power, compliance is based instead on respect for and belief in the leader. Coercive power means doing things *to* others. Utility power means doing things *with* others. Principle-centred power means doing things *for* others. These terms are defined in more detail in Tables 5.4–5.6.

In contrast to contingency models of leadership, these three paths to power are not presented as situationally appropriate leadership styles. Lee criticizes situational leadership models for viewing behavioural styles as merely alternative means for obtaining employee compliance. Following the 'servant leader' model of Greenleaf (1977), principle-centred leadership involves a new type of relationship between leaders and followers, based on mutual trust and respect. This involves three types of activity: pathfinding, team building and gardening:

- *pathfinding*: recognizing and accommodating the legitimate needs of all stakeholders by clarifying vision, context, direction, location, goals, strategy, purpose and pace;
- *team building*: helping others to work together to create healthy, safe conditions for risk taking, helping others to become leaders, providing resources and being a resource, helping others move from dependence to independence, to move from independence to interdependence, helping others get things done, and getting out of the way;
- *gardening*: working behind the scenes to create a culture that embodies core principles and values, determining how everyone works together, helping everyone agree on worthwhile purposes, creating enthusiasm and understanding in a critical mass of followers, identifying and removing obstacles, providing support, recognition and reward systems, procuring raw materials, pruning when necessary, planning for harvest.

Drawing on Helgesen (1990) and Godfrey (1996), Lee explicitly links this new style of leadership to traditional female approaches to family life and

Table 5.4 **Coercive power**

What we do when we are coercive		What we get when we are coercive
in the Hard approach	in the Soft approach	
suppress	mislead	an adversary
force	beguile	a fight
control	deceive	compliance
intimidate	seduce	opposition
bully	deter	dependence
threaten	divert	high risk
scare	sadden	revenge
belittle	discourage	negative external control
prohibit	inhibit	sabotage
disparage	trick	malicious compliance
emasculate		distrust
disenfranchise		win/lose relationships
		quick fixes
		transitory results
		revolt

Source: Lee, 1997, p. 75. © 1997 Franklin Covey Co. Used with permission. All rights reserved.

Table 5.5 **Utility power**

This is what we do	This is what we get
deal	a deal
bargain	a transaction
argue	a compromise
dicker	low risk
exchange	positive, external control
settle	situational ethics
concede	independent relationships
debate	temporary solutions
contend	performance agreements
quarrel	partial win/win relationships
compromise	

Source: Lee, 1997, p. 98. © 1997 Franklin Covey Co. Used with permission. All rights reserved.

childrearing. He concludes, 'To lead with honour and power challenges the best in us all; there is little room for the small-mindedness of parochial or gender-biased thinking and acting' (Lee, 1997, p. 270).

The moral maze

Machiavellian politics creates ethical and moral dilemmas for change drivers. On the one hand, there is a danger that those who readily engage in political action become manipulative and careerist, sacrificing themselves,

Table 5.6 **Principle-centred power: living with honour**

This is what we do	These are the results we get
persuade	partners and partnerships
be patient	a mutual transformation
be gentle	synergy
teach	calculated risks
accept	increased capacity
be kind	positive, internal control
love	ethical behaviour
learn	interdependent relationships
discipline	proactivity
be consistent	trust
live with integrity	win/win solutions
	partnership agreements
	deep satisfaction
	long-term relationships

their families and others to personal definitions of 'success'. On the other hand, political entrepreneurs can also become perceptive, flexible and effective political players, consistently attentive to their own needs and agendas and to the perceptions and needs of those around them. This tension can be set out in the form of a costs and benefits comparison:

Costs of political engagement

- Your ideas, manners and attitudes become adapted to what is 'required'. What is left of the 'real' you? Concerned with expediency, you may end up being corruptible. As the saying has it, 'Those who think it permissible to tell white lies soon grow colour-blind.'
- Your perception of others and the world around you becomes dominated by the 'needs' of your project and your own 'success'. Other people are only instruments to be used, and even though the world may not be out to 'get you', it may begin to seem that way.
- Your worries and anxieties increase. As you adapt yourself to other people, or your perceptions of their views, you see yourself through their eyes – and you begin to get more concerned about how they see you, and whether your perceptions are right. In the classic aphorism of Jean-Paul Sartre, 'hell is other people', and you may find yourself developing an excessive need for confirmation from significant others.
- Despite a demeanour of addressing the wants of others, you ultimately become mean and stingy towards yourself, family and friends as you desperately attempt to maintain the illusion and reality of success.
- You become increasingly subject to a nagging sense of self-betrayal and concerns about whether your private life has become sacrificed to the needs of the organization.

- You discourage deep personal relationships at work and at home as they get in the way of your struggle to get ahead and achieve your goals in the organization.
- Your relative lack of sincere warmth and affection in interpersonal relations begins to worry you as you appear incapable of developing meaningful long-term friendships.
- Your lack of concern with conventional morality often leaves you uncertain about how to act and with insufficient time and energy to consider what you believe to be the right way of behaving.
- Your attempts to motivate and enthuse become more apparent to yourself and others as a subtle form of manipulation. Getting others to commit themselves to helping you or the organization begins to seem more like exploitation than empowerment. A cycle of distrust and confusion begins to develop in your relations with work colleagues.
- Your maintenance of a 'macho' management image and complete self-sacrifice to the organization allows you little room to express emotion or reveal signs of weakness and doubt.
- Your lack of real commitment to the organization becomes increasingly apparent to others as your manoeuvrings begin to appear more like self-interested games-playing.
- You find that you are tending to resort prematurely to coercion and manipulation in the face of potential opposition, setting off cycles of conflict and distrust.
- Your personal and family life is beginning to collapse and your enjoyment and success at work has begun to decline.

Benefits from political engagement

- You develop the ability more accurately to assess yourself and others.
- You dramatize issues, and enthuse and entertain others in a manner that gets and keeps their interest.
- You are proactive in dealing with problems and crises and do not relapse into moaning and complaining about what is being 'done' to you.
- You are relatively non-ideological and liberal as a leader in comparison to previous bosses.
- You are not hostile and vindictive towards other people, even those who oppose you and win. Such attitudes and actions would be the sign of a loser.
- You are not aiming to build empires, or to dominate others ruthlessly to that end.
- Your finances and your career are progressing well.
- You adapt flexibly to changing circumstances and situations.
- You resist unthinking or crude pressures by individuals or groups to perform unkind or corrupt acts.
- You inspire admiration in others for your technical and interpersonal accomplishments and successes.

As our discussion of hero entrepreneurs and new leaders suggests, it is possible to challenge the dominance of 'turf protection', and obtain co-operation from others in creating a more innovative organizational culture. Champions of such a change may be proactive, inspirational and collaborative. They may have a realistic understanding of the dynamics of what Nalebuff and Brandenburger (1996) call 'co-opetition'. This means co-operating with superiors, colleagues and subordinates who may at different times play the role of co-operators (or 'complementers') and competitors, as well as suppliers and customers. On the other hand, such champions of innovation may also appear to be exploitative, competitive and insidiously intrusive ideologues. They may not genuinely empower employees or really contribute to organizational success. In fact they may be acting immorally or illegally, entrapping employees within systems not of their choosing, or creating the illusion rather than the reality of success. An insight into how the activities of political entrepreneurs can take, or be interpreted as taking, either form can be obtained by considering how the hero entrepreneur and new leader traditions interpret the activities of political entrepreneurs in contrast to the description provided by Punch (1996) of 'dirty business' and Jackall (1988) of the 'moral maze' within which managers operate.

Working the bureaucracy – another shadow side

The hero entrepreneur tradition interprets the modern era as a transition between the Machiavellian politics-ridden bureaucratic organization of the past, and the new, empowered, integrative, organic organization of the future, with hero entrepreneurs driving the transition. In contrast, Punch (1996) argues that the 'casino capitalism' of the 1980s and 1990s created the irresponsible corporate 'yuppie'. The environmentalist cry that, 'There is no such thing as a free lunch', was replaced by Michael Douglas' slogan from the film *Wall Street*: 'Lunch is for wimps!' This world, Punch argues, bred a 'shadow' organization, unlike the innovative adhocracy documented by Kanter (1983) and by Peters and Waterman (1982). He uses the fate of Robert Maxwell and of Barings Bank to illustrate the way in which a competitive market economy that supports the pursuit of legitimate self-interest may systematically institutionalize and accept 'deviant' activities. Punch points in particular to: shadow corporate strategies (bribing your way into markets); shadow organization structures (units set up to conduct deviance, such as Revco); shadow financing (smokescreen offshore accounts); shadow accounting (creation of false accounts in many scandals); and shadow personnel management (selecting pliant managers ready to cut corners, as in heavy anti-trust cases). Organizations with such a shadow side seek to maintain the appearance of legality and probity, even while engaging in sophisticated, subtle and carefully constructed alternative strategies and structures in order to achieve corporate or group goals by illicit means. This 'shadow boxing' requires skill, ingenuity and cunning. It can range from managers merely trying to meet organizational goals and expectations, to the criminal empire of BCCI which operated a 'black bank'. In many of these cases, managers were at pains to conceal their real motives, conduct and performance from both internal and external scrutiny, and were prepared to cover up shadow systems if threatened. In this way, managers constantly juggle a form of 'mental and moral double bookkeeping' as they come to terms with the 'dark' side of life in what Bowles (1991) also called the 'organization shadow'.

Workable illegalities

The hero entrepreneur perspective focuses on the use of informal influence to get things done that cannot be achieved through formal authority. In so doing, it points to the importance of an informal world that makes the formal world 'work'. This has long been recognized. As Jacobs (1969) and Gouldner (1954) observed in their critique of public images of 'symbolic' or 'mock' bureaucracy, the 'real' activities are always performed in an inherently non-bureaucratic manner. This has been a common theme in classic studies of 'what managers actually do' from Dalton (1959) to Watson (1994). In *Men Who Manage* (1959), Dalton revealed managers working on two levels – one for the records and appearances, and one submerged but acknowledged for 'real' simply in order to get things done. Some of the practices Dalton uncovered while working as a manager were, however, far from the honourable heroic entrepreneurial activities outlined by Kotter. For example, he pointed to:

- records being 'lost' to someone's advantage;
- the manipulation of accounts with non-existent personnel on the payroll to fund secret operations;
- informal bargains repaid with informal favours (such as redecorating offices);
- people being informed beforehand when inspections were coming;
- failure to record many accidents so as to improve safety records;
- guards on the gates colluding in the removal of the firm's goods.

Dalton (1959, p. 31) argues that managers are inevitably coached in a multiplicity of such 'finesses of workable illegalities', in the normal course of their routine and legitimate business life. Punch (1996) puts an even more 'deviant' slant on the working of this informal world. He cites Bensman and Gerver (1963), who show the links between the formal and informal organization in a study of criminal practices in a factory. The personnel involved maintained public values while at the same time performing those actions necessary to attain public or private ends. Similarly, Punch cites cases of commercial bribery where there exists a 'myth system' that publicly bolsters institutional values, and the 'operational code' which is covered in secrecy and which is concerned with how things are actually done. Bribery, for example, may deviate from the myth system, but may be seen as appropriate under an operational code that provides a set of private and unacknowledged rules that selectively tolerates extraordinary payments as part of ordinary business.

High-impact deviance

While advocates of the heroic entrepreneur point to the democratization of organizations and the increasing openness of politics, Punch (1996) points to the new opportunities being opened up for high-impact corporate deviance through the globalization of the world economy, the spread of rapid and advanced information and communication technologies, increasing economies of scale and industrial concentration, and the reduced power of governments to control such activities. He points to the use of power and resources, not just for trivial activities such as fiddling expenses, but for the serious business of bribery, secrecy, deception, falsification, industrial espionage, black markets, intimidation, conspiracy, price-fixing and so on (Punch, 1996, p. 57).

Punch (1996, p. 5) argues that management

> remains locked into an ostensible concern with strategy formulation and planning related to survival, long-term continuity, return on investment, a reputable image and the application of the latest and most sophisticated techniques of managerial practice. But under that coherent and apparently rational effort there is a world of power struggles, ideological debate, intense political rivalry, manipulation of information, and short-term problem-solving. Viewed in this light, managers emerge as something of amoral chameleons, buffeted by moral ambiguity and organizational uncertainty, and they survive this 'messy, not to say dirty' environment by engaging in Machiavellian micro-politics.

The principle-centred leadership of Covey and Lee appears thoroughly naïve and ineffectual against this backdrop.

This image is supported by Jackall (1988) in his extensive interview-based study of 'ethics in action' in four American organizations. Claims to be creating a 'positive' world of politics are seen by Jackall as merely another 'rehearsal of legitimation'. In the search for 'defensible' rationales, the first rehearsal commonly involves casting around for different viewpoints to 'cover all the bases'. The second rehearsal shifts to a more focused discussion by testing out the consequences of different rationalities. The final rehearsal is when a certain viewpoint seems convincing and a more formal rationale is usually elaborated and disseminated. The morality involved is one of appearances alone. As he argues:

> [M]orality becomes one's personal comfort zone in relation to the anticipated views of others. The measure of that comfort becomes a confidence in the casuistry necessary to persuade others that one's stories are plausible and one's

choices reasonable . . . rehearsals also encourage the most subtle form of hype, namely convincing oneself of one's own rectitude. (Jackall, 1988, p. 189)

Deviant practices and dirty business

Punch (1996) outlines a range of 'deviant' activities that are informally institutionalized:

- Informal rewards: perks, fiddles, discounts, presents.
- Work avoidance/manipulation: arriving late, seeking 'cushy numbers'.
- Employee deviance against the organization: stealing, absenteeism, neglect and sabotage, embezzlement.
- Employee deviance for the organization: bend rules, avoid safety regulations, institutionalize 'indulgence patterns' (Gouldner, 1954).
- Organizational deviance for the organization: serious and deliberate practices with a measure of acceptance in relation to internal and external formal controls in order to achieve formal or informal organizational goals.
- Managing deviance against the organization: victimize own company and loot it in your own interests.

Heroic drama, last act

Advocates of the hero entrepreneur place their innovator among a cast of characters that includes the powerless, the naïve, cynics, cowboys and corpocrats. The outcome of the drama is that the shining hero entrepreneur appears as an empowering realist, possessing the entrepreneurialism of the cowboy and the attention to people of the corpocrat. Sarah Bernhardt is famous for having told Bernard Shaw that they should have a baby because, with her body and his brains, it would be a wonderful child. Shaw's equally famous retort was, 'What if the baby has my body and your brains?' What if the hero entrepreneur has the ideological rigidity of the corpocrat and the disregard for other people of the cowboy, without the positive qualities of either? An alternative picture is presented by Jackall (1988, p. 204):

> For those with the requisite discipline, sheer dogged perseverance, the agile flexibility, the tolerance for extreme ambiguity, the casuistic discernment that allows one to dispense with shopworn pieties, the habit of mind that perceives opportunities in others' and even one's own misfortunes, the brazen nerve that allows one to pretend that nothing is wrong even when the world is crumbling, and, above all, the ability to read the inner logic of events, to see and do what has to be done, the rewards of corporate success can be very great. And, of course, those who do succeed, those who find their way out of the crowded, twisting corridors and into the back rooms where the real action is, where the big games take place, and where everyone present is a player, shape, in a decisive

way, the moral rules-in-use that filter down through their organizations. The ethos that they fashion turns principles into guidelines, ethics into etiquette, values into tastes, personal responsibility into an adroitness at public relations, and notions of truth into credibility. Corporate managers who become imbued with this ethos pragmatically take their world as they find it and try to make that world work according to its own institutional logic. They pursue their own careers and good fortune as best they can within the rules of their world. As it happens, given their pivotal institutional role in our epoch, they help create and re-create, as one unintended consequence of their personal striving, a society where morality becomes indistinguishable from the quest for one's own survival and advantage.

The point of these contrasts between the heroic entrepreneur and the shadow organization is to emphasize the different forms that innovative activity can take, and the different moral evaluations that can be brought to those actions. There is ambiguity and tension in the way in which hero entrepreneurs and new leaders are being advocated. While appearing to present a 'win-win', participative and harmonious view of power, there is recognition of the need for diagnosing and carrying out a variety of different forms of politics, including a more ruthless and coercive dimension. If we return to McClelland (1970, 1975, 1995), while he points to the importance of the power motive, and its indispensable presence in effective leaders, he is ambivalent about its character. There is a 'danger in this motive profile; empire building can lead to imperialism and authoritarianism. . . . The same motive power which produces good power management can also lead a company or country to try to dominate others, ostensibly in the interests of organizational expansion' (McClelland, 1975, p. 109). McClelland consequently stresses the central importance of 'safeguards', based on internal psychological restraints (a lack of egotism, and a strong faith in people), and external social constraints (democratic structures and a participatory coaching style of management).

Similarly, while Kotter (1985) gives a positive and constructive view of the hero entrepreneur, he emphasizes that his is not a claim about the 'end of politics' or a simple appeal for 'soft' participative management, nor is it restricted to the use of 'informal' methods. Political diagnosis may indicate the need for rapid decision making and 'hard' forceful, if not directly coercive action. Action involves using all possible methods and resources, whether these are hard or soft, formal or informal. Kanter (1983) also shows that this is no simple appeal for 'participative management'. She points, for example, to managing the complex politics of teamwork. While arguing for the formation of innovation teams, she observes that these teams still have 'politics'. The knowledge and information necessary to participate is unequally distributed, as are the requisite skills and personal resources. Seniority patterns are established within a team. The external hierarchy continues to influence team activities as many members have to return to that hierarchy after the project concludes. Within teams there is a

Leadership as a balancing act

In real life the actual leader balances on a knife edge between expressing personal dominance and exercising the more socialized type of leadership. He may show first one face of power, then the other. The reason for this lies in the simple fact that even if he is a socialized leader, he must take initiative in helping the group he leads to form its goals. How much initiative he should take, how persuasive he should attempt to be, and at what point this clear enthusiasm for certain goals becomes personal authoritarian insistence that those goals are the right ones whatever the members of the group may think, are all questions calculated to frustrate the well-intentioned leader. If he takes no initiative, he is no leader. If he takes too much, he becomes a dictator, particularly if he tries to curtail the process by which members of the group participate in shaping group goals. There is a particular danger for the man who has demonstrated his competence in shaping group goals and in inspiring group members to pursue them. In time both he and they may assume that he knows best, and he may almost imperceptibly change from a democratic to an authoritarian leader. (McClelland, 1970, p. 42)

politics of interest maximization, characterized by jockeying for status, and by the diverse backgrounds of and historic tensions between members. New oligarchies or tyranny by the group may emerge. 'Soft' skills contribute to resolving these tensions, but have to be combined with a broader approach to politics using a set of power tools and skills.

This 'harder' edge to politics can also be found in the principle-centred leadership studies. While Lee (1997) talks of the new roles in terms of pathfinding, team building and gardening, this pleasant 'nurturing' image is also accompanied by references to the need for drastic 'pruning' when needed to bring in the 'harvest'. When Lee addresses the issue of how the principle-centred leader deals with challenge from the more ruthless and coercive organizational politician, he includes such actions as: 'get help – join with others for support and possible resistance'; 'do not take it lying down . . . there may come a time for you to do something, to stand up and be counted, to make the tough decisions, to find your way through corporate or private moral mazes'; 'go underground' (Lee, 1997, pp. 282–3).

The picture that emerges from these exceptions to the general tenor of Lee's text is one of the political entrepreneur using a variety of tactics to deal with different political contexts – not so dissimilar to the more complex picture of tactics and morals advocated here.

Perspectives on culture

Martin (1992) distinguishes between 'integration', 'differentiation' and 'fragmentation' approaches to culture. This can provide a platform for the critical assessment of political behaviour in organizational change. The leadership and change approaches discussed in this chapter adopt an integration perspective which approaches moral and ethical issues in terms of the consequences of a universal 'character type' or leadership approach. In the case of the hero entrepreneur, or the new leadership, this means using the informal 'shadow' organization to achieve corporate and personal objectives. This assumes the desirability of 'instrumentalizing' the 'informal' organization, in much the same way that teamwork initiatives seek to get workers to use their social networks and peer pressure to reduce 'anti-company' work practices and to mobilize their efforts for 'pro-company' activities. As Martin observes, however, the validity of such an approach is thrown into doubt by proponents of the 'differentiation' and 'fragmentation' perspectives.

The differentiation perspective views culture in pluralistic terms, consisting of a variety of sub-cultures, each with its own beliefs and values. Here one expects to find conflicting views on the goals and practices of innovative activity. Part of the task of the political entrepreneur is to understand and address this diversity. There is no simple or universal set of costs and benefits, for any such analysis would be contested. Kanter (1997) recognizes this complexity, and this informs her more complex model of the political manoeuvrings of 'change masters'. However, the overall tone and political orientation of her analysis of the transition from 'segmented' to 'integrative' organizations is closer to the value position of the harmonious 'integrative' view of culture than it is to pluralistic 'differentiation'.

The fragmentation perspective emphasizes the uncertainty, the ambiguity and contradictory nature of cultural beliefs and values, even within sub-cultures, and the thinking and activities of managers themselves. This reinforces the complexity of the political entrepreneur's role. It is not simply a question of taking a stand, and supporting the values and beliefs of particular groups, for these may be, at least in part, shaped by the change process and the activities of political entrepreneurs themselves. It would be naïve, and dangerous, to employ different political strategies on the assumption of fixed and stable beliefs, values and goals among change participants.

Situational legitimacy

> *Texan sales and loans consultant*: If you didn't do it, you weren't just stupid – you weren't behaving as a prudent businessman, which is the ground rule. You owed it to your partners, to your stockholders, to maximize profits. Everybody else was doing it. (Punch, 1996, p. 20)

Organizations seem to be characterized by a 'moral schizophrenia'. Morality, on the one hand, is defined by formal systems of authority and control. These systems sanction, as 'good behaviour', actions that contribute to profitability and growth and conform to corporate regulations and codes of conduct. This cannot, however, be simply equated with the 'legitimate' aspect of organizational life. Within the formal world of corporate decision making, determining 'good behaviour' and legitimate practice is not a simple matter. Corporate goals may clash with social values and legal sanctions over such matters as environmental sustainability, employee health and safety, community welfare, distribution of wealth. This raises political questions about the appropriate nature of corporate control and regulation, ranging from laws requiring media to be owned by 'fit and proper' individuals, to more broad-ranging debates over worker democracy and corporate governance.

The pursuit of corporate objectives may also clash with established practices. A Western corporation entering an Asian economy might, for example, be forced to modify practices concerning 'kick backs' and 'bribes' in order to support its growth objectives. A policy of 'employment for life' may be sacrificed in the face of a major loss of global competitiveness. Different sub-units may have formal goals and embedded structures and practices that conflict with the goals and practices of other sub-units, or even the sustainable competitiveness of the organization as a whole. Accountancy and finance may, for example, have return on investment criteria that clash with those of industrial engineering, and either may be seen as threatening to organizational innovativeness. Such ambiguities and conflicts in the formal organization are inherently political in nature. Their resolution involves uncertainty and conflict, and impacts on the distribution of rewards. Such ambiguities also have political implications for authority and decision making.

On the other hand, organizations have a set of informal, shadow, back-stage and sub-group moralities that are often more pressing and real to their members. These are the informal systems made up of different sub-cultures and networks of power and influence. These informal systems sanction as 'good behaviour' actions that contribute to particular individual and group success (career advancement, group resources) and conform to the codes of conduct of group sub-cultures (peer group values, professional ethics, departmental style).

Organizations both create and deny the reality and morality of these informal worlds. On the one hand, the dominant formal culture is rationalist and unitary. Efficiency, profit and viability are the only legitimate public criteria to apply to decisions. Attempts are made to represent informal goals and activities as at best 'non-legitimate' (not the legitimate concern of the organization), and at worst 'illegitimate', insofar as they act against or distract attention from the pursuit of sanctioned objectives. On the other hand, both labour markets and individuals are assumed to be driven by self-interest. When Knights and Murray (1994, p. 30) place 'the pursuit of career in the boiler room of organizational politics', they are pointing to the central nature of this tension between public and shadow worlds.

Conventional wisdom views the formal organization structure as a mechanism for securing *organizational* goals. From an individual perspective, however, this structure is also a career ladder, a mechanism for securing *personal* welfare and advancement. Insofar as individual interests and careers are bound up with the interests of organizational sub-units or professions, self-interest becomes a driving force of cross-departmental and professional politics. The legitimate pursuit of individual and group goals is situational in character. For some, the defence of professional codes of practice or departmental resources is seen in terms of 'higher purpose', rather than simply self-interest. In some settings, the blatant and aggressive pursuit of self-interest and advancement may be acceptable. Elsewhere, individuals are expected to be committed to organizational visions and ideals, and some settings even encourage respect for personal and family life.

Moreover, the corporate ends of profit and growth can often be used to justify activities that would normally be regarded as immoral or illegal. This can cover a range of activities from illicit bribery and golden handshakes to the selective release of information in public relations statements. Similar kinds of justifications can be provided for activities carried out to ensure job security and support a family, preserve professional integrity and ethics and defend the interests of departments that perceive themselves as performing a valuable service for the organization and its customers. The informal means selected to pursue different goals may also be perceived as moral or immoral depending on the context. For organizations where the 'male macho management style' predominates, for example, coercion and fear may be tolerated and even respected. In more bureaucratic settings, the manipulation of group dynamics in meetings may be expected.

There can be no absolute separation between individual and group self-interest, on the one hand, and organizational goals and purposes, on the other. Formal and informal, public and private, goals and objectives are intertwined. Just as the formal cannot be simply equated with 'legitimate', the 'illegitimacy' of the informal cannot be presumed. In Dalton's words, people pursuing private objectives are not 'bad men performing dubious activities'. They are 'often promoters and reorganizers as they do not see the firm as static. Rules and procedures are not sacred guides but working tools to be revised . . . or dropped as required in striking successive balances between company goals and the personal ends and claims of themselves and their supporters' (cited in Punch, 1996, p. 218). In recognition of this interdependence, organization design and human resource management have advocated numerous mechanisms for aligning the formal and the informal. Whether or not one sees this as a 'positive' force depends, at least in part, on the legitimacy accorded to formal corporate goals compared to the informal goals of individuals and groups. When these systems are in alignment, then there may be limited conflict. Individual or group motives and activities reinforce and support performance and the pursuit of organizational success. The formal system is regarded as legitimate by employees, and sanctions the activities undertaken in the formal world. Where these systems are out of alignment, then the legitimacy of the formal system is brought into question; the formal system defines as illegitimate 'deviant' informal goals and activities.

The moral matrix

We must conclude that the moral discourse surrounding organizational politics is complex – a moral maze with many entrances and criss-crossing pathways, but no clear centre or exits. Political behaviour cannot readily be sectioned into a morally benign 'high road' and a morally repugnant 'low road'. We are faced instead with a spaghetti junction of intertwined means and ends, formal and informal systems, legitimate and illegitimate behaviours.

Despite this complex set of advantages and disadvantages of Machiavellian political behaviour, it is possible to discern a number of underlying themes to the general moral discourse on politics. Discussions centre on judgements on three dimensions:

1   the appropriate *degree* of politics;
2   the acceptability of political *means*;
3   the legitimacy of political *goals*.

Questions of *degree* are related to how far political behaviour is perceived as necessary and valuable. Rational and consensual views of organizations see politics as an unnecessary and disruptive distraction from 'real work'. Pluralist and conflict views of organizations see political behaviour as inevitable, and see political mastery as an essential management skill. But 'degree' is a problematic concept, with connotations of 'more' and 'less' which, considering political behaviour, are difficult to apply to practice.

The acceptability of political *means* refers to the extent to which the strategies and tactics employed are not sanctioned. This involves evaluation of formal legitimation or informal justifications (accounts) of the tactics used, particularly when this involves more controversial, extreme and ruthless forms of coercion, deceit and manipulation. This concept is also problematic. As Chapter 2 argued, establishing what is and what is not 'sanctioned' in most organizational settings can be extremely difficult.

The legitimacy of political *goals* raises issues such as whether or not the goals are formally sanctioned, the degree to which political activity involves the pursuit of individual or sectional interests, and the degree to which sanctioned goals or individual or sectional interests are perceived to be valuable and legitimate in social terms. Once again we run into the question: is it sanctioned? We also encounter the difficulty of relating change initiatives exclusively to either organizational or individual purposes. In most instances these goals, as indicated earlier, imply each other and are inextricably intertwined.

Political entrepreneurs are advised, in the framework of Chapter 1, to be clear about their warrant to initiate change, and about implicit warrant for political behaviour. This entails an assessment of the context, and the anticipated responses of stakeholders, as well as personal goals, expertise and reputation. The costs and benefits of political behaviour may be assessed from a number of perspectives, to arrive at decisions concerning appropriate degrees, means and goals. The critical perspective here, concerns an individual's assessment of the implications of their actions for the change agenda, and for their reputation. Decisions about appropriate ploys and accounts flow from this personal assessment.

The change driver is advised either to abandon, or to treat with caution, 'universal' normative ethical principles of the kind outlined in Chapter 3. Such principles fail on contact with reality. The change driver seeking practical guidance should perhaps resort to a *situational ethic*. What is appropriate and acceptable in this context? What is justifiable and defensible in this context? Disputes over these questions can be resolved in the court of public debate. In other words, for the change driver, these questions attract specific, concrete, local responses. Disputes over universal principles are dealt with in the court of intellectual discussion. Such questions generate endless and irresolvable dispute.

Situational ethics may appear untidy and controversial. The advantage of using this framework is that it leaves open what is regarded as ethical and legitimate in different contexts, while offering the political entrepreneur a model for interrogating the moral issues involved in the change process. The ethical and moral perspectives explored here present a set of costs and benefits, and views of what constitutes legitimate political activity. These should not, however, be taken as rigid guidelines for a political entrepreneur who will inevitably have to fashion his or her own situationally specific code of ethics and legitimatory accounts. In addition, advocacy of a situational ethic is only one dimension of the perspective of the political entrepreneur, explained in more detail in Chapter 7.

Before leaving the arguments of this and the previous chapter behind, you may find it useful to reflect on your personal position with respect to the following issues:

1 To what extent do my personality and behaviour correspond to the Machiavellian, or the corporate gamesman?
2 In relation to my organizational political behaviour, where do I currently stand on a personal cost–benefit calculation?
3 How do I and my colleagues use terms like 'Machiavellian' or 'negative politics' or 'playing games' to discredit the behaviour of others? And how do I attempt to avoid such 'accusations' myself?

4 How do I view 'the shadow side' of organizational life? A seedy, nasty underworld of illegitimate 'dirty business' and corruption? An inevitable, legitimate underworld of conflict and tension, source of the dynamics of change, exploitable and manageable?

5 Is there an alternative to involvement in organizational politics? Is there a 'higher moral ground'? Or is that 'high ground' illusory?

6 The politics of failure and the failure of politics

Failing fashions

> Globalization. Information technology. Total quality. Benchmarking. Best practices. Customer focused. Micromarketing. Flexible manufacturing. Value creation. Core competence. Competitive advantage. Strategic intent. Strategic alliances. Partnering. Outsourcing. Networks. Time-based competition. Continuous improvement. Concurrent engineering. Computer-aided design. Computer-aided engineering. Computer-aided manufacturing. Computer-integrated manufacturing. Cross-functional teams. Downsizing. Rightsizing. Flattening. Delayering. Information. Revitalization. Restructuring. Re-engineering. Organizational transformation. Business process redesign. Mission statements. Organizations as orchestras. The new organization. The information-based organization. The knowledge-intensive organization. The learning organization. The network organization. The informated organization. The cluster organization. The adaptive organization. The post-industrial organization. The transnational organization. Knowledge workers. Empowerment. Pay-for-performance. Diversity. Entrepreneurs. Intrapreneurs.
>
> (Eccles and Nohria, 1992, p. 1)

During the 1980s, the CEO of a major international bank announced a company-wide change effort. He reviewed the bank's purpose and culture with his senior management team. He published a mission statement, and hired a new vice-president for human resources (HR) from a company with an excellent HR reputation. He established company-wide programmes to push change. He created a new organization structure, performance appraisal system, pay for performance compensation plan, training programmes to turn managers into change agents, and quarterly attitude surveys to chart the progress of the change effort. There was one problem. Two years after the CEO launched this programme, virtually none of the desired changes in organizational behaviour had occurred (Beer et al., 1990).

There are many such 'war stories' concerning large-scale change, usually involving one or other of the currently fashionable TLAs: TQM, BPR, CIM, AMT, FMS or AWGs. A TLA is a Three-Letter Acronym – an indispensable accompaniment to any 'best practice' reorganization doctrine. A similar pattern may be cynically predicted with respect to more recent fashions for the 'virtual corporation', 'intelligent manufacturing systems' and the 'learning organization'.

A large American financial institution committed itself in 1988 to a total quality management (TQM) programme. The company trained hundreds of employees and communicated the programme's intent to thousands more. After two years, they had 48 teams, and morale was reported as very positive. However, no bottom-line performance improvements were reported – because there were none. The vice-president of a large mineral extracting corporation described the results of his three-year old TQM programme: 'We have accomplished about 50 per cent of our training goals and about 50 per cent of our employee participation goals but only about 5 per cent of our results goals' (Schaffer and Thomson, 1992, p. 81).

Illustrative cases of the failure of advanced manufacturing technology (AMT) and computer-integrated manufacturing (CIM) are also common. In 1990, a large computer manufacturer reported that a $6 million robotics line capable of producing keyboards was sitting idle, and that 20 operators, trained in automation, were building the keyboards manually. An industrial hose maker implemented a materials requirements planning (MRP) system which actually increased the time to process orders rather than reducing it (Majchrzak and Gasser, 1991, p. 321).

The picture is similar for business process re-engineering (BPR). One computer company re-engineered its finance department, reducing process costs by 34 per cent, but operating income stalled. One insurer cut claims-processing time by 44 per cent, but profits dropped. Another insurance firm decided to re-engineer its personal insurance lines, but ended up only re-engineering a process that contributed 3 to 4 per cent to business unit costs, with a negligible effect on overall performance (Hall et al., 1993).

Stories of failures to achieve the predicted benefits of innovation and change are widespread, and are regularly confirmed in surveys. For example, 86 per cent of CEOs in America were reported in 1991 as believing that TQM was likely to remain a top priority in the year 2000, yet in the same year a survey of more than 300 electronics companies reported that 63 per cent of those undertaking TQM (73 per cent of the sample) had failed to improve quality defects by even as much as 10 per cent (Schaffer and Thomson, 1992, p. 81). The evidence suggests that overall success rates with TQM are below 25 per cent (Spector and Beer, 1994). A similar picture emerges from recent surveys of BPR projects. These have revealed that in America, up to 88 per cent of large corporations are involved in such projects (Clemons et al., 1995), and in the UK at least 59 per cent were either planning or undertaking BPR projects (Willcocks and Grint, 1997). Yet, a recent survey of over 500 chief information officers by Deloitte-Touche ended up rating their success in improving customer service and process timeliness as only 5 out of 10, with effects on increasing revenue only obtaining a rating of 2 out of 10. Even one of the original re-engineering gurus, Michael Hammer, acknowledges that as many as 70 per cent of projects fail (Moad, 1993). Surveys of AMT and CIM have obtained similar results. In a 1990 survey by the Society of Manufacturing Engineers of 363 users and vendors of advanced manufacturing technology, 57 per cent of respondents reported that AMT systems installations were over schedule by as much as 50 per cent. A study of 2000 American firms developing information systems revealed that at least 40 per cent of these systems failed to achieve the intended results (Majchrzak and Gasser, 1991).

The politics of failure

Why such high failure rates? A number of explanations have been offered. Advocates frequently argue, somewhat predictably, that their methods have not been properly understood, or have been partially applied. Many quality programmes are criticized by their guru designers for implementing bureaucratic quality controls, rather than creating a culture of commitment to quality and the customer (Dawson and Palmer, 1995). Business process re-engineering projects are frequently condemned for their partial, incremental and narrowly focused cost-cutting – in stark opposition to the strategic and radical restructuring that the originators recommended (Willcocks and Grint, 1997). Self-managing work team initiatives are criticized for their frequent lack of real empowerment, and the failure of senior management to make the changes in middle management and support structures necessary to make teamwork a reality. Zealous supporters of advanced manufacturing technologies often argue that they have only been applied in a narrow fashion to improve the efficiency of particular individuals, operations and sub-units (Bessant, 1991). It is claimed that there has been a consistent failure to exploit the boundary-spanning and integrative potential of new technologies to support radically new forms of work and organizational design (Kaplinski, 1984).

It is not surprising that those directly responsible for change implementation often blame combinations of personal and local factors: individual failings, inadequate knowledge and skill in the organization, the weak 'people skills' of change agents, resistance by particular individuals, a lack of senior management commitment etc.

There is, however, an alternative explanation that does not rely on individual and organizational failings, but which attributes high failure rates to the political difficulties inherent in major change initiatives. Simple changes, introduced slowly and incrementally, are typically not characterized by high degrees of tension, conflict or debate. Complex changes which require rapid and radical changes in behaviour, on the other hand, are highly vulnerable to political disruption. A major structural, cultural or procedural change may be only partially realized as departments, sections and other interest groupings in the organization 'translate' broad recommendations into a package acceptable to them. This typically involves ensuring that changes do not threaten vested interests and privileges. Major changes rely on the contribution, compliance and co-operation of a range of groups and departments with different values, perceptions and goals. It is hardly surprising that combinations of inexperience and resistance severely disrupt implementation.

Radical projects and inter-departmental politics

Many large organizations, despite the predictions of 'airport lounge' management books, are still characterized by complex hierarchies and functional differentiation, creating the 'functional stovepipe' model organization chart. This is what Kanter (1983) calls the 'segmentalist' organization (see Chapter 5), in which status, hierarchies, and professional, occupational and departmental sub-cultures are well established and resistant to change. Segmentalist organizations suffer from 'structural inertia' (Hannan and Freeman, 1984). They provide reliability through routine and institutionalized patterns of activity. Change is inevitably perceived as hazardous. Yet the segmentalist organization is the primary target for initiatives such as TQM, BPR, CIM, self-managing teams and other 'best practice' initiatives.

In this context, radical organizational change increases political vulnerability for two reasons:

1 *Breadth*: Recommendations are typically portrayed as central to the organization's strategy and survival, involving modifications and adjustments to established structures 'across the board'.
2 *Depth*: Change involves attempts to introduce radical departures from established ways of doing things.

The Scope of Change

The plant manager of an Australian plastics irrigation equipment company slammed his fist on the table and proclaimed, 'The project was *not* just about creating teams. It meant changes to computer systems, databases, accounting, even the building for God's sake! And their problem: "Theory X" was not just an attitude of mind. It was embedded in the systems around us.' This plant had been successful. In an Australian aeroplane manufacturer, changes had been slower and more painful. When interviewed, the CEO sadly reflected, 'The old culture was so strong. It was in the walls, in the pictures, behind the curtains. It takes decades to change'. The need for change was most dramatically presented by an Australian air conditioning company. Their CEO, when asked by government officials about 'payback' on their computer technology project, walked around behind them, poured himself a coffee, then shouted, 'Payback! Payback! That's like asking a heart attack victim what the payback was on bypass surgery. It's a matter of life or death. We cannot survive without this change.'

As major, fashionable, organizational restructuring recommends flattening the hierarchy and redistributing tasks and resources, those affected typically see a threat to their traditional resource bases, and conflict ensues. Even where that conflict is not a zero-sum game, in which one department's gains are another's losses, competing interests are usually required to co-operate more closely than they have done in the past. The breadth and depth of major organizational changes make substantial demands on interdependent departments and levels in the organization, with diverse goals, perceptions and modes of operations – some of the traditional triggers of organizational politics (see Chapter 8). Competing departments and hierarchical levels now have to share information, to allow access to work sites, to work longer hours to support change implementation teams, to change attitudes and behaviour patterns, perhaps even to change to another organization.

Conflict is fostered by interdependence *and* diversity. Interdependence, and the need for co-operation, do not necessarily lead to heightened politicization. Organizational politics only become more predominant when interdependence is accompanied by diversity. Diversity here refers to heterogeneous or inconsistent goals, and to differences in modes of operation and points of view. Different departments and levels often have widely variant sub-cultures and work practices, and can pursue very different goals in radically different environments. As outlined in the classic study by Lawrence and Lorsch (1967), for example, departments such as sales and marketing, research and development, and production and operations have:

- different time horizons, ranging from the short-term orientation of production to the long-term orientation of research and development;
- different goals, in new technology, market growth, production costs and quality;
- different degrees of structure, more formal in production, more informal in R&D.

These differences are encouraged and exaggerated by the fact that these units have different tasks, operate on the basis of different information, have members with different educational and training backgrounds, and have conflicting prior experiences. As a result, when faced with major restructuring, with new work practices, new cultures and new career paths, different units inevitably look at such initiatives from different viewpoints and want different outcomes. There is also likely to be disagreement over which initiatives are appropriate in the first place, and over how and when they should be implemented. As Fisher et al. (1994, pp. 21–2) note:

> There is a Russian saying that everyone looks at the world from the belltower of his own village. Perceptions differ because our experiences differ, and because we select from among our experiences. Each of us observes different data in part because we are all interested in different things. Depending on our specific perspective, our perceptions vary. Terrorists are seen as freedom-fighters by those who would like to be free. Freedom-fighters are seen as terrorists by those who are terrorized.

Complexity and the politics of restructuring

The conflicts and disputes surrounding radical change projects are supported and encouraged by the complexities and uncertainties of the change.

As these are complex multi-faceted projects, there is a large degree of uncertainty about what is to be done and how to do it. In contrast to what McCalman and Paton (1992) describe as 'mechanistic' projects, complex projects can have disputed objectives, imprecise resource requirements, ill-defined activity boundaries, frequent changes in direction and schedule, and high dependence on motivated participants. They note that, in such conditions, it is harder to establish shared perceptions of the project's goals and to sustain commitment to providing solutions. Uncertainty allows and encourages disagreement, and conflicts emerge from a variety of different quarters. In what is already a pressured environment, more time and effort has to be spent ensuring effective communication, addressing people's perceptions, encouraging flexibility, and generating and regenerating involvement in the face of new problems, setbacks and opportunities.

The polyfilla role of socio-technical change agents

In a series of workshops in the Netherlands, Denmark and Britain in 1995, over 50 socio-technical researchers and change agents were questioned about the politics of the projects on which they had been engaged. One of the main conclusions of these workshops was that socio-technical change processes were not simple and linear in character. In contrast, they involved an endless 'circuit' of change activities to ensure that senior management, middle management and operational staff remained committed to the project and were performing the necessary activities. Leadership, drive and communication were continual requirements at every level of the organization when moving towards a more 'empowered' workplace. In order to keep the change programmes going, change agents were forced to play a continuous 'polyfilla' role: identifying cracks and weaknesses in the change programme and attempting to resolve problems. This ranged from resocializing new senior managers, through training technicians to play a more proactive leadership role, to resolving union disputes and lobbying for support for personnel swamped by the demands placed upon them by the change process.

The character of major change initiatives gets defined and redefined in the process of addressing these complexities and uncertainties. Universal recipes and guidelines for 'TLA' initiatives (TQM, BPR, AWGs [autonomous work groups]) are generic in orientation. Yet through implementation, generic principles come into conflict, ambiguities are revealed, trade-offs need to be made, and initiatives are adapted to the resources, constraints and objectives in hand. Change drivers have a significant range of 'action space' in determining how generic models are to be interpreted, how they are to be selectively developed, and the degree to which they are to be introduced.

Political behaviour thus plays a crucial role in translating generic packages into locally workable solutions. As recognized in nearly all

---

The devil in the details

In an Australian white goods company, a year's deliberations on the introduction of 'just-in-time' scheduling systems for manufacturing cells had not
resulted in common agreement about what just-in-time 'really' was. For some,
it was production for customer demand, 'pulled' by empty 'kan-ban' containers supplied to the production cell. However, decisions about the size of
these containers were guided by a 'supply' approach (economic order quantity)
that defined the 'optimum' number of parts in a production run. This was the
opposite of what many meant by 'just-in-time'. Manufacturing engineering
was concerned with implementing a 'practical' just-in-time system that
embodied their ideas of 'optimum' production runs. Was such a system 'just-
in-time', or its opposite? Another engineer, having read a magazine article by
an authority on 'period batch control' for manufacturing cells, spent six
months developing a rigid system for the regular planning of production. This
clashed with the production supervisor's desire to follow the cellular principle,
allowing as much autonomy as possible for the new cell teams.

---

studies of organizational politics, uncertainty in cross-functional projects
feeds insecurities, allows vested interests to impose different definitions of
the situation, fuels the political process, and heightens the political intensity of such projects.

Desperately seeking legitimation

One of the authors was recently contacted by a design engineer in an
Australian white goods plant inquiring what he knew about 'lean production'.
When told that there were some European socio-technical critics of lean
production, the engineer was delighted and requested copies of the papers to
use as intellectual support in an internal battle that he was waging. He
admitted that he wished to preserve the strength of the manufacturing engineering department that was under threat from a new plant manager who
wanted to implement lean production. As a product design engineer, he
wanted the manufacturing engineers retained as support for his design teams,
contributing to a new 'concurrent engineering' initiative. The plant manager,
however, wanted to break up manufacturing engineering and place the
engineers under the control of production team leaders and supervisors,
supporting lean production. The battle over which approach to adopt had only
just begun.

It is rarely possible, for example, to implement a 'generic' total quality
management (TQM) package of philosophies and techniques. In a recent
workshop with an Australian steel company, disagreements emerged over
the 'real' nature of TQM. It was apparent that there were sharp differences
between TQM as represented in the work of academic gurus (such as

Demming and Juran), the TQM packages of consultancy companies (such as McKinsey and Arthur Anderson), and specific company-based TQM change programmes (such as Motorola and Toyota). There are different philosophies of TQM, with Demming and others diverging over matters such as the use of bonuses and job descriptions. There are also a diverse range of forms (some would say levels) of TQM from which to choose – ranging from the implementation of bureaucratically defined quality controls and procedures, to the creation of new organizational cultures and structures oriented towards continuous improvement of excellence in satisfying customers. Different groups in the steel company favoured different interpretations, for a variety of personal and institutional reasons.

TQM in the Asia-Pacific region

Some light may be thrown on the role of organizational actors in promoting different orientations by a recent survey of team-based cells in different Asia-Pacific countries. Common across each country was a general reduction of middle management numbers with the introduction of team-based cells, with one exception: that of manufacturing and industrial engineers. A tentative explanation for this was that the companies had simultaneously initiated TQM practices, and more manufacturing engineers were required to help document, standardize and operate the new quality control systems. In these cases, manufacturing engineering had a clear and immediate vested interest in a more bureaucratic approach to TQM.

As observed earlier, traditional functional departments and hierarchies have strong vested interests in weakening the cross-functional orientation of much organizational restructuring, and interpret such propositions in a manner that strengthens rather than weakens their own area (Amburgey et al., 1993). BPR, for example, has been widely promoted, and in some cases implemented, as radical organizational restructuring. Yet, as a result of the fears of senior managers, or the lobbying of different organizational groups, many companies have only initiated incremental or medium-level changes and have used BPR process redesign techniques to address far more limited objectives – in direct contrast to the proclaimed radicalism of the BPR gurus (Willcocks and Grint, 1997). Computer-based technologies such as robotics, flexible manufacturing systems and computer-aided design and manufacture have been promoted as building blocks for the integrated and automated 'factory of the future'. As such, it is argued, they should not be used merely as sophisticated computer-based tools within existing operations (Kaplinski, 1984). The reality is often different, with expensive computer-aided design and manufacturing equipment, for example, being used as 'electronic drawing boards' with existing structures, rather than as integrative automation (Badham and Wilson, 1992).

A similar degree of local 'configuration' is apparent with self-managing and cross-functional teamworking (such as new product development teams, concurrent engineering teams, innovation teams). In the face of increasing costs, departmental interests and strategic corporate goals, organizations are obliged selectively to develop specific aspects of team-work, to increase autonomy or cross-functionality in particular areas, defining the appropriate levels and directions that they are able and willing to reach. Should, for example, a press shop that has allocated control over scheduling to self-managing cell teams also have these teams responsible for moving materials into and out of the cells (Badham et al., 1997a)? How much autonomy in making marketing decisions should be given to the marketing member of a cross-functional product development team, and how much participation is required by this member at different stages of the development process (Jürgens, 1997)? Resolution of these issues is affected by the interests of the departments and hierarchical levels responsible.

Concurrent engineering and departmental perspectives

The implementation of concurrent engineering provides a useful illustration of the issues that need to be locally resolved, and how outcomes affect the interests of participating departments. Concurrent engineering involves the reorganization of product development from a sequential process in which departments hand on responsibility at different stages of the process. It involves instead the formation of product-based cross-functional teams with representatives from each of the functional departments working together on the whole development process. Functional departments thus have to relin-quish monopoly control over their particular stage of the development process, but the balance of power and control between functional and cross-functional structures is variously interpreted. In practice, the tension between the functional departments and the new product development team (or its 'heavyweight' leader) is resolved in a number of ways. Members of different functions may be more or less involved in the team at different stages. One representative may or may not be empowered to make decisions for the functional department. The product team leader may have different degrees of authority over final product decisions. Team members may be co-located in a specific product development area or remain in their base departments. Performance assessment and career paths may be more or less tightly controlled by functional departments, or by product development personnel, and so on (Moffat and Gerwin, 1994).

How these issues are resolved may be partially, and aptly, determined by appropriate efficiency considerations. They are, however, also the subject matter of political conflict and dispute – especially given the ambiguity and uncertainty among concurrent engineering philosophies about how such issues are to be resolved.

The politics of best practice

They may only be experts, but they are our experts

In Wombat Plastics, an Australian motor car components supplier, a project to break up an instrument panel assembly line into autonomous model-based cells was opposed by a number of production engineers committed to traditional Taylorist assembly line concepts. Within a few weeks of the start of the project, these engineers sought to discredit the project by circulating a *Sloan Management Review* article criticizing the celebrated assembly cells at Volvo's Uddevalla plant in Sweden, in favour of the 'democratic Taylorism' of the American GM–Toyota joint venture NUMMI. While the academic debate was real, the main concern of the plant engineers and their suppliers was not to address the issues. It was, rather, to find (in the inevitably uncertain and controversial higher level debate about 'best practice') some 'expert' support for their traditional perspective: the design of Fordist-style mass assembly lines.

Innovation processes resemble what March and Olson (1983, p. 286) have described as the 'garbage can' model of reorganization, which relies on, 'highly contextual combinations of people, choice opportunities, problems and solutions'. The complex and lengthy nature of implementation means that management attention is difficult to sustain. This is apparent in many 'best practice' initiatives. Most commentators stress the importance of senior management commitment, but the average tenure of senior managers (at least in English-speaking countries) is normally less than the time required effectively to implement major reorganizations. The socialization of new senior managers into the objectives and purpose of projects is of crucial importance, but faces the inherent problem of those new managers wishing to make their own mark on events.

The difficulty of sustaining management attention, combined with the ambiguous nature of problems and solutions, allows less central actors to move into the foreground and inject competing definitions of the situation. Projects then become, 'collections of solutions looking for problems, ideologies looking for soapboxes, pet projects looking for supporters, and people looking for jobs, reputations, or entertainment' (March and Olson, 1983, p. 286). In such conditions of disagreement, complexity and uncertainty, the players and their sections begin to pay attention to the use of power and influence to press their case. For Pfeffer (1981), this results in the use of two main types of power strategy: unobtrusive tactics and legitimating activities. These are exemplified in attempts to influence the use of measurement criteria, the selective perception and use of facts, choice of outside experts, and control of the change agenda. It also spills over, however, into two other strategies: the co-optation of key players, and the building of coalitions amongst affected interests.

While interdependence and diversity tend to encourage organizational politics and the use of power and influence, this is not necessarily always the case. The issues involved may be regarded as trivial and as not worth fighting about, or the power inequalities may be so great that the relatively powerless simply accede to the planned changes. However, this is rarely the case with major restructuring initiatives. These typically generate fundamental threats and opportunities affecting the survival and strength of different sections and groups, and they depend heavily on the compliance of a variety of actors whose information, expertise and support is required if the projects are not to bog down in a mass of internecine rivalries and technical disasters. The stakeholders thus have to be cajoled, bribed, enthused, threatened and otherwise persuaded to support the change. The importance of recognizing and addressing the interests and sub-cultures of different organizational units is thus crucial for major projects.

Departmental power

In his classic argument about departmental power, Charles Perrow (1970, pp. 59–60) observed that,

> for all the discussion and research regarding power in organizations, the preoccupation with interpersonal power has led us to neglect one of the most obvious aspects of this subject: in complex organizations, tasks are divided up between a few major departments or subunits, and all of these subunits are not likely to be equally powerful. Top management, like social scientists, like to avoid issues of power such as this and deal instead with individual, or face-to-face power. The literature on power in organizations is generally, though not always, preoccupied with interpersonal or intragroup phenomena, or else it takes as the major dimension of power the relative and absolute power of levels in the hierarchy.

Interdepartmental rivalry is widely regarded as the very stuff of organizational politics. Gandz and Murray (1980) found 'interdepartmental co-ordination' to be the area in which power was perceived to be most frequently involved. This was closely followed by 'promotions and transfers' and 'facilities and equipment allocation', both factors that are closely tied into established hierarchies and departmental structures. Madison et al. (1980) similarly identified 'reorganizations', 'personnel changes' and 'budget allocations' to be most highly vulnerable to politics and power. For Kanter (1983, pp. 80–1), this is ' the "opposition" that American managers describe receiving as they try to develop innovative projects . . . non-receptive systems nearly always include turf issues: ownership of issues, jealousy of a manager's visibility to higher levels'. Kanter (1983, p. 81) cites one manager as commenting:

> You have to be a good hair parter or bouncer to persuade them. You have to crank tails to get their attention. I don't pull out a gun and shoot, but I've thought

about it. I sometimes need to explain, 'Look, we have this date scheduled. I can't perform unless you get off your dead ass.'

What does this mean for major organizational change? A recent survey of BPR implementation in Britain found that the main project design problem was in gaining 'buy in' from stakeholders, and resistance to change was the main problem in implementation. Gaining and sustaining senior management support was consistently ranked as the major critical success factor. Middle and line management vested interests and resistance, and prevailing culture and political structure, were two of the four most significant barriers (Willcocks and Grint, 1997, p. 99). From American case studies, Douglas (1993, p. 6) concluded that, 'the CEOs we spoke with say they have spent a year or two just trying to soften up defences formed by business unit heads and top-level management to the point that they can begin discussing re-engineering'. In researching a BPR project in the British national health service (NHS), Willcocks and Currie (1996) report a senior clinician's comments: 'End-games are difficult in the NHS . . . you get political opposition, given the range of professional groups and stake-holders. In information systems there are many interests to look after.'

The failure of politics

There is frequently no shortage of political speculation surrounding major innovation and change. Political discussion, innuendo, claim and counter-claim are common elements of what March and Olson (1983) refer to as the '*realpolitik*' dimension of 'reorganization rhetorics'. However, a recognition of organizational politics is not the same as developing an approach capable of guiding and enhancing the effectiveness and reputation of change drivers. One reason for the failure of major change initiatives may concern the dominance of approaches to organizational politics that do not effectively provide such guidance. While capturing some aspects of the politics of change, each approach neglects other important elements. Predominant amongst these approaches are: traditional project management, organization development and cynical 'black art' views of organizational politics.

Project management

The traditional project management approach focuses on what Buchanan and Boddy (1992) call the 'content' and 'control' agendas of change. The content agenda concerns technical expertise in the substance of an innovation. The control agenda concerns establishing, monitoring and controlling project resources and schedules. Effective change thus depends on rational project management techniques. It would be a mistake, however, to see this approach as neglecting or failing to recognize politics, for at least two reasons.

First, project management makes unitarist assumptions about organizational goals. Organizational processes are seen as neutral instruments to achieve these shared goals, and reorganization is interpreted as a way of improving organizational efficiency. While this rhetoric appears to be non-political, it has embedded within it a particular set of political positions and practices. Pichault (1995) argues that, behind the technical language lies a 'panoptic management' (see Chapter 8), seeking to exert total control through rationality and transparency. Project management texts, however, typically fail to admit openly the implications of power distribution and influence on structures and change programmes. This literature thus legitimates the agendas of dominant groups, invalidates discussion of political options, and recognizes no limits on acceptable means to achieve pre-determined goals.

Second, project management approaches still have to address the conflict and resistance that they face. On the one hand, project management is often presented as working to create an 'apolitical utopia', transcending the disruptive politics of the present. But this is a utopia of authoritarian politics, in which dissent is not permitted (Willcocks and Grint, 1997). On the other hand, project management does recommend tactics for overcoming resistance. This may involve the use of time-consuming (and possibly superficial and mechanistic) stakeholder analysis methods (Mintzberg, 1994). Given the 'irrationality' of opposition to 'progressive' change, further information, communication and rational persuasion is frequently also recommended. Where this does not work, however, there is a tendency to lapse into more or less open coercion as employees are 'let go' or, as one computer-aided design and manufacturing consultant bluntly put it, 'neutralized' (Badham, 1989, p. 47). In many cases, the solution to resistance is seen in terms of strengthening the formal authority and powers of sanctioned change drivers, becoming increasingly harsh and dismissive towards 'irrational' or 'personally motivated' resistance.

This approach is exemplified in many BPR projects. Tinaiker et al. (1995) found that 96 per cent of published articles on BPR dealt exclusively with technical issues. BPR is also commonly depicted as a top-down approach to restructuring to increase efficiency on the basis of technical design criteria (Willcocks and Grint, 1997, p. 106). Where political factors are recognized, the response has often been mechanistic and authoritarian in character. As Hammer and Stanton (1995, pp. 174, 183) observe:

Dramatic improvement has to be paid for in some way, and the coinage is usually denominated in units of suffering. . . . it is necessary to deal with them [resisters] gently but insistently by pointing out the gaps in their understanding and the errors of their ways. By means of repeated communication and clarification they can be brought onto the straight and narrow. However, those who are deliberately trying to obstruct the re-engineering effort . . . need the back of the hand.

There are three problems with this model. First, the dynamics of organizational change are not adequately captured by a simple equation of formal goals with rationality and reason, and of opposition with irrationality and personal failings. The need to build informal support for change is marginalized, and deep-seated opposition embedded in the organizational sub-cultures and practices is also ignored. Second, the full cultural and structural consequences of major change are dependent on the political nature and implications of alternative organizational designs, and these implications are not considered. Short-term technical or financial achievements may be gained in the absence of any consideration of longer term effects on motivation, skills and experience, innovativeness and flexibility. Third, the sources and consequences of controversy and opposition, and how these lead to frustration, anger and resentment, are sidelined. This can fuel incomprehension and despair, or an unthinking authoritarian backlash – which detract from rather than promote successful innovation.

In contrast, the change driver as project manager needs to:

- maintain tight control, wherever possible, over project resources and schedules, while being prepared to change course, renegotiate resources, and reschedule when contexts and goals change;
- create and legitimate shared 'win-win' agendas for change, while being aware of the constructed and reconstructed nature of these agendas and their coercive implications;
- concentrate on establishing efficient and effective organizational redesign, while also remaining flexible enough to introduce compromises to incorporate different views and interests where necessary;
- be tough and forceful in pursuing a change agenda, yet be sympathetic and compromising whenever possible with respect to other interests and sources of concern.

Organization development

The organization development model is more subtle in its approach to politics. A similar unitarist view is often adopted of the overriding goals of the organization. However, organizational processes are not perceived just as neutral instruments, but as the lived reality of organization members. Reorganization is, therefore, not only about making these processes more efficient, but also about ensuring the satisfaction and motivation of employees. This approach emphasizes the importance of involvement, consultation, information sharing, the creation of trust, continuous multi-level, multi-media communication, counselling, obtaining 'buy in' from those affected, and expert 'process' advice where necessary. The 'positive' politics of this process – using rational persuasion, knowledge, information and genuine caring – is contrasted with the 'negative' politics of 'empire builders' and authoritarian 'coercive' managers.

This approach is typically advocated by TQM consultants, but is a common theme across the organization development intervention toolkit. It has also gained prominence in concurrent engineering research on the 'apolitical manager'. McDonough and Griffin (1997) argue, from an in-depth study of seven firms, that successful cross-functional product development arrangements ('holistic innovation teams') require 'apolitical leaders' as well as 'strategic rationalization' as necessary infrastructural supports. These apolitical leaders disseminate information widely, make decisions on the basis of reason and facts, are non-judgemental and supportive listeners, and set realistic expectations. This type of leadership is seen as necessary at senior, middle manager and team leader levels in order, 'to prevent game-playing and scape-goating that can lead to project delays, wasted resources, and missed product specifications' (McDonough and Griffin, 1997, p. 12). Moreover, 'Because information is widely shared across the firm, basing decisions on facts is less difficult than in firms where information provides personal power and thus is less broadly shared' (McDonough and Griffin, 1997, p. 13).

This view of change is often combined, particularly in America, with the 'apolitical utopia' perspective mentioned earlier. Thus, for example, Johansson et al. (1993, p. 202) present this glowing view of the post-BPR organization:

[Managers] should measure everything they can. Once managers know what changes have to take place, they will start to influence the behaviour of staff, focus on results, and release their creative talent. They also start changing their roles, becoming less concerned with control and instruction, and more concerned with challenge and discussion. With this change of management style, organizational politics can be cast aside.

Kanter (1983, p. 179) provides a similar utopian view of the effectively restructured 'integrative' organization:

'[O]pponents' are won over by persistent, persuasive arguments; open communication is used to resolve debates, not back-stabbing. Perhaps the very publicness and openness of the battlegrounds – if that word even seems appropriate – makes 'reason' prevail. It is hard for back-room bargaining or displays of unilateral power to occur when issues are debated in group settings. Public meetings require that concerns be translated into *specific* criticisms, each of which can then be countered by data or well-mounted arguments. And the heavy reliance on informal communication networks as a source of reputation places a check on dirty dealing. 'Bad press' would ensure that such a person gets frozen out. An innovating company, then, begins to substitute a control system based on debate among peers for one based on top-down authority.

This approach incorporates a potentially insidious political posture. By presenting major organizational change initiatives exclusively in the light of reason and rationality, it seeks to 'persuade' those affected of this 'fact'. The various techniques of information, communication and counselling can be regarded as politically inspired rhetoric, presented with a rationalistic voice, and not just as the embodiment of neutral reason and rationality. Moreover, the flavour of 'human relations' rhetoric comes up against a number of harsh realities. Many organizational restructuring projects result in unemployment – whether this is middle managers displaced as a by-product of self-managing team operations, routine and craft work taken over by computer-based technologies, or jobs 're-engineered' out of existence. When the organization is affected by new waves of technology or competitive threats, the demands of competitiveness often impose job shedding and restructuring on even the most collaborative high-trust work environments (Friedmann, 1977).

A related critique is that an emphasis on involvement, consensus and alignment may impose a conformism that stunts imagination and creativity, and prevents organizations from adapting to changing circumstances. More directly, however, there is evidence that this kind of 'participative' and 'soft sell' approach to change does not work well in contexts that are highly conflictual (Reason, 1984), or where large-scale changes have to be implemented rapidly (Dunphy and Stace, 1993). Kotter (1985) adds that the extensive use of persuasion techniques is extremely time-consuming. Dunphy and Stace (1993) endorse this point, arguing that dictatorial methods are necessary to achieve large-scale and rapid change. These conditions are, of course, frequently present in major organizational restructuring that consumes considerable amounts of time and money, and cuts across established structural interests and cultures. The organization development models of change offer little advice or assistance on these matters, other than deploring the legacy of 'negative politics' or handing such 'difficult issues' to the client rather than to the change driver.

In contrast, the change driver as OD practitioner needs to:

- assume and build on the potential for communication and co-operation in the change setting, but yet also realistically assess the sub-unit change context and stakeholders in order to identify real and enduring sources of conflict;
- accommodate change to the needs and interests of affected groups and sub-units, and implement information sharing, open communication and co-operative problem-solving structures, but also develop flexible strategies adapted for different groups and different waves of activity in the change process, allowing for greater or lesser accommodation to individual or group needs and more or less use of forceful and coercive influence tactics;
- create, where feasible, a shared vision for change as an inspirational 'gyroscope' to guide co-operation between different levels and departments, but also monitor continuously changes in the context and content of the innovation process, such that previous strategies, tactics

and resource allocations can be fluidly adapted to changing pressures, demands and problems – involving, for example, more or less authoritarian and decisive actions, and a greater or lesser sharing of information.

Cynical black art

Kotter (1985) contrasts the project management and organization development approaches to change with what he describes as the 'cynical' or 'black art' model of politics. In this view, changes will always be contested, championed by one set of interests over another and, ultimately, represent the triumph of particular groups and interests over others. It identifies issues in terms of 'win-lose' situations, encourages distrust within and towards change participants (Morgan, 1989), and tends to look behind the search for non-zero-sum 'win-win' solutions to the careers, interests and hidden sub-texts of change initiators. 'Cynics expect destructive power struggles, bureaucratic infighting and parochial politics to be almost everywhere almost all the time' (Kotter, 1985, p. 17).

While on the surface the cynical perspective appears to capture the dynamics of organizational politics, it is ultimately inadequate and self-defeating as an approach for informing change drivers introducing major change. Bolman and Deal (1991, p. 238) summarize the two main weaknesses of what they call 'the political frame'. The first lies in underestimation of the significance of rational and collaborative processes. The second concerns the overstatement of the inevitability of conflict and understatement of the potential for effective collaboration. Kotter (1985, p. 17) makes a related but different point. The cynic, in his view,

> is unable to explain or predict where and when episodes like these [destructive power struggles, bureaucratic infighting, etc.] will be found, and where and when they will not. The cynic, much like the naïve (ironically), attributes organizational outcomes to forces inside individuals – the cynic assumes evil forces are usually at work, the naïve assumes good forces are the norm. At the same time, both are almost blind to the social milieu surrounding people inside organizations and how that milieu can shape behaviour, systematically create conflicts among people.

In contrast, the change driver as political entrepreneur needs to:

- recognize the centrality of the political dimension of change, yet also keep a balanced focus on the technical content of the change agenda, particularly given the cross-functional nature of changes and the need to cross traditional knowledge boundaries in organizational redesign;
- prepare for self-interested opposition and conflict between vested interests, yet also critically assess how sources of conflict and co-operation

are rooted in departmental structures and organizational hierarchies, as well as with the stakeholders;

- recognize and address the demands created by zero-sum conflicts, while also maximizing the potential for collaborative 'win-win' outcomes by, wherever possible, improving career paths, enabling a concentration on the more valued and creative tasks carried out by functional units, and the removal of commonly recognized frustrating, bureaucratic and conflict-inducing procedures;

- create feasible strategies for minimizing as well as addressing destructive zero-sum conflict situations created, for example, by the removal of resources from sub-units as inefficient procedures and duplications are eliminated, and the creation of new technical and cultural demands on employees requiring retraining and redirection.

The political entrepreneur

In other words, the change driver, as argued earlier in this book, must become a political entrepreneur, creatively and proactively working in and with the political system of the organization, rather than attempting to work against it, or worse, ignoring it. The successful implementation of major organizational change means overcoming not only powerful vested interests, but also the powerlessness that seems to dog many change initiatives (Kanter, 1983; Pfeffer, 1992a). The exercise of formal authority, or initiatives to create 'strong cultures', are unlikely to be sufficient to overcome opposition and inertia. As Pfeffer (1992a, p. 12) puts it,

> unless and until we are willing to come to terms with organizational power and influence, and admit that the skills of getting things done are as important as the skills of figuring out what to do, our organizations will fall further and further behind. The problem is, in most cases, not an absence of insight or organizational intelligence. Instead the problem is one of passivity.

To overcome this passivity, the political entrepreneur has to work the content and control agendas, and also the power-political processes of influence and legitimacy building that determine whether an initiative is given organizational space and resources (Buchanan and Boddy, 1992). The political entrepreneur must be able and willing to manage interdependencies between different sub-units (Kotter, 1985) in waves of cross-functional agenda setting, coalition building, mobilization and completion that make up a complex change project (Kanter, 1983). In managing these processes, political entrepreneurs draw on their track record and established working relationships. Reputation is only sustained and enhanced, however, if the political entrepreneur manages the exercise of power and influence with both strength and sensitivity.

Managing interdependencies

Kotter (1985) emphasizes the importance of managing peers and colleagues from different social backgrounds, understanding and obtaining the support of senior management, and motivating and directing those at lower organizational levels. The establishment of such 'broad-band' relationships is now widely recognized. In project management research, a three-level model of action is often employed: senior management; middle or project management; and lower management and shopfloor (Burnes, 1992). In the literature on project management structures, reference is frequently made to senior-level steering committees or stakeholder groups, middle-level project or design teams, and lower-level problem-solving or issue groups (Benders et al., 1995; Wellins et al., 1991). Similarly, in research on change champions and change management, the focus is frequently on top management strategic support and commitment (on 'patriarchs' and 'sponsors'), design and implementation teams or coalitions ('evangelists', 'drivers', 'change agents', 'visible' and 'invisible' project teams), and lower-level adopters and resisters ('user champions', 'targets', 'subversives') (Beatty and Gordon, 1991; Davenport, 1993; Geddes et al., 1990; Hutton, 1994). Technology management studies, meanwhile, focus on global resource networks and local design networks that enrol technical and organizational actors (Clegg, 1989; Law and Callon, 1992).

In three international workshops with socio-technical change drivers, it was found that activities at all three levels are crucial to the success of change projects. In the classic SAPPHO study of innovation, a senior-level 'business innovator' was found to be the strongest predictor of success (Freeman, 1982). Beatty and Gordon (1991) confirm the importance of high-level 'patriarchs' and 'godfathers' to advanced manufacturing technology applications. As the time of senior management is limited (and their changeover often rapid), Beatty and Gordon argue that their main tasks occur at the 'genesis' stages of change. Hammer and Champy (1993, p. 107) stress the key role of strong leadership at a senior level:

> Without strong, aggressive, committed and knowledgeable leadership there will be no one to persuade the barons running functional silos within the company to subordinate the interest of their functional areas to those of the processes that cross their boundaries. No one will be able to force changes in compensation and measurement systems, no one will be able to compel the human resources organization to redefine its job rating systems.

As Beatty and Gordon argue (1991, p. 93), senior managers may continue to play a crucial support role in these areas throughout a change project. Lower-level 'evangelists' 'will need approval, empowerment and active support and often protection from top management to effectively promote AMT across organizational boundaries. Otherwise they may get bogged down in "turf wars"'. Studies of business process re-engineering

(Davenport, 1993) and total quality management (Hutton, 1994) have argued for the central role of a senior management 'sponsor', 'someone who has the authority to legitimize the change' (Hutton, 1994, p. 3).

> Ultimately it falls to the change leader or sponsor to create and maintain strong commitment and consensus among the executive team members with respect to the need and vision for change and the plans for creating radical improvement in strategic processes. Failure to achieve executive team consensus can prevent a business unit's process innovation efforts from ever getting off the ground, and failure to maintain commitment and consensus will diminish the degree of change that is achievable and delay progress and the realization of benefits. (Hutton, 1994, p. 181)

Stjernberg and Phillips (1993, p. 1212) also emphasize the legitimacy issue in their study of socio-technical projects: 'In our experience,' they claim, 'resistance may come from superiors and peers as often as from subordinates. Moreover, this kind of resistance is more difficult to challenge and convert into support, since the change agent seldom has access to these external resisters.' The 'hard part' for the change driver was thus dealing with attacks from outside their own department. Middle-level champions of organizational change are at the mercy of such attacks if a senior management coalition has not given external legitimacy to initiatives by treating them as central to strategic goals. This external legitimation is central, as the existing culture is likely to be critical of the change, by definition, as that is often the object of change.

The importance of middle management change activities is increasingly being recognized. A Netherlands study reveals that what defines 'front runner' companies from the 'rest of the pack' is their more frequent use of cross-functional design and operation teams – and the degree to which they effectively delegate design and implementation responsibilities to these teams (den Hertog et al., 1994, p. 7). In their study of CAD/CAM implementation, Beatty and Gordon (1991, p. 86) argue that the role of middle management change evangelists is more important than the senior 'Business Innovator' identified by the SAPPHO study. This is crucial, they argue, because the central project requirement is typically to 'see it through', sometimes over a number of years. Given the long, slow process of major change, the importance of a middle management evangelist often proves crucial. As documented by Ashridge Teamworking Services, multi-skilled leaders are required for cross-functional projects as they have the difficult and crucial task of both mobilizing the 'visible' project team actively to run the project, and influencing the 'invisible' coalition on whose contribution the success of the project depends (Geddes et al., 1990).

Finally, at the level of lower middle management and the shopfloor, 'user champions' are of central importance in training, providing assistance and winning over 'converts'. For some, this function merges with middle management as 'process owners' need to be identified who can accept responsibility for the project and act as lower-level drivers of change (Davenport, 1993, p. 182). This also involves the mobilization of enthusiasm and managing an increasing adopter/user role in change – a necessary transition in the move to self-regulating work structures. Friis (1988), for example, notes that in a number of computer system projects there was a move from a 'traditional user role' (no knowledge of design and computers), to 'interested user role' (curiosity and interest awakening), to 'analyzing user role' (wants to participate in analysis and influence change – maybe recognize necessary change), to 'designing user role' (understand what is going on, build prototypes, wants last word on potential to computerize'), to 'evaluating user role' (considered as systems owner and wants to evaluate, test and modify – with 'experts' assisting). This is a change agency dynamic similar to the 'situational leadership' model of developing work teams (Hersey and Blanchard, 1988), as higher-level change drivers move from a 'traditional analyst expert role' to 'collaborating expert role' to 'teaching and consultative expert role' in the change process.

As Kotter (1985) describes, political entrepreneurs should, therefore, take active responsibility for developing relationships across structural levels. With bosses, this involves collecting information about strengths, weaknesses, work styles and pressures, honestly appraising their own skills and motives, and forging a relationship that matches these conditions. These relationships must be maintained by keeping bosses informed, retaining a reputation for dependability and honesty, and using the time and resources of senior management selectively.

Managing relations with peers and colleagues across organizational units requires detailed information about social relations and a keen understanding of diverse and interdependent groups whose co-operation or compliance is required. There is a need to know the parties, their perspectives, and where there are likely to be conflicts, as well as obtaining the necessary power and influence and being willing to use it. This involves answering such simple questions as: Whose co-operation is necessary? Will they resist and why? How strong are they? Can I reduce or overcome their resistance? With major organizational change, particular sensitivity is needed towards those in different departments whose co-operation is necessary. Ongoing assessment and the development of good working relationships are essential. This requires particular skill and effort given that so many major initiatives involve working with people at a distance, through infrequent contacts, and often in rushed and pressured circumstances. The political entrepreneur may also need to be prepared, when appropriate, to go beyond communication, education and negotiation to include more subtle and forceful methods to overcome resistance. As Kotter (1985) notes, diversity creates a multitude of causes of resistance. It may occur because people have no time or resources, because they are limited in their abilities, because they have different assessments of the help that they are given, because they are unaware of what they need, because they do not trust us, or they are angry with us because they believe we have

different interests at stake. The establishment of good working relationships is an essential part of discovering the source of opposition, minimizing it, and finding solutions.

Good working relationships

At a meeting of an industry–university research institute, the new director
talked of the need to build good working relations with people in the associated company as well as in the university. Later in the meeting, a younger
member of staff exclaimed, 'One of the main problems is politics. The heads of
department have control over staff and material resources, and institutes are
attempting to take some of this control away. How do you deal with that?'

'That', said the director, 'is what I meant by "establishing good working
relationships!"'

The effective management of one's superiors and peers ('managing up')
helps with the mobilization of support from lower organizational levels.
Credibility and reputation are of major use, as is the collection of information about the interrelation of subordinates in complex social systems. It
is important to create an environment for the positive resolution of conflict
and to make targeted interventions for inspiring motivation and ensuring
direction – whether these interventions are direct or indirect, hard or soft.

Waves of activity

The political entrepreneur has to be able and willing to manage these
interdependencies in different ways at different times. Bolman and Deal
(1991) stress three sets of activities: 'agenda setting', 'coalition building' and
'negotiation'. Kanter (1983) defines the first wave of change activity , agenda
setting, as one of appropriate 'problem definition'; making your project
realistically appear to be trialable, reversible, divisible, concrete, familiar,
congruent and appealing. After the initial stage of establishing a sense of
urgency, Kotter (1995) places the creation of a powerful guiding coalition as
the second key step. He argues that this must include a percentage of
powerful senior executives, but also recognizes that a number may not 'buy
in'. How is the opposition of senior managers overcome? Beer et al. (1990)
show how the defined business need and senior management coalition have
to combine into a shared vision of change and the fostering of a consensus.
However, as they argue, 'some people, of course, just cannot or will not
change, despite all the direction and support in the world' (Beer et al., 1990,
p. 163). The resisters should not be replaced too early, as the change process
has not yet gained sufficient legitimacy. Dismissal would appear unfair, they
would not be seen as having been given a chance, and people don't have a
clear understanding at the outset of what is required. However, as the
change continues, replacing or moving people who resist can be more readily

understood. At this stage replacing people can reinforce commitment to change by visibly demonstrating senior management's commitment. A tactic reminiscent of the British Navy's classic execution of one admiral for failure '*pour encourager les autres*'. There may need to be an iron fist, but, as Beer et al. (1990) put it, perhaps it should be in a 'velvet glove'.

Accommodation and influence

In an Australian chemical company, the change driver responsible for building a new factory and implementing self-managing work cells emphasized the key role of politics in ensuring the success of the project. The project involved setting up a cross-functional team to design the new factory and work arrangements and to run the factory once it was completed. In the early stages of the project, much time was spent accommodating the interests of different managerial groups in order to get 'buy in' to the project from the different functional areas. However, the change agent and senior sponsor (the manufacturing director) also exerted substantial influence in encouraging the development of a radical and inspirational vision of change. Once resources had been committed, schedules determined and financial objectives set, accommodation was more restricted and the change driver adopted a tougher and less accommodative stance, using every political tactic and manoeuvre available to ensure that the change programme was driven through on time and within budget. Political style was adapted to circumstances and project requirements at different stages of the change process.

Kanter's (1983) view of coalition building as the 'second wave' of innovation activity focuses on obtaining cheerleading peers and blessings from the top, clearing the investment, preselling and making cheerleaders, horsetrading, securing blessings and formalizing the coalition. Clearly agenda setting and coalition building are interactive processes that occur in different sequences or iterations in different contexts. Finally, Kanter stresses the importance of a third wave of activity – mobilization and completion, where there is a need to: handle opposition and block interference; maintain momentum and build teams; undertake secondary redesign and rule bending; and provide ongoing external communication of results and deliverables. The advocacy of 'results-driven' in preference to 'activity-driven' change (Schaffer and Thomson, 1992) stresses the significance of focusing change and maintaining momentum by ensuring that there is a set of 'accountable managers' with defined 'responsibility for results'. Kanter emphasizes the importance of a participative style in order to persuade, build teams, obtain needed input, show political sensitivity and reveal a willingness to share rewards and recognition. This is, however, not a 'soft' option as it involves setting rigorous standards for subordinates and entering into sometimes tough negotiations with peers and superiors.

In this context of uncertainty, and ambiguity, organizations are only able to innovate if they can consistently commit to change over the long term, learn from experiences, apply that learning, and manage the complex technical, cultural and organizational factors that are an inevitable part of the change process. It is not surprising, therefore, that there is now a growing interest in organizational learning, change management, 'new project management' and implementation as key factors in achieving context specific innovation (Badham et al., 1997a; Buchanan and Boddy, 1992; Frame, 1991; Geddes et al., 1990). In *Beyond the Hype*, Eccles and Nohria (1992, p. 6) condemn the 'desperate search for quick solutions to eternal management challenges, "new" ideas presented as universally applicable quick-fix solutions – along with the obligatory and explicit caution that their recommendations are not quick fixes and will require substantial management understanding and commitment'. Their solution? To restore the central concern of management with *action*: 'In recent years, there has been an amazing amount of verbiage instructing managers on how to become "leading-edge", "excellent" or "innovative" – yet little of it attends to the practical questions of how to actually get things done in organizations' (Eccles and Nohria, 1992, p. 1). In *Management Redeemed*, Hilmer and Donaldson (1996) continue this theme in their critique of the 'quick-fix and fad mentality'. From a practitioner perspective, they note that firms such as General Electric, Motorola and Procter and Gamble have achieved success because of their commitment to a few simple themes, and the fact that they have refined their practices over several decades. They are characterized by 'excellence in the doing', rather than 'the cleverness of their ideas or nifty jargon' (Hilmer and Donaldson, 1996, p. xi).

We have tried to demonstrate that managing the complex politics of change is a key component of this 'excellence in doing'. Its importance increases in direct proportion to the radical and complex nature of the changes being introduced. Traditional models of project management and organization development help in managing the content of change, controlling projects and improving communication and involvement in the change process. However, these perspectives provide little systematic advice on how to manage the diverse and interdependent players or stakeholders in the change process. Cynical models of politics capture some of the dynamics involved, yet are unable to provide practical advice on how constructively to address the conflicts and dilemmas that emerge. If change drivers are to achieve effective change and enhance their skills and reputations, they need to act as political entrepreneurs in the innovation process. This chapter has demonstrated the significance of political factors in causing and overcoming resistance from functional structures and bureaucratic hierarchies. It has also introduced some of the methods and types of political action involved in dealing with senior and middle management as well as shopfloor employees. It has shown how these tactics need to be deployed in setting change agendas, building coalitions and maintaining the momentum of change. This 'perspective' of the political entrepreneur is extended in the next chapter.

7 Power-assisted steering: maxims for Princes and Princessas

CONTENTS

funny **Business**

THE CITY BAR + GRILL

by MORRIS

"Stop worrying Harry, youth and enthusiasm can always be beaten by treachery and cunning."

Positioning: pitch and players

Interviewer: What do you see as the advantages to the individual of being able to use political behaviour?

Manager: The key advantage, I think, is that you can more successfully achieve the outcomes that you personally are looking for in the process. I think there is an ability to understand the visible and invisible parts of the organization, and I think the skilled political operator is able to tap into those invisible aspects far more easily. So they will be exposed to a different series of information sources and they'll be able to get information to different people far more easily.

The other advantage I think is that you can disproportionately . . . to work to your position with the organization . . . attract attention and support if you martial your campaign well. And I think if you can tap in to the sympathies people have for a particular function, or the fact that other senior managers have worked in that function in the past, and use your network of people, you can actually seek to develop quite a strong case for protecting or developing your part of the organization.

Numerous writers have sought to offer guidance on the appropriate use of power and political strategies and tactics. This tradition dates at least from the work of Niccolò Machiavelli (*c.* 1513) and his well-known work *The Prince* (but see Chapter 4), to Rubin's *The Princessa: Machiavelli for Women* (1997). With almost 500 years' worth of commentary, there is no shortage of advice in this area. Here we assume that change drivers can usefully be regarded as the aspiring new Princes and Princessas of our time. The literature of power and politics does not directly address the interests of organizational change drivers. The literature on change management adopts a spread of unsatisfactory perspectives on the issues of power and politics.

How should change drivers be advised to address the political dimension of their role? What maxims should guide them? How can political strategies and tactics be deployed to shape the nature, direction and outcomes of change? How is the change driver to balance the progression of the change agenda with the interests of the organization and with personal reputation and career aspirations?

The degree of political intensity varies from one organizational change setting to another. Figure 7.1 captures this variation by plotting change on two axes. The vertical axis runs from 'challenged' at one extreme to 'accepted' at the other. Change proposals that are well understood and welcomed are likely to generate less conflict and political behaviour than ambiguous changes which are controversial and hotly contested. The horizontal axis runs from 'marginal' to 'critical'. Change which is radical and rapid also heightens uncertainty, which, as already noted, is a major trigger of political behaviour.

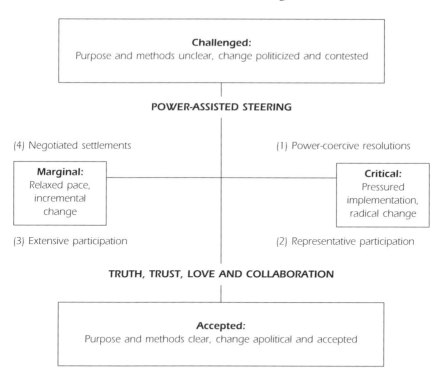

Figure 7.1 **The change driver's context**

Change proposals which are critical to the organization, but which meet with broad acceptance, may be implemented quickly with representative (as opposed to all-inclusive) participation (quadrant 2). Change which is more marginal to the success of the business and which can be implemented at a more relaxed pace allows for extensive participation (quadrant 3). The lower half of the figure is the domain of traditional organization development, of 'truth, trust, love and collaboration' approaches to change.

Change proposals which are critical and challenged may have to be driven using power-coercive solutions (quadrant 1). Dunphy and Stace (1988, 1990) argue from their Australian research that major changes that have to be introduced quickly are more likely to succeed if the management style is what they describe as 'dictatorial transformation'. The problems with change which is marginal, but is also challenged, may be resolved through negotiated settlements between advocates and opponents (quadrant 4). The upper half of the figure is thus the domain of 'power-assisted steering'.

One implication of this analysis concerns the choice of initiatives that the Prince or Princessa wishes to be seen driving. The problem here is that very few managers have developed an ambitious, fast-track, high-flying career by implementing at a relaxed pace minor and uncontroversial changes that had little impact on the organization. Career advance depends on high visibility and high impact (Rein et al., 1987). This means positioning oneself in a change agency role with respect to major, highly visible, high-impact initiatives. The additional problem is that such changes are inevitably controversial and contested, highly politicized, and also, therefore, risky. The risk extends to organizational performance, and to the change driver's reputation.

We are concerned with the domain of power-assisted steering. However, a note of caution is in order, to set this argument in a wider context. Change which is politicized is not going to be driven exclusively by power-political behaviour. The conventional apparatus of project management, participative methods and organization development interventions still applies. A focus on the less well-explored political aspects of change implementation does not deny the continuing relevance and importance of more traditional or conventional methods. Political behaviour must be regarded as complementary to those methods.

Who are the new Princes and Princessas anyway? We argued earlier that the concept of the singular 'change agent' is problematic. It can be difficult to pin this person down. Chapter 1 argued that the concept of *change agency* is of more value, in highlighting the fact that change is typically dependent on a number of interacting agents or players, or by what Hutton (1994) calls 'the cast of characters'. His 'cast' includes sponsors (who legitimize and protect the change), advocates (who initiate proposals and convince sponsors) and change agents formally responsible for planning and orchestrating the change, once the mandate has been granted. For Hutton, the term 'change agent' can apply to an officially designated person, and also to *anyone who chooses to take the lead in this way*.

We escaped from this definitional problem in Chapter 1 by following the fortunes of one particular member of the cast – the change driver. This individual can have many titles, formal and informal. Many commentators adopt the term 'change champion'. It is interesting to note Schon's (1963, p. 84) argument about the major 'themes' that appear to develop from his analysis of accounts of radical innovations:

1   The new idea meets with indifference or active resistance, because it appears to counter established practice, and it also looks expensive and unworkable.
2   The new idea gets vigorous and active promotion, to advocate, sell and otherwise fight for the concept.
3   Advocates use informal personal networks rather than 'official' channels to introduce and disseminate the new idea, particularly during the early stages.
4   One individual typically 'emerges as champion of the idea'. Schon regards it as a requirement that somebody is prepared to put themselves 'on the line for an idea of doubtful success'; he claims, 'the new idea either finds a champion or dies'.

The static notion of a change driver or a champion does not adequately capture the dynamics of Schon's analysis. The point is that the concept of the change driver is an *emergent* one, depending on the cast of players. This conceptualization also recognizes considerable *fluidity* in the notion of change driver. The players who 'take the lead' change over time, as an initiative develops and matures, as other initiatives and actors come into play, as events deflect planned progress, and so on. In an organizational world in which change drivers emerge, maxims for the effective use of political behaviour could be of value to *anyone who chooses to take the lead in this way*. It is therefore not possible to legislate on who the new Princes and Princessas might be, or could become, or will remain, in a given context. The advice on offer may apply to those formally appointed to change driving roles, and to those self-appointed; to those driving a particular initiative, and to those seeking to block or subvert that project and to promote an alternative. This advice applies equally to internally and to externally appointed change agents.

The question here (to use a sports analogy) is: what positions do you want to play? The question of defining the 'change driver' is of some theoretical interest. What is more significant, from analytic, explanatory and practical perspectives, is how the players in the turf game position themselves, and the ways in which they take, define and change those positions in relation to change as it unfolds through time. The change driver must be able to change position, to maximize personal advantage, to progress the change agenda.

Buchanan and Storey (1997) refer to this as 'role taking and role switching'. Consider Schon's requirement that somebody be prepared to put themselves 'on the line'. Let us presume that one wishes to be perceived as effective, competent, credible and successful. Positions in relation to change initiatives that enable one to take credit for outcomes will be desirable. Positions in which one could potentially attract blame for mistakes and failure are to be avoided. Positioning, with respect to type of change, and to roles in relation to change, can thus have significant implications for the change driver's reputation.

The ability of the change driver readily to switch roles will depend largely on the substance and goals of the change initiative in hand, the formal position, power base and personal attributes of the change driver, and the positions adopted by other players in the game at any one time. The manner in which the individual change driver takes and switches roles will thus rely on a judgement of the context and of the way in which events are unfolding. But even the change driver ostensibly 'trapped' in a formal position, which may have undesirable consequences, can adopt 'distancing' strategies to indicate, for example, lack of agreement with the way in which proposals are being advanced, or implementation is being progressed.

In a seminal article, Ottaway (1983) establishes a taxonomy of change agents, and this is summarized in Table 7.1. Ottaway distinguishes change *generators* from change *implementors* from change *adopters*, identifying

Table 7.1 **A taxonomy of change agents**

Group	Category	Description
Change generators	Key change agents	The first, or primary, converter of an issue into a felt need – their methods, style and values dominate the change process.
	Demonstrators	Visibly show their support of the process of change set in motion by the key change agents – the first line of confrontation between agents and resisters.
	Patrons	Have the task of generating financial and other public support for the change process.
	Defenders	Defend the change process at the grass roots, keep the issue alive, help work out the implications and consequences of proposals for change at the lowest levels.
Change implementors	External implementors	Brought in from outside to assist development of the change process.
	External/internal implementors	Brought in to help develop internal implementors, acting perhaps out of 'head office' in an advisory or training and development capacity.
	Internal implementors	Responsible for implementing proposed changes in their own groups, briefed to do this as a full-time activity – may work with other categories of implementors.
Change adopters	Early adopters	First adopters of the change and thus the prototype for further adoption – high in commitment, change advocates, self-nominated, the link between implementors and other adopters.
	Maintainers	Adopt change while retaining their commitment to maintaining the organization, committed to work roles even while these are changing – if the maintainers don't change, there is no change.
	Users	Get into the habit of using the products or services of the changed organization – if there are no users, there will be no change – at this level most of us are change agents.

Source: Based on Ottaway, 1983

three or four 'sub-roles' under each of those main categories. Some of Ottaway's labels map onto language which we have already used. His 'key change agents' can be viewed as 'advocates' or 'initiators', the 'patrons' as 'sponsors', and his 'internal implementors' are change drivers. In contrast to the scheme presented in Chapter 1, Ottaway's taxonomy has a chronological basis, running from key change agents or initiators to end users. This usefully reinforces the point that the change driving role is both emergent and fluid, shifting position through time, as change initiatives unfold in some predictable and some unanticipated ways.

The maxims for Princes and Princessas which can be derived from this argument so far concern *positioning*, and appear to include the following:

- Position yourself in the domain of major, radical, significant, high-impact, high-visibility change for maximum career advantage.

- Recognize the balance of risks and rewards involved in this positioning strategy. Some high-impact change may carry unacceptably high personal and organizational risk.
- Do not abandon project management, organization development and participative change implementation approaches. Political strategies must be used to complement conventional methods when necessary.
- Carefully select the change agency role or roles that you wish to adopt in relation to particular initiatives, given the cast of characters around you. These choices have implications for your developing reputation.
- Switch and redefine your roles as the change unfolds, to achieve maximum organizational and personal advantage. This also has implications for reputation.

Beyond the recipe: a creative perspective

The six phases of a project:

1 enthusiasm
2 disillusionment
3 panic
4 search for the guilty
5 punishment of the innocent
6 praise and rewards for the non-participants

(Source unknown)

Pettigrew and Whipp (1991), among others, criticize the prescriptive litera-ture in this area for offering over-simplified 'recipes' for effective change. This criticism appears to be widely shared by practising managers who find it difficult to translate these recipes into specific organizational contexts (Buchanan et al., 1997). What are the problems with these recipes, and how can we both use and move beyond them?

A major British telecommunications organization uses an eight-stage 'problem-solving process' for change implementation, following these steps (Buchanan and Boddy, 1992, p. 10):

1 identify problem;
2 gather data;
3 analyse data;
4 generate solutions;
5 select the solution;
6 plan for implementation;
7 implement and test;
8 continue to improve.

This is a typical project management recipe, and there are many such rational, logical, linear, stepwise models available. One of the most fully developed of these rational approaches is PRINCE 2, which stands for PRojects IN a Controlled Environment. This methodology was developed by the British Central Computer and Telecommunications Agency, and can now be accessed at the following website: http://www.prince2.com/. Successful change from this perspective depends on the clarity with which change objectives are stated, and on the effectiveness of monitoring and control to ensure that the project stays on target with respect to time and money. Ineffective change is thus blamed on a failure to specify goals, tasks, milestones and budgets clearly, and on poor project control. The change driver in this model needs two areas of expertise: first, with respect to the content of the changes being introduced (a new information system, office building, payment system); second, with respect to project control, defining goals and tasks, monitoring progress, and taking remedial action to reduce and avoid deviations from plan.

Project management models of change have one striking feature in common: they rely on the assumption that change unfolds in a planned and logical sequence. Solutions are not identified until the problem has been clearly defined. The 'best' solution is not chosen until the options have been compared and evaluated. Implementation does not begin until there is agreement on the solution. Key actors each have clearly defined roles and responsibilities. Plans unfold more or less as they were originally specified. Implementation is closely monitored and any deviations from plan are detected and corrected. The implementation process is bounded in terms of resources and time, with a clear project completion date. This 'logical unfolding' implies a rational-linear model of change. The assumptions concerning rationality and linearity have attracted significant criticism, much of which has already been noted in this and earlier chapters. Organizations rarely operate in such a tidy and predictable manner, particularly with respect to strategic (major, messy, radical) change.

Continuing with this 'recipe' theme, Eccles (1994) identifies 14 factors in successful change, in four categories, as shown in Table 7.2. The premise underlying this and similar approaches to change implementation is that the presence of these ingredients will promote success, while their absence promotes difficulties and possible failure. While advocating 'truth, trust, love and collaboration' in part, Eccles is also sensitive to the need for 'impression management' as an aspect of organizational change, and to the manipulation involved in this approach. The impression management theme is most evident in his remarks on 'concordance and trust' and on 'building on action and success'.

Here are three more, typical, change recipes from the literature of the 1990s. Burnes (1992) advocates a nine-element approach: create an ambitious vision, develop a catalogue of strategies, create the preconditions for change, create a flexible culture, assess the type of change required, plan and implement, involve those concerned, keep up the momentum, and seek continuously to improve. Kotter (1995) outlines 'eight steps to transforming your organization': establish a sense of urgency, form a guiding coalition,

Table 7.2 **Eccles' 14 ingredients for a recipe for successful change**

(1) Purpose and initiative	
The pregnant executive	There has to be a champion who embodies and lives the new dream.
The single goal	There has to be a clear and sustained purpose to which people can commit.
Clarity of purpose	There has to be a defensible, unambiguous reason for the change.

(2) Concordance and trust	
The illusion of unity	Don't expect everybody to back the change.
How open to be?	Tell people as much as practicable, taking some risks by being candid.
Communication	Effective communication is vital, and almost impossible to over-do.

(3) Leadership, capabilities and structure	
The rule of proportionate responsibility	The more senior you are, the more responsibility you must take.
The limitations of empowerment	Even enterprising employees need to be led.
Teams and leaders	Good teams and leaders support each other.
Structure and culture	Use structure to change culture.

(4) Building on action and success	
Creating winners	Personal success is a great motivation.
Fast change and initial acts	Early successes create productive momentum.
Caring for casualties	Caring for people is both morally and organizationally commendable.
Minimizing unintended consequences	You cannot avoid all the errors; but you can organize to anticipate some and to recover from others.

Source: Eccles, 1994

create a vision, communicate the vision, empower people to act on the vision, create 'short-term wins', consolidate improvements to produce further change, and institutionalize new approaches. Finally, Dawson (1994, p. 179), writing from a processual perspective, and drawing on a number of case analyses, offers the following change implementation advice:

1 Maintain an overview of the dynamic and long-term process of change, and appreciate that major change takes time.
2 Recognize that the transition process is unlikely to be marked by a line of continual improvement from beginning to end.
3 Be aware of and understand the context in which change takes place.
4 Ensure that change strategies are culturally sensitive and do not under-estimate the strength of existing cultures.
5 Consider the value of having a champion of change.
6 Affirm that the substance of change is fully understood.
7 Train staff in the use of new equipment, techniques or procedures.

8   Ensure senior management commitment and support.
9   Develop a committed and cohesive local management team.
10   Ensure that supervisors are part of major change programmes.
11   Gain trade union support.
12   Spend time developing good employee relations.
13   Clearly communicate the intentions of change to employees.
14   Provide appropriate funding arrangements.
15   Take a total organizational approach to managing transitions.

Dawson's advice draws particular attention to some of the untidy aspects of major change. Otherwise, these 15 guidelines share many ingredients with other recipes from the change management field: have a clear vision, communicate it properly, involve those affected, have adequate resources and training, and so on. Much of this advice appears unremarkable, common sense and uncontestable. Imagine advocating 'short-term losses', 'lack vision', 'avoid training', 'ignore communication and understanding', 'be inflexible'.

> *Manager*: Can I just talk about the context here? In trying to create change in a healthcare environment, understanding the kind of political issues and being able to work with the political issues is absolutely critical. Because the politics largely defines what you can enact and you can't enact as change. When we first started, we had a typical linear-rational change methodology – the typical management consultancy approach – you follow step 7A, followed by step 7B. You set your terms of reference, then you analyse, then you redesign, then you pilot, then you implement. And after about three months of trying that, we had to chuck it out the window. The major reason for that was the methodology took no account of the political set-up and the political behaviour in the organization. We had to design a completely different methodology, that took account of the politics of the organization. It was just so naïve to assume that one could just go in and create some fabulous redesign for a new service, and just be able to implement it, if you had good planning. What it exposed was how deep and fundamental a lot of the political structures of the organization are, and how incredibly difficult those are to change.

There are several reasons why these recipes might be difficult to apply in practice. First, they identify a more or less comprehensive 'ideal' agenda which management may not have the time and resources to address. Second, they are generic and offer little or no guidance on how they might be effectively 'translated' into specific organizational contexts. Third, the relationships between the ingredients, and the relative emphasis which each deserves, are not explored. Fourth, these approaches typically adopt the organization development perspective that conflict in the organization is caused by failures in interpersonal communications. Many OD interventions are designed to address this apparent failure by creating contexts for sharing information and perceptions. The pervasive political nature of change is denied. The political dimension of change is repressed. Finally, these recipes are presented in a universal, mechanical style. Translating that advice into specific contexts requires local knowledge, informed managerial judgement and intuition, and creativity.

Change is untidy, and major change can be particularly messy. Methodologies and recipes are invaluable tools in this respect, in serving to bring order and structure to that complexity. Planning is much easier when the dimensions of the problem can be clearly plotted. Decision making is more straightforward when relevant information can be presented in a manner that permits options to be compared and assessed systematically. Communication is easier when goals and visions have been articulated precisely and without ambiguity. But as noted earlier, planning and decision making and communicating in the real world are socio-political processes, not rational-empirical. It is not 'the information' that reaches decisions but the players with their competing interpretations, and different values, interests and preferences.

These methodologies are at the same time valuable and incomplete. They lack *perspective*. They lack the creative, reflective perspective of the *political entrepreneur*. Methodologies such as these cannot be 'followed' in any meaningful prescriptive sense; see, for example, the above quotation from a management interview. They can, however, be 'used' by the change driver to legitimate change, as tools to guide the implementation process, and as tools in the turf game. Despite what we know about the untidy realities, change has to *appear* in our culture to be rational and linear. These are as much 'recipes for how the change implementation should appear to be' as for how it should be managed in the first place.

Maxims from this section for Princes and Princessas appear, para-doxically, to include:

- Beware the simple recipes for effective change management. These are not accurate reflections of real change processes, and are thus not good guides for appropriate action, particularly political action.
- Embrace the simple recipe for change management. This is how the organizational change process should appear in public both during and after implementation. These are accurate guides to the 'politically correct' representation of change implementation processes.

Playing the turf game: strategies and tactics

Pfeffer (1992a, p. 27) provides a 'seven-point plan' for getting things done through power and influence in the organization:

1 decide your goals;
2 diagnose patterns of dependence and interdependence in the organization, including which individuals are influential;
3 establish their views of your goals;
4 identify their power bases;
5 identify the bases of your own power and influence;
6 determine effective strategies and tactics for the situation;
7 choose a course of action.

This approach, like many others, relies on stakeholder analysis as a
decision-making and action-planning tool. Egan (1994) offers somewhat
more detailed advice on choosing a political strategy. His starting point
concerns what he calls 'the practice of positive politics'. In other words, the
change driver should begin with a legitimizing, institution-building agenda.
This represents a positive, desirable 'facilitative' view of power (Clegg,
1989) in which the function of political activity is to 'shepherd' agendas
through the organizational maze. The change driver should, in Egan's
view:

• welcome open scrutiny and entertain competing agendas;
• promote positive political values, recognizing the value of competition
  and collaboration;
• acquire the power to compete with other players;
• conduct a stakeholder analysis;
• choose viable political strategies;
• organize the political campaign;
• audit the organization's politics and decide what kind of player one
  would like to become.

Egan's detailed advice for actually choosing a viable political strategy
echoes Jackall's (1988) comments about the 'maze bright' manager, and is
as follows:

• learn the name of the game in your organization; how are politics
  played here?;
• get to know the playing field, the informal organization, the communication networks;
• identify the key players (not always obvious) and their main interests;
• get organized; enlist your supporters at an early stage; form alliances
  with powerful groups, form coalitions to establish a powerful group
  voice;
• use informal networks to gather intelligence, and to send unobtrusive
  messages;
• develop relations with those who you know will support you;
• know who owes you favours, and call these in when necessary;

- balance overt and covert action, know when to go public and when to work behind the scenes;
- learn how to use trade-offs effectively; maximize flexibility without becoming 'slippery';
- use drama and theatre, but sparingly; use stirring gestures that don't cheapen the agenda.

There is a lot of advice similar to this in the literature. Martin and Sims (1964, pp. 218–19) summarized many of these ideas some decades ago. They asked:

> How can power be used most effectively? What are some of the political stratagems which the administrator must employ if he is to carry out his responsibilities and further his career? This is an area that has been carefully avoided by both students and practitioners of business – as if there were something shady about it. But facts are facts, and closing our eyes to them will not change them. Besides, if they are important facts, they should be brought into the open for examination. There follows an account of certain tactics which we have found to be practised by most men whose success rests on ability to control and direct the actions of others – no doubt, raw and oversimplified when reduced to a few black-and-white words, but for this very reason more likely to be provocative.

They proceed to identify nine commonly practised tactics, defined in Table 7.3. About 10 years later, *Harvard Business Review* published an article on 'power and the ambitious executive' by McMurry (1973), who argued that:

> The methods of holding top-management power in a company strike many people as devious and Machiavellian. They involve calculated alliances, compromises, and 'deals' – and often they fly in the face of practices advocated by experts on organizational behaviour. . . . Such strategies are not always noble and high minded. But neither are they naïve. From the selfish standpoint of the beleaguered and harassed executive, they have one primary merit: they enhance his chances of survival. (pp. 140, 145)

McMurry also offered a number of maxims on the use of power and political tactics:

- Use caution in taking counsel.
- Avoid too close superior–subordinate relationships.
- Maintain manoeuvrability.
- Use passive resistance when necessary.
- Not hesitate to be ruthless when expedient.
- Limit what is to be communicated. Many things should not be revealed.

Table 7.3 **Common political tactics**

Taking counsel	The able executive is cautious about how he seeks and receives ideas.
Alliances	In many respects, the executive system in a firm is composed of complexes of sponsorship and protégé relationships.
Manoeuvrability	The wise executive maintains his flexibility, and he never completely commits himself to any one position or programme.
Communication	It simply is not good strategy to communicate everything one knows. Instead, it may be advantageous to withhold information or to time its release.
Compromising	The executive should accept compromise as a means of settling differences with his tongue in his cheek. While appearing to alter his view, he should continue to press forward toward a clear-cut set of goals.
Negative timing	He initiates action, but the process of expedition is retarded. He is considering, studying and planning for the problem; there are difficulties to be overcome and possible ramifications which must be considered.
Self-dramatization	Dramatic art is a process by which selections from reality are chosen and arranged by the artists for the particular purpose of arousing the emotions, of convincing, of persuading, of altering the behaviour of the audience in a planned direction.
Confidence	Once an executive has made a decision, he must look ahead and act decided. Thus, the man who constantly gives the impression of knowing what he is doing – even if he does not – is using his power and increasing it at the same time.
Always the boss	Warm personal relations with subordinates have sometimes been considered the mark of a good executive. But in practice an atmosphere of social friendship interferes with the efficiency of an operation and acts to limit the power of the manager. Thus, a thin line of separation between executive and subordinate must always be maintained.

Source: Based on Martin and Sims, 1964

- Recognize that there are seldom any secrets in an organization.
- Learn never to place too much dependence on a subordinate unless it is clearly to the latter's personal advantage to be loyal.
- Be willing to compromise on small matters.
- Be skilled in self-dramatization and be a persuasive personal salesman.
- Radiate self-confidence.
- Give outward evidence of status, power and material success.
- Avoid bureaucratic rigidity in interpreting company rules.
- Remember to give praise as well as censure – frequently.
- Be open-minded and receptive to opinions which differ from yours.

Pettigrew (1974) lists 10 'defensive tactics' used by senior executives to block advice from staff specialists:

1 straight rejection;
2 'bottom drawer' it;
3 mobilize political support against the specialist;

4   the 'nitty gritty' tactic, criticizing detail to frustrate and annoy the specialist;
5   the emotional tactic, to induce guilt in the specialist;
6   'but in the future' things will be different, so your recommendations won't apply;
7   the invisible man, avoiding all personal contact with the specialist;
8   'further investigation is required', to create delay;
9   the scapegoat, who will make implementation impossible;
10 deflection, onto issues where the specialist is less well-informed.

From a processual-contextual perspective, Pettigrew (1985) offers the following guidance for intervention in the organization's political system:

• Set up management development initiatives which challenge existing thinking.
• Alter administrative mechanisms and career paths and reward systems.
• Form task forces around issues and problems.
• Fragment a global vision into manageable bits.
• Exercise patience, repetition and perseverance.
• Back off and wait until the time is right, for other reasons.
• Replace those who leave (the 'creative retirals') with known supporters.
• Change the organization structure and procedures to shift emphasis.
• Promote key individuals or 'role models', changing their responsibilities at the same time.

Pfeffer (1992a, p. 273) demonstrates how organizational design can be used in power plays. He notes that, 'Power is built by ensuring that you control as much territory as possible, and this control is obtained by placing your allies in key positions and by expanding the activities over which you have formal responsibility.' The tactics he discusses are:

1   Create domains with defined responsibilities. Fragment established entities to reduce their power.
2   Expand your own domain, through access to resources, information, formal authority and sphere of influence.
3   Use task forces and committees. These are vehicles for driving plans and for co-opting others. Choose people you can influence and control to populate these groupings.

Pfeffer (1992a, p. 207) also offers advice on the politics of interpersonal influence. Affecting the way in which decisions are viewed early in the process can be critical in affecting the outcome, particularly where a 'social consensus' for a particular initiative or direction can be demonstrated. Pfeffer refers to this as 'the principle of social proof'; as individuals, we are more likely to accept a view when we believe that it is shared with others. Pfeffer emphasizes the effect of physical attractiveness, positive association, flattery and working through friends and acquaintances to influence third parties. He also advocates the controlled use of visible emotion as a tactic in influencing others.

Furthermore, Pfeffer points out the importance of clever timing in the use of political behaviour:

- It can be appropriate in some settings to *be early and move first*, particularly when, once started, it will be difficult to stop.
- Use deliberate and accidental *delay*. It is often wise to call for further study; the proponents get tired of waiting and give up. Backers may move on to other projects. Deadlines and windows of opportunity may be missed.
- Play *the waiting game*. Make others wait for you. This demonstrates your power and emphasizes your importance.
- Use *deadlines* carefully. Always favour the side that has the momentum. Use deadlines to convey a sense of urgency and importance. Use deadlines to counter delaying tactics.
- Manipulate the *order of consideration*. Committees often choose the good candidate or proposal that follows a string of weak contenders. Launch two proposals and let the weaker get trashed first, so that the second looks stronger by comparison – and the group doing the consideration may be reluctant to trash the advocate twice. Also, by the time the second proposal is reached, there is less time left for detailed debate. In reverse, squash an issue by not putting it onto the agenda.
- Choose *propitious moments*. Other events and coincidences can create 'ripeness'. So, find circumstances in which particular proposals will find and attract attention.

This kind of advice has a number of interesting characteristics. One finds the same maxims being restated in subtly different and sometimes not so different ways by different authors. Many of these maxims draw from Machiavelli's advice to the aspiring sixteenth-century Prince. And we also seem to be repeating the 'recipe-based approach' criticized in the previous section. Change cannot be managed from a checklist of action steps. Political behaviour cannot be deployed from a checklist of political tactics.

Another feature of this advice is that it is male-oriented, a politically incorrect aspect of 1960s and 1970s writing on Machiavellianism and related themes noted in Chapter 4. We appear to be dealing, as Chapter 4 also noted, with *men* behaving badly. To what extent does this advice travel across the gender divide?

Tannen (1990, 1995) argues that boys and girls acquire different linguistic styles in childhood, and that this affects their respective working styles and career prospects. Girls tend to learn conversation rituals that focus on the rapport dimension of relationships, while boys focus on the status dimension. Men thus tend to think more in hierarchical terms, and of being 'one up', are more likely to jockey for position by putting others down, and appearing confident and knowledgeable. Women are more likely to avoid putting others down, and in ways that are face-saving. Women can also appear to lack self-confidence, according to Tannen, by playing down their certainty and expressing doubt more openly. Women adopting a 'masculine' linguistic style can be regarded as aggressive.

Kanter (1979) argues that women are typically rendered 'structurally powerless' in being restricted to routine, low-profile jobs, as well as facing male discrimination in promotion decisions. Mann (1995) similarly argues that women are under-represented in management ranks because they are less successful in acquiring power in the organization. Mann argues that it is easier for men to acquire power, for several reasons. Organizations which encourage long hours of work disadvantage women with family responsibilities. Failure to participate socially – the late drinks evenings – can also lead to exclusion, exacerbated by inadequate childcare facilities. Meetings can thus be scheduled at times inaccessible for women, who can also be excluded from informal male meetings in inaccessible locations (the golf course, the locker room at the gym). Male conversation can often be dominated by topics in which women do not share an interest.

Mann thus argues that many women fail to recognize the significance of political competence, and deny its value and relevance. 'Innocent' behaviour can simply be read as political naïveté, while 'passive strategies' are not as effective as self-promotion in terms of career progression. Arroba and James (1988) similarly argue that women have innate attributes that can be exploited to political advantage. These include intuition, sensitivity, observation, and a willingness to engage with feelings. Women, they argue, should put to one side their distaste for politics and discomfort with the concept of power. Getting involved in the politics game, they note, is tough, but not getting involved means staying put.

In *The Princessa: Machiavelli for Women*, Rubin (1997) argues that women should not rely on 'feminine' tactics such as nurturing, compromise and negotiation, but should welcome and use conflict to establish their authority and make an impact in pursuit of their goals. Rubin offers a somewhat rambling, paradoxical and mystical account of the strategies and tactics of the Princessa: 'how to be brilliantly disruptive', 'enlarge the space in which you can be strong', 'the paradox of power anorexia', 'know your shame, love your power', 'on the use of men as weapons'. One underlying theme concerns an attempt to distance this advice from that of the original Machiavelli, which is concerned with strategy, and with winning by crushing opponents (who are then in no position to exact revenge). Rubin is concerned instead with 'win-win' approaches, with the emotional dimensions of organizational conflict, and with what she calls 'the lover/fighter or collaborative antagonist' (p. 10).

We thus need to move beyond checklists and recipes, and to consider how this advice can be creatively deployed by a range of change drivers in practical settings. One alternative approach is to consider how different

Table 7.4 **A phase model of political strategy and tactics**

Phase	Political strategies/tactics
(1) Conception	The politics of project presentation, selling, positioning, justifying
(2) Launch	The politics of project definition, recruiting support, coalition building
(3) Delivery	The politics of driving, steering, keeping momentum, blocking resistance
(4) Completion	The politics of termination and withdrawal, reporting back, moving on
(5) Afterlife	The politics of representation, tales and myths of problems and success

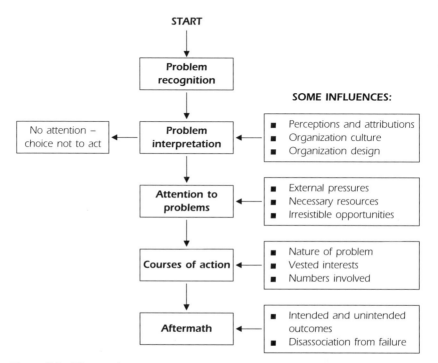

Figure 7.2   **Phases of management decision making**
Source: Based on McCall and Kaplan, 1990

kinds of political strategies and tactics might be appropriate at different stages of the change implementation life cycle. Pettigrew (1985) describes a model of change with four overlapping phases: developing concern, acknowledging the problem, planning and acting, and stabilization. The change agency task changes with the phase of development of implementation. Table 7.4 offers one account of how the political dimension of change agency may need to alter in this respect.

Most of the literature which we have considered so far seems primarily concerned with the politics of delivery. Various commentators, however, have been concerned with the politics of conception and launch. McCall and Kaplan (1990), for example, offer a model of the phases of management decision making outlined in Figure 7.2. The argument of this model is that problems not only have to be recognized as such. Problems also have to be interpreted and they have to get management attention. The factors influencing problem interpretation include the perceptions and attributions of those involved, organization design and culture, the availability of resources, external pressures and the promise of irresistible opportunities. A problem may not gain attention where those in positions of influence do not recognize the issue as significant, or attribute the causes to transient factors beyond their control, or see a solution benefiting only some other (competing) function, or feel that resources need to be deployed elsewhere to higher priority tasks, or feel that the opportunities are minimal.

One key political task at conception may simply be to get the issue onto a management agenda which is crowded with other competing projects, initiatives and problems. March and Olson (1983, p. 292) refer to this as the 'organization of attention'. Dutton (1988), in exploring how attention becomes allocated to strategic issues, identifies specific tactics for 'orchestrating the impressions' attached to management proposals. These concern the management of *issue salience*, *issue sponsorship* and *agenda structure*.

Interviewer: Can you give me some examples?

Manager: Yeah, sure. The first year of the re-engineering programme, we had a situation where we had a directors' group who are all the senior managers of the organization. They met every week in this meeting called the directors' group. There was this huge re-engineering programme, 50 people seconded full time, nearly 100 re-engineering projects, and yet if you looked at what those senior managers spent their time doing, you'd think re-engineering wasn't happening. OK, there were all sorts of horrendous things going on for the organization. There was a severe financial crisis. There was somebody potentially doing a [sabotage] job in the operating theatres – it wasn't that bad in the end, but at the time. . . . There was winter bed crises. There was an impending industrial dispute over staff salaries. And meant that the senior managers in the organization were all engaged in things that were very urgent, but not necessarily important. So you have this huge programme going on, and to judge from what the most senior managers in the organization were doing at that time, you might not even have known it was happening. So it was a question of how to engage those people with the change process at the same time.

Dutton presents four tactics for manipulating *issue salience*. The *magnitude* of an issue can be influenced, by describing it as critical to the organization's survival, competitiveness and profitability. The *abstractness* of an issue can be altered either by grounding or clouding it, by generalizing the issue to broaden support, or by making the issues more specific and focused. The *simplicity* of an issue can be altered either by 'going to the heart of the matter', or by linking it in more complex ways to related concerns. Finally, the *immediacy* of an issue can be manipulated. It may be a pressing concern requiring immediate action, or the urgency can be played down. The required shade of meaning is achieved through the style of language and presentation used to articulate and communicate proposals.

Dutton identifies similar tactics for influencing *issue sponsorship*. The *location* of an issue can be manipulated by attaching a powerful individual to it in some way, or by recruiting influential friends to its support. In the same way, *attachment* can be altered, through allowing more people to participate and to get involved to increase their commitment. Finally, Dutton identifies tactics for modifying *agenda structure*, through the *size* or length of the current agenda (depending on what is realistic and manageable), and by changing the agenda *variety*, which can help to determine support for or resistance to new items.

The *direction* of manipulation in each case will depend on the issue and on the context in which it is being pursued. This is a matter of judgement for the change driver. While conceding that the agenda-setting process is a conservative one, Dutton also argues that such conservatism can be defeated by new and influential managers who have a mandate – implicit or explicit – to change the agenda structure. These tactics, which 'represent attempts to manage an issue's meaning for other organizational members' (Dutton, 1988, p. 138), can be effective because the issues often constitute uncertain and ambiguous developments and are not concrete, at least in initial stages when subjective impressions can be more easily orchestrated.

A discussion of political strategies and tactics would be incomplete without consideration of the problems of resistance to change. Eccles (1994) lists 13 sources of resistance (Table 7.5).

In keeping with the theme of this book, however, Eccles also identifies a hierarchy of five anti-resistance techniques:

1 Convince your critics of the selfless validity of your chosen strategy. If they can be brought on side without having to pay them a price, then that must be the most cost-effective strategy, if it works.
2 Demonstrate that the behaviour you want will have a track to the top, and that it is in their interests to climb aboard.
3 Buy their support, or flatter them – as with the British health minister who, when asked how he would get the support of complaining medical consultants for the creation of the National Health Service, replied, 'we will stuff their mouths with gold'. That worked.
4 Marginalize your critics and use their skills for the benefit of the rest of the organization. They can be 'exited' later if they remain a nuisance.
5 Neutralize or 'exit' them. Termination may be the only effective way to neutralize.

The 'meta-maxims' that can be derived from these lists of strategies, tactics and maxims for Princes and Princessas appear to include:

• Stakeholder analysis is an old but valuable tool for surveying the organization's political landscape.

Table 7.5 **Sources of resistance to change**

Ignorance	Failure to understand the problem.
Comparison	The solution is disliked as an alternative is preferred.
Disbelief	Feeling that the proposed solution will not work.
Loss	Change has unacceptable personal costs.
Inadequacy	The rewards from change are not sufficient.
Anxiety	Fear of being unable to cope in the new situation.
Demolition	Change threatens destruction of existing social networks.
Power cut	Sources of influence and control will be eroded.
Contamination	New values and practices are repellent.
Inhibition	Willingness to change is low.
Mistrust	Motives for change are considered suspicious.
Alienation	Alternative interests valued more highly than new proposals.
Frustration	Change will reduce power and career opportunities.

- From the checklists presented here, the change driver should seek to develop a wide behaviour repertoire of political strategies (overall approaches to the turf game) and tactics (specific ploys and methods).
- Develop the political sensitivity to detect when other players are using such strategies and tactics against you. Keep your political consciousness, your political 'antennae', switched on.
- Be aware of how the game changes with the stage of project development: conception, launch, delivery, completion and afterlife involve different tactics.
- Seek to orchestrate the impressions and understandings of others, particularly in the early stages of implementation, through agenda management tactics.
- Accept that, on occasion, ruthless tactics may be required to deal with resistance.

Accounting: the politics of completion and afterlife

> We exercise power and influence, when we do it successfully, through the subtle use of language, symbols, ceremonies, and settings that make people feel good about what they are doing. A friend once remarked that it is management's job to make people do what they need or have to do in order to make the organization prosper. In a similar fashion, it is the job of people interested in wielding power and influence to cause others to feel good about doing what we want done. This involves the exercise of symbolic management.
>
> (Pfeffer, 1992a, p. 279)

We argued in Chapter 1 that the *reputation* of the change driver is a key factor in understanding the shaping role of political behaviour in organizational change. Our concept of reputation equates closely with

Interviewer: How do you define the acceptable boundaries or the limits in this area?

Manager: The unacceptability is not necessarily in the tactics but in the outcomes. If you accept that the political manager has a role to play, then it's quite difficult to set boundaries around the tactics they can use. I'm not sure we came across any tactics that were unacceptable. I think we came across a number that were disappointing in terms of the impact they had. For me, it was very disappointing that one of the members of our senior team chose to sit on the sidelines and not be involved in the process until it was much further down the road. I would say that was unacceptable.

I would find that unacceptable because what they chose to do was to undermine the impact of the whole process. If they had reservations and concerns, then I'd rather they openly discussed that at the beginning. And if those had shaped the terms of reference of what we were doing, I think that would have been more useful. One of the consequences of that was, perhaps we created more fear of the impact of change in the organization, because the proposals which we developed were dragged back towards something more moderate. I think that was unfair for those people who experienced the fear, of change, redundancy, loss of job, or whatever. If we'd been more honest about the extent to which we were prepared to accept change, then we wouldn't necessarily have had to put those people through that. So in terms of the impact, a number of people were living with a very stressful process of change, had more stress than necessary, that was slightly unacceptable.

I haven't got strong views about the unacceptability of the tactics. I think if you accept you're going to play the game, you might as well use all the abilities open to you to play it. The only rider to that is perhaps, that can become uncontrollable from the organization's point of view. It exists, but it's not talked about; if you're prepared to be more open about accepting it as a process, you're then going to create something that runs and runs and will be hard to control. If you're talking about this as a fairly difficult process to understand and work out why individuals have this ability, where they attract their influence from, to then say, you can use it but only within certain parameters, is naïve.

what Wight calls 'prestige' – a concept around which he notes there is much confusion. Wight (1978, p. 97) defines prestige as 'the halo around power', as 'the influence derived from power', and as 'the recognition by other people of your strength'. Noting the ambiguities in this term, Wight (1978, p. 99) comments:

Thus prestige, like honour, is an ambiguous term. It may mean deliberately refraining from exercising your power because you prefer the advantages of not having done so; and in this sense it comes very near to being magnanimity, which as Burke said is not seldom the truest wisdom in politics. Or it may mean forcing other people to admit your power on every occasion; and in this sense it is simply an extreme policy of asserting your 'honour' and interests . . . one is 'power based upon reputation', and the other is 'reputation based upon power'.

The framework presented in Chapter 1 also emphasized the link between reputation and *accounting*, in explaining, justifying and defending the actions of the change driver. The 'language game' discussed in Chapter 2 reflects what Burns (1961, p. 262) refers to as the 'dual code', moral and linguistic, surrounding the exercise of political behaviour in organizations. From this linguistic perspective, 'the moral legitimacy of action is a relative matter', depending on the context and the goals being pursued. What can be presented as legitimate in one context may be unacceptable in another. Burns points to the discrepancies between the public and private terminologies surrounding political behaviour. Players can be represented as collaborators in a common enterprise, while at the same time being rivals for rewards, resources and progression. Both values – collaborative and competitive – are socially valued. However, there is a clear distinction between the issues that are discussable backstage, and the language that can be used, and what can be aired and admitted in public.

March and Olson (1983) similarly draw attention to this dual linguistic and moral code in their distinction between the rhetoric of administration and the rhetoric of *realpolitik* in discussions about reorganization. The rhetoric of administration speaks of structures, procedures, efficiency, effectiveness, planning, economy and control. The contrasting rhetoric of *realpolitik*, on the other hand, speaks of political struggle, competing interests and dominance. The rhetoric of administration emphasized management control, while the rhetoric of *realpolitik* emphasizes political control. March and Olson (1983, p. 291) argue that these twin rhetorics work in parallel in analyses of the 'ritual of reorganization':

> On the one hand, a commitment to administrative purity is made tolerable by an appreciation of realpolitik, much as a commitment to personal purity is made tolerable by an appreciation of human weakness. At the same time, a commitment to realpolitik rhetoric is made consistent with human hopes by a faith in the imaginability of improvement through human intelligence. It should not be surprising to find that both rhetorics survive and thrive, and that both find expression in the symbols of reorganization.

March and Olson (1983, p. 288) also note that the interpretation and reception of proposals for change can alter through time. They argue that:

> [P]ersistent repetition of similar ideas and similar arguments over a relatively long period of time appears to make some difference. Persistence both increases the likelihood that a proposal will be current at an opportune time and creates a diffuse climate of availability and legitimacy for it. Recommendations that produce a storm at one time are later accepted without opposition . . . different times, different meanings.

Does this once again turn the management of change in general, and accounting for the behaviour of the change driver in particular, into a game of impression management, in which illusion and form are more significant than substance and achievement? Must organizational change merely follow cultural norms in sustaining the cosmetic of rationality, even when this is not an accurate representation of events? March and Olson (1983, p. 290) ask if the ritual of reorganization is simply, 'a tactic for creating an illusion of progress where none exists'. Their defensive response draws from an analysis of government changes in America this century, but is relevant to contemporary organizational change:

> Any effective deceit is testimony to a belief deeply enough held to warrant the costs of hypocrisy. If we observe that everyone says the same thing while doing different things, we are observing something important about the political system, the beliefs on which it rests. Virtuous words sustain the meaning and importance of virtue, even among sinners. To view the symbols of politics as intentional efforts by sophisticated actors to deceive the innocent is likely to exaggerate the extent to which things as fundamental as optimism that mankind can direct and control its environment for the better can be manipulated arbitrarily as a tactic. Leaders need reassurance too. More generally, organization and reorganization, like much action, are tied to the discovery, clarification, and elaboration of meaning as well as to immediate action or decision making.

Evidence for a dual linguistic code, for twin rhetorics, is thus no platform for simple manipulation by false information and other deceits. The accounts offered by politicians, and by change drivers, are reflections of their own beliefs, sometimes deeply held. We are assuming that change drivers are concerned with making a difference, with making an impact on the organizational setting in which they operate. And as we have tried to demonstrate, efficacy in that regard involves a broad combination of skills and abilities, one of which is the ability to provide, when asked or challenged, an acceptable account of their actions.

Pfeffer's argument (1992a, pp. 248–54) that decisions must appear rational in the circumstances is key here. He notes that, with complex, multidimensional issues, rational analysis rarely helps determine the option to select. This means that there is ample scope for advocating criteria and presenting information in ways that favour one's personal position. This relates to the tactic of selective use of information. Decision quality is difficult to assess, notes Pfeffer, and so is rarely pursued. Is it unseemly to be 'caught out' doing this kind of thing? Pfeffer suggests that one can hire an outside consultant to do this, and then rely on their impartial (but carefully briefed) judgement.

Read (1992) outlines a model of how we construct accounts for social actions, when for some reason we are challenged. The central feature of an acceptable account, in Read's perspective, is the coherence of our account, the extent to which it 'hangs together' in the perception of its audience. The construction of a 'good' account must therefore consider both the circumstances of the case, and the perspectives of those constituents whom the account is designed to sway.

Table 7.6 **The construction of accounts**

Category	Construction
The excuse	Admit that damaging behaviour has occurred, but that you are not responsible; negative consequences were unforeseen, you were under considerable pressure at the time, the damage was actually caused by something, or someone, else.
The justification	Admit responsibility but claim the behaviour was justified in the context; because no harm was done, because positive outweigh negative consequences.
The concession	Admit to the offence, expressing apologies and remorse, and offer restitution; may seek to deflect censure and blame as well.
The refusal	Deny that the damaging behaviour ever happened; claim that the challenger's version or perception of events is incorrect; or deny that the challenger has a right of reproach, because they are not involved, suffered no damage themselves.

Read (1992, p. 5) demonstrates the central role of goals in constructing coherent accounts. The primary goal is to construct an account that will be believed and honoured. The problem is that the secondary goals of truthful representation and avoidance of blame may often conflict. The person constructing the account must decide which goals take precedence:

> If our primary goal is truth, then our focus is to develop the most accurate account possible. However, if our primary goal is to justify or excuse our behaviour we must focus on how to do this. And, if in constructing such an account, we must be less than faithful to the facts, we must ensure that the reproacher does not find out . . . this suggests that often we may be quite concerned with what the reproacher knows so that we can know whether and how the facts constrain us.

Read identifies four major types of accounts, with different implications for how the account is constructed (Table 7.6). The main consideration when constructing an account is the perspective of the person delivering the challenge. How much does that person already know? What is their current interpretation of events? What are their general beliefs and perceptions about how society and organizations work? How are they likely to respond to one particular type of account or another? For Read (1992, p. 9) the account construction process must then consider:

1   the kind of account we wish to construct;
2   our desire to have the account honoured;
3   what we know of the facts of the case;
4   what the reproacher knows, or is likely to learn, of the facts;
5   the reproacher's beliefs about social and physical causality;
6   our own beliefs about social and physical causality.

The aim is to, 'evaluate the account we construct from the perspective of the reproacher so that we can judge the likelihood that the account will be honoured' (Read, 1992, p. 9). The more coherent the challenger judges our account to be, the more likely it is to be honoured. The main point here is that it does not much matter how convincing the person presenting the account believes it to be; what matters is how compelling the audience judge it to be. Bies and Sitkin (1992) reinforce this point, arguing that our goals when we offer excuses to others in the organization include making our behaviour intelligible and understood, and making that behaviour appear warrantable, or justified in the context. The adequacy of the account and the sincerity of the communicator are also key variables, according to Bies and Sitkin, in determining whether the account will be accepted.

The maxims for Princes and Princessas which can be derived from the argument in this section thus concern *accounting*, and include the following:

- Be sensitive to the moral and linguistic codes of your organization; know what is acceptable and legitimate, in terms of behaviour and language in different settings.
- Be attuned to the different codes and values of different groups, departments, sections and occupational sub-groups in the organization.
- Recognize and accept that the representation of political behaviour as reasonable in the context is a critical dimension of political efficacy.
- Be prepared to provide coherent, sincere and compelling accounts to justify political behaviour in the change process, taking into consideration how such accounts will be interpreted and judged by their audience.
- Recognize and accept that accounts may not always be entirely faithful to the facts, but that this is not a licence for deceit for its own sake.

The perspective of the political entrepreneur

> Bureaucracy poses for managers an intricate set of moral mazes that are paradigmatic of the quandaries of public life in our social order. Within this framework, the puzzle for many individual managers becomes: How does one act in such a world and maintain a sense of personal integrity?
>
> (Jackall, 1988, pp. 193–4)

The checklists and maxims presented here are of little use on their own. They perhaps convey a sense of the number of interacting variables involved in change implementation, and of the rich variety of political behaviour that can be observed and used in an organizational context. It is worth repeating, however, that change cannot be managed by reference to a checklist. There is a key ingredient missing.

How can the change driver address Jackall's puzzle? The answer, we propose, lies in the development of an appropriate frame of reference, or perspective, to guide practice in this potentially controversial area. Such a perspective is missing from the change management literature. For example, one can convey a knowledge of paint, the history of art, the use of the brush, and different types of media, but the reader would still be unlikely to produce canvases comparable with those of, say, Manet, Lowry or Hockney. This analogy implies that one's perspective is uniquely personal. However, in the context of the shaping role of political behaviour in organizational change, it is possible to sketch in general terms what kind of perspective might be valuable to the change driver.

The term 'perspective' is used here to refer to a set of considerations, or convictions, which are used to inform the change driver's decisions and actions. At least seven sets of considerations seem to emerge from the issues and arguments raised here. This perspective is offered as a 'totality' and these points appear in no particular order.

(1) 'Reality' is illusory

Constructing convincing and acceptable accounts of our actions is particularly important when political behaviour is potentially concerned (Chapter 1). Reality is socially constructed (Chapter 2) rather than 'given'. Organizational reality is what we define it to be, is what we represent it to be. From this point of view, 'political' is a category of behaviour used by players in the turf game for different purposes. The ability to represent 'your' behaviour as non-political while accusing 'me' of blatant politicking can be a critical skill in establishing legitimacy for some actions while challenging the legitimacy of others. This position taken alone leads to accusations of 'all form without substance'. However, this dimension of organizational reality is inescapable, and this is only one dimension of the perspective offered here. How will political actions be regarded and assessed? What form of accounts will be appropriate if challenged? Can political behaviour be represented as reasonable in the context? Is it possible to weave the cloak of defensibility? Dealing effectively with these issues is central to the change driver's reputation, which must be considered here in a broad social sense, and not merely in relation to a narrow group of constituents in the current organization. A concern with personal reputation can be seen as a factor triggering and sustaining organizational political behaviour, and also as a factor restraining such action.

(2) Game on

The turf game involves continuing interaction and exchange, and rarely involves 'single plays'. There are typically a limited number of players active at one time, but the 'cast of characters' can be fluid depending on the flow and outcome of events. The concept of 'change agency' is an *emergent* one and is not static. This is a dynamic game of action and response, of anticipating how others will react to one's behaviour and position, and of then acting accordingly. Players are not always well informed about each other and their respective plans and intentions. This is a game played in a mist or fog most of the time. Some of the 'moves' in the game are substantial, some are symbolic, but both can be significant. There are no time limits; there is almost always a rematch available.

(3) The credibility factor

This is a game of credentials, in which reputations established through time are important assets. The credibility of the players is crucial; will individuals keep to their goals and agendas and promises? Are threats and actions credible? What kind of reputation as a change driver do you want to build? The 'right' reputation enhances personal career, and improves one's ability to obtain resources and organizational support for change.

(4) In context

Political behaviour is one particular variety of change implementation tool. The concept of power-assisted steering implies that organizational change has motive forces behind it other than political goals and aspirations. Conventional change management methods (project management, organization development, planned strategic change) still apply. What matters is: What factors in this context are significant? What is the political climate, the political temperature? What approaches will work in this context given past experience, current stakeholders and future aspirations?

(5) A situational ethic

There are severe problems in attempting to apply normative universal ethical principles to political behaviour in an organizational context. Decisions thus have to rely on an informed judgement of what is possible, of what is acceptable, of what is justifiable, and of what is defensible in the situation – which returns us again to the notion of accounts. 'Merely accounting' can be seen as an insubstantial, cosmetic position. It can be valuable to work through a 'cost–benefit' analysis to inform a situational ethic.

(6) The reflective practitioner

Schon (1983) argues that the decisions and actions of the professional are informed by a considered combination of theory, evidence and past personal experience. Each new situation or problem is conceptualized as unique, for what it is, but in the light of relevant theoretical frameworks and previous experience. Decisions are thus based on a combination of knowledge and conceptualization of the context, managerial judgement and creativity. In this view, practice is improvisatory, and is sometimes experimental. The change driver is a *bricoleur*, using whatever resources are to hand in the pursuit of objectives, including opportunity, luck and accidents of good timing. This will sometimes involve the use of complicating strategies, with multidimensional, multifaceted approaches, to deal with different stake-holder constituencies and to confuse and block interference and subversion from different sources. The reflective practitioner is also self-conscious, self-aware and self-critical, learning from experience – and from mistakes when necessary. This type of 'self-monitoring' is particularly valuable in a context where the boundaries of acceptable behaviour are approached, and in some instances crossed, in the pursuit of change agendas.

(7) Risky shift

The change-driving role is not an easy one. Major change makes the driver more visible, and more vulnerable. The role requires a behaviour repertoire that extends into various forms of 'Machiavellian' actions, and other managerial character styles. This can involve the conscious switch from one position in relation to change implementation to another, to reduce risk and maximize personal advantage. It also requires energy and commitment – perhaps even passion – as well as creativity. It involves the acceptance of personal risk in career terms. The penalties for mistakes or failure can be high, while the rewards for success are sometimes intangible if significant. This can be more of a lifestyle than a job. Without energy and commit-ment, stamina and good health, the change driver is likely to struggle. It is this particular combination of characteristics that renders the label 'politi-cal entrepreneur' particularly apt in these circumstances.

What of the criticism that, if everyone in the organization is sensitized to and trained in the use of political behaviour, and approaches this domain from the same perspective, the result will be 'chaos on a higher plane'? This is unlikely to happen, for a number of reasons. First, natural selection plays a part here. The weaker players quit. The cast of active characters is self-limiting to this extent. Skilled players, as in any sport, interact more effectively, recognizing, for example, when players are matched, or when others have the advantage. We have also noted that 'the rules', such as they are, change with time. Players who have an advantage at one point may thus lose this through circumstances outside their direct control, and play switches to others. The turf game is dynamic, indeterminate and creative. Training and education in this field has to be based, as it is here, on broad approaches, modes, style, illustrations and exemplars. As indicated already, you can learn to mix the paint and use the brush, but still not be able to produce a masterpiece. Training will not bring everyone involved to the same level of expertise.

A final comment is required on the sub-title of this book. The concept of 'winning' carries a number of connotations, with differing implications.

Major change often creates 'winners' and 'losers'. The strategies and tactics explored here can be used to maximize the probability that one belongs to the former group more often than to the latter. In the context of individual conflicts of interests, or the competition between ideas, or clashes of wills and personalities, these tactics can again be deployed in order to win. But in the context of considering one's reputation, the concept of winning can assume a broader definition. This may mean simply achieving and sustaining the position to which one personally aspires in the organization and in the community at large. This may also mean deliberately choosing, in a particular context, not to 'win', but to concede or to lose in the interests of longer-term personal, interpersonal and organizational goals.

In other words, 'winning' is also a socially defined and constructed concept, depending on what one wants to achieve, depending on how one wants to perceived. This may involve actions of which one is not always proud, and to which one might not always want to admit publicly. Jackall (1988, p. 196) eloquently describes the advantages, ambiguities and costs of 'winning' the turf game:

> On the other hand, winning carries with it the knowledge of others' envy and the fear that one's defeated opponents are lying in wait for an opportunity to turn the tables. One adopts then a stance of public humility, of self-effacing modesty that helps disguise whatever sense of triumph one might feel. Moreover, winning, say, on a policy dispute carries the burden of implementation, sometimes involving those whom one has defeated. One must then simultaneously protect one's flanks and employ whatever wiles are necessary to secure requisite co-operation. Here the disarming social grace that is a principal aspect of desirable managerial style can be particularly useful in making disingenuousness seem like 'straight arrow' behaviour. Finally, winning sometimes requires the willingness to move decisively against others, even though this might mean undermining their organizational careers. These may be neighbours on the same block, members of the same religious communion, longtime work colleagues, or, more rarely, members of the same club. They may be good, even excellent, employees. In short, managerial effectiveness and others' perceptions of one's leadership depend on the willingness to battle for the prestige that comes from dominance and to make whatever moral accommodation such struggles demand. In the work world, those who adhere either to secular democratic precepts as guides or, even more, to an ethic of brotherly love, run the risk of faltering in those struggles. But those who abandon the ethics of *caritas* and hone themselves to do what has to be done must accept the peculiar emotional aridity that is one price of organizational striving and, especially, of victory.

The perspective set out here is not definitive, but is intended to serve as a guide to the individual change agent, to the political entrepreneur, in establishing their own personal sense of morality and integrity, in acting effectively to establish and to develop their own reputation, in defining their own understanding of what it means to 'win the turf game'.

8 The triggering factors

DB

'I don't have so many people to push around since we downsized, and since we delayered I don't have that overwhelming sense of management superiority. How boring.'

Personal, decisional and structural triggers

The aim of this chapter is to explore in more detail the factors which trigger political behaviour. We have argued throughout that political behaviour is an aspect of organizational life that can be managed, in some sense, but it is not a phenomenon that can be 'managed away'. Political agendas provide the motivation, drive, energy and enthusiasm for organization development and change. Organization without politics would surely be an exceptionally dull, boring, lifeless, static affair. This is not to deny that some political behaviour is extreme, unethical, unacceptable, even illegal and thus damaging. Between that extreme, on the one hand, and unremarkable day-to-day actions, on the other, lies a vast, murky and unclassified range of behaviours that can potentially be represented as political.

What factors, then, give rise to the phenomenon of political behaviour in an organizational setting? There seem to be three main sets of factors at work: *personal* characteristics, *decisional* characteristics and *structural* characteristics (Chanlat, 1997).

Personal characteristics

As Schon (1963; see Chapter 2) argues, significant change is often driven by a 'champion', who is in turn driven by personal values and beliefs which can extend to passionate commitment. That commitment can be attached to a new corporate strategy, to a shift in organization culture, to the redesign of work, to a new payment system – whatever. Individuals with strong convictions can be expected to use their skills in persuasion and influence, and other techniques. These other techniques may become more extreme, to the extent that challenge and resistance are regarded as unwarranted, ill-founded, or perhaps motivated by personal agendas irrelevant to organizational processes and outcomes.

Political behaviour is also the natural consequence of ambition and the desire for career advancement. The more ambitious you are, the more likely you are to argue and lobby for your ideas, your innovations, your projects and your goals. Organization populations usually contain a significant proportion of ambitious people whose ideas naturally and necessarily compete with each other. Tension and conflict are thus central features of all organizations. The 'reasoned case' is a weak weapon in the war of ideas. A range of other political techniques is helpful in recruiting allies, marginalizing opponents, forming coalitions and sustaining attention on your idea, agenda or project.

Political behaviour is thus a direct consequence of organizational recruitment, appraisal, training and promotion policies. When did you last see a recruitment advertisement asking for people without ambition? How many favourable appraisals rely on the appraisee having no ideas of their own?

Who got promoted precisely because they were lacking in drive and creativity? (Of course, individuals are favourably appraised and promoted for lacking these features. But usually these are moves in a political game, which is not made public.)

Political behaviour can also be triggered by the desire for retribution and revenge. Where we have been the targets of what we believe to be political tactics, reciprocity may appear to be an acceptable and satisfying option. This can, of course, become extremely damaging, to the players and to the organization. However, it is necessary to recognize the enjoyment of power play that many managers experience. Many find it challenging, exciting, thrilling even. This is a game often, but not always, carried out by 'consenting adults'. Losing this time around is not a disaster, the experience can improve awareness and skill, and losing can be an invitation to, or an excuse for, a 'rematch'.

Decisional characteristics

Decisions vary on the extent to which they are structured, on the one hand, or unstructured on the other. Structured decisions are 'programmable', which means that they can be resolved using known decision rules. Deciding how many kilometres you can drive before you need to stop to buy more petrol is a structured, programmable decision. Unstructured decisions are unprogrammable, and cannot be resolved using decision rules. Examples include:

- What organization culture will be most appropriate for us in five years' time?
- How should the role of the human resource management function develop?
- Would it be more appropriate to use a work redesign or a process re-engineering approach to resolve quality and employee morale problems?
- Which of these three different lines of product innovation should we pursue?
- Should we upgrade our management information system now, or delay for two years until improved hardware and software are available at lower cost?

Routine, day-to-day decisions tend to be more structured. Significant strategic decisions tend to be unstructured. To make matters worse, unstructured decisions typically have to be reached in the face of change and uncertainty. Who knows what size the organization will be in five years' time, or what the composition of the workforce will be like? What are the main factors affecting product quality and employee morale, and can we be sure that work or process redesign will really address these? How can the balance of costs and benefits of organization restructuring be assessed? Who knows what product or service innovations the competition are about to launch? Who knows what developments will or will not take place in computing hardware and software – and prices – over the next two years?

The number of management decisions that can be reached unambiguously on the basis of information, analysis and logical reasoning is thus limited. Major decisions are value-laden. Information and analysis may point in particular directions, but information alone is usually inadequate to resolve an unstructured decision. In these circumstances, one expects reasonable people to disagree. It cannot be undesirable that two managers, say, with different past experiences and current preferences, argue the merits of work redesign and process re-engineering solutions. That debate is normal and valuable.

But we are not talking just about the value of information sharing and open discussion. We are dealing with the possible deployment of a range of other political tactics to encourage support, and to deflect resistance, to win the debate. The consequences of the turf game concern individual positioning, reputation and career progression, and the status of sections, departments and occupational groups. Organizations are not debating societies operating to a set of polite and structured rules. To win the competition of ideas in an unstructured decision situation, players will do whatever they can, within the constraints imposed by social norms and considerations of personal reputation, to ensure that their ideas prevail over others.

Political behaviour is thus a direct consequence of the numerical superiority of unstructured decisions over structured ones. It is also a consequence of the tendency for informed and interested parties to disagree with each other, partly on the interpretation of information and analyses, and partly because they are likely to hold differing beliefs, values and preferences.

Structural characteristics

As organizations grow in size, separate functions and departments emerge, specializing in distinct activities: purchasing, production, sales, distribution, accounting, human resource management. This horizontal differentiation, between functions, creates legitimate interest groupings, which naturally develop differing goals, priorities and world views. They are also likely to make competing calls on the organization's resources, particularly in the context of generating innovative and creative initiatives for change and development in their respective areas. The concept of organization as united community in pursuit of shared goals is a fiction of the management literature and of corporate publicity. Vertical differentiation creates the need to control and co-ordinate the work of others, and generates resistance from those in subordinate positions. This need to control generates resistance while simultaneously stimulating the aspirations of some of the controlled to enter the ranks of the controllers.

Political behaviour is thus an inevitable consequence of structural differentiation (Johnson and Gill, 1993). This structural view may be seen to imply that power relations are frozen in some manner by organizational arrangements. Some functions, or particular levels in the organization hierarchy, may then dominate in perpetuity. As individuals, the extent to which the organization dominates is easy to identify, over matters such as recruitment, reward, status, training and development opportunities, promotion, and working conditions. However, it is also possible to argue that as individuals we can exploit employing organizations in the pursuit of our immediate need satisfaction and longer-term career progression. As individuals, we have countervailing power. So-called 'lower-level' participants in the organization structure can have power through (Batstone, 1978):

- possessing skills that cannot readily be replaced;
- occupancy of positions crucial to the workflow;
- the ease with which they can disrupt operations;
- creating or resolving uncertainty in work processes.

This combination of personal, decisional and structural triggers of political behaviour thus reinforces the argument that organizational politics is an *autonomous* domain. Political behaviour is inevitable, and occurs regardless of management attempts to reduce or eliminate it. Pfeffer (1992a) lists a number of conditions that determine the *politicization* of issues and decisions. These conditions include personal, decisional and structural factors:

- the involvement of large numbers of people;
- decisions involving interdepartmental co-ordination;
- decisions about promotions and transfers;
- decisions about resource allocation;
- decisions at higher organizational levels;
- interdependence between parties combined with differing views;
- scarcity of resources;
- disagreement on goals;
- importance of the issue.

Pfeffer (1992b, p. 37) notes that:

[P]ower is more important in major decisions, such as those made at higher organizational levels and those that involve crucial issues like reorganization and budget allocations; for domains in which performance is more difficult to assess such as staff rather than line production operations; and in instances in which there is likely to be uncertainty and disagreement.

Given what we think we know about trends in organization design and functioning, is the significance of power and politics diminishing or increasing?

Politics in the postmodern organization: has the ground moved?

Was organizational life really more peaceful in the 1950s and 1960s? It is tempting to argue that, in the period which saw the rise of socio-technical systems thinking and the organization development movement, the organizational political climate was less significant, less pressing, less volatile, less hostile. Research into management character types (Chapter 4), such as the obedient 'organization man' and 'his' more devious cousins, the 'gamesman' and the 'Machiavellian', suggests some concern with organization politics. But the change management literature from that period (Burns and Stalker, 1961, is an exception) presents a picture which is virtually politics-free. This relative tranquillity does not appear to characterize the experience of organizational research and consultancy in the two closing decades of the twentieth century. Has 'the political' become more prevalent?

A change in context, actual or perceived, implies a change in the behaviours required to operate effectively in that context. Chapters 4 and 5 explored arguments concerning how organizational characteristics apparently encourage particular character types and associated behaviour. These arguments apply to management in general. What are the implications of a change in context for the change driver, and for the role of political behaviour in change?

Particular problems confront those responsible for implementing change in contexts where 'the arena resembled a battleground, in which a function committed to improving performance could not become associated with openness and participation as it would be less able to sustain itself or influence the course of events' (Charlton and Herlihy, 1982, p. 34). Reason (1984) discusses the different role and contribution of organization development in a 'power culture'. Stjernberg and Philips (1993) document how the context of organizational change can shift during the course of project implementation. Buchanan (1997) explores the way in which political agendas influenced the definition of goals and methods of an organizational change project in a British hospital, concluding that the change driver requires a combination of sector knowledge, technical expertise, and political sensitivity and skill. Badham et al. (1997a) discuss how action researchers had to adopt differently politicized change strategies in each of three organizations involved in an Australian project to implement team-based cells.

In other words, if the organizational climate has become more turbulent, then the change driver may now require political skills to a degree not previously required. However, the political dimension is probably a perennial feature on the terrain of the change driver, even if political factors have not figured prominently in earlier theoretical frameworks or practical guides. Several factors may simply have heightened awareness of political agendas, rather than generated a fresh set of issues. The scope of organizational change strategies appears to have widened. Buchanan (1994a, 1994b) notes a shift from work design to organization design, and identifies inconsistencies concerning different applications of 'teamwork'. The development of all-embracing strategies for manufacturing system development finds support in the work of, for example, Drucker (1990) and Parnaby (1988). This trend also finds expression in the work of Dutch theorists in the development of a new paradigm of 'integral organizational renewal' (de Sitter and den Hertog, 1990). Writing in the organization development domain, French and Bell (1995) note an increased concern to 'get the whole system in the room' when analysing change initiatives.

This widening of scope, and the almost frantic search for novel techniques, have in combination increased concern with the complex politics of multiple constituencies, particularly when dealing with radical organization redesign proposals. Various threats to job security in industrialized economies appear to be changing perceptions of the meaning and significance of work. The management of diversity and the need to consider the rights of minority groups attract regular media attention. The production of management fashion has become an increasingly significant commercial enterprise in its own right, creating fierce inter-consultant rivalry (Micklethwait and Wooldridge, 1996; Shapiro, 1996).

A shift in the moral terrain of management is more difficult to substantiate. Jackall (1988) demonstrates the morally contingent nature of managerial work, interpersonal relations and corporate decision making. In other words, definitions of 'acceptable' and 'ethical' and 'legitimate' depend on the organizational context, and in particular on the views and behaviour of senior management. But Jackall does not explore the implications of this argument, in general or in the context of organizational change. Hughes (1993) argues that minority voices now claim exaggerated attention precisely because they are and have been minority voices deserving, by definition therefore, favoured treatment. Hughes thus writes about the development of a 'culture of complaint' in American society. Many managers may recognize this culture of complaint in contemporary organizations.

Table 8.1 offers an exaggerated portrayal of these trends, comparing the 1960s with the 1990s. This table is offered in the knowledge that it is potentially an artefact of bias in published work, and also that it is empirically untestable. However, this can be read either as a real shift, or as a *shift in perceptions* of organizational trends. In other words, this is probably an idealized picture of trends through time, but one which highlights current preoccupations and perceived priorities. Thompson and Davidson (1995) argue that the theme of 'turbulent times' is a creation of

Table 8.1 **Has the ground moved?**

	1960s–1970s It was all so simple then	1980s–1990s Uncertainty rules
Context factors	Job redesign, local technology and shopfloor-level change Local implementation, with predictable ripples Recruit organization members Apparent system stability Narrowly defined gains – gimme productivity	Organizational transformation, multiple levels of change Systemic, with many unpredictable ripple effects Redesign the whole activity chain Apparent system instability Broad and rapid gains – gimme speed
Technique factors	Unambiguous paradigm Clear exemplars 'Dry', unfashionable management theory Few competing fads and techniques (what's BPR?)	Competing versions of 'teamwork' Contradictory exemplars (e.g. Japanese and Scandinavian) Heathrow organization theory is 'HOT' Guru worship (what's next?)
Moral factors	Management licence, operating behind closed doors Managing 'the voiceless' Quality of working life Managerial humanism Premium on involvement Social responsibility, ethical clarity	Management visible, open to scrutiny and challenge Managing a 'culture of complaint' Competitive advantage Moral relativism Premium on exclusion Change politically charged; postmodern uncertainty and confusion

the 'pop management' literature and that, moving beyond the cosmetic surface of organizational transformations one finds deep continuities in organization structures, work design and managerial styles.

If the management media are to be believed, the character of many organizations in the early decades of the twenty-first century is widely perceived to be quite different from that experienced during the second half of the twentieth century. Bureaucracy and hierarchy have been replaced by empowered, multiskilled teamwork. 'Due procedures' have been cast aside in the interests of speed and flexibility of response. Change, revolution and discontinuity are the norm; stability, evolution and consistency imply commercial suicide. The concept of 'the' organization is an anachronism in a world of partnerships and networks and other forms of collaboration. The traditional notion of 'career' has little currency in a world in which many individuals regularly switch between jobs, occupations and organizations.

Our organizations thus appear to be becoming faster, flatter, and more flexible (three Fs) – or, as Thompson and Davidson (1995, p. 17) note, decentralized, disaggregated, disorganized and delayered (four Ds). Given what we know about the triggers of political behaviour, what will be the impact of these trends? In an unpredictable organizational context in which the traditional procedural rules and career ladders have gone, individuals become more dependent on their own resources and interpersonal skills. Regular personal advance based on 'time serving' cannot be taken for granted. The competition of ideas becomes an even hotter competition for promotion. Increased uncertainty increases the prevalence, and the significance, of unstructured decisions. Organization structures become more differentiated, fragmented and fluid. The relatively stable coalitions and interest groups of the past are replaced with transient alliances. The personal, decisional and structural triggers of change are thus intensified in the ambiguous, so-called 'postmodern' organization. We seem to be looking at a future in which political behaviour will play an increasingly significant role in organizational decision making and management careers.

This view of a politicized future is inconsistent with some contemporary thinking about management and organizational trends. Handy (1997) argues that organizations should be conceived as communities, and that employees should be considered and treated as citizens. He argues that commercial success depends on consistency of values, identity and purpose. This view can be regarded as naïve, perhaps dangerous. Naïve because it ignores the realities and implications of organizational power-inequalities and power-plays. Dangerous because it ignores the potential benefits of tension, conflict and political behaviour. Dangerous also because this perspective puts ideological constraints in the path of those who would resist and challenge and otherwise seek to subvert an organization's purpose. The harmonious community of citizens, neither questioning nor challenging their purpose, is unlikely to be an effective or successful venture in the twenty-first century.

Machiavelli in a new millennium

No contemporary treatment of power is complete without reference to the work of the French philosopher and historian Michel Foucault, who died in 1984. Foucault was concerned with the development of the human sciences since the eighteenth century, and with the evolution of forms of discipline and control. His best known writings deal with prisons, punishment and the evolution of sexuality (Foucault, 1977, 1979). As a homosexual in France in the mid-twentieth century, Foucault was no stranger to prison life. While his work is not directly concerned with the politics of organizational change, his analysis offers novel insights.

Popular notions of social and organizational power have two significant features. First, power is generally regarded in *negative* terms. Power corrupts, political behaviour is counter-productive. Second, power is typically regarded and defined as *episodic* in nature. Power is a resource possessed by some individuals who exercise it over others through social interaction. We have consistently in this book sought to extend these notions. We have argued that power and political behaviour, in organizational change, cannot realistically be regarded in a wholly negative light, and that political behaviour is inevitable, necessary and desirable. We have also demonstrated how power inequalities are embedded in social and organization structures. Power can be exercised through 'non-decision making' and through the 'mobilization of bias' as well as in face-to-face episodes of interpersonal influence. Foucault also argues for the productive and pervasive aspects of power, but his work brings radical and fresh conceptualization and force to these arguments.

Foucault's writing style often makes severe demands on the reader. One is therefore drawn either to 'edited highlights' (Rabinow, 1984), or to the extensive 'secondary' literature produced by his interpreters and commentators (Burrell, 1988; Clegg, 1989; McKinlay and Starkey, 1998). Much of this secondary literature adopts a style at least as opaque as the original, and interpreters tend to disagree over 'what Foucault said'. In addition, Foucault produced a vast and related body of work that resists fragmentation into 'topics' such as a narrow focus on power. A brief treatment is thus open to accusations of oversimplification. It is necessary to offer this 'interpretation' warning before we proceed.

Two concepts are central to Foucault's notions of power: *bio-power* and *disciplinary power*. Bio-power operates through establishing and defining what is normal or abnormal, and thus what is socially deviant or acceptable in thought and behaviour. Bio-power is targeted at society as a whole, and is achieved through a variety of *discursive practices*: talk, writing, debate, argument, representation. The media thus play a significant role in sustaining and altering what we conceive as socially normal and deviant. Bio-power exercises control over us through 'constituting the normal'. For most of the twentieth century in Britain, for example, it has not been 'normal', and thus barely acceptable, for women to aspire to senior managerial positions. Bio-power thus operates through our individual cognition and understanding. Assuming you accept without challenge the 'constitution of the normal', as this is currently represented, bio-power assumes a self-disciplining role as far as your thinking and behaviour are concerned. No powerful superior managerial or supervisory figure is necessary to keep you under control. This is a long way from an 'episodic' conception of power, but reinforces the need to question the 'constitution of the normal', rather than tacitly accept current and taken-for-granted definitions and representations.

Disciplinary power operates through the construction of social and organizational routine, and is targeted at individuals and groups. Foucault thus regards power as a set of techniques whose effects are achieved through *disciplinary practices*. Disciplinary practices are simply the tools of surveillance and assessment used to control and regiment individuals, to render us docile and compliant. The social and organizational control of the individual, from this perspective, relies on a 'micro-physics' of cultural practice. This involves practical, sometimes taken-for-granted, techniques of discipline, surveillance and coercion. The techniques or mechanisms which achieve compliance include (Hiley, 1987, p. 351):

- the ways in which the allocation of physical space (in a prison, office or factory) establishes homogeneity and uniformity, establishes individual and collective identity, locates the individual in terms of rank or status, and fixes the individual in a network of social relations;
- the control of behaviour through timetables, regimentation, standardization of work routines, repetitive activities;
- the 'composition of forces' in which individuals become elements in larger aggregates, part of the assembly line, one of the company workers, member of the team, and so on;
- the use of job ladders and career systems, and their attendant future promises, to encourage consent to organizational demands (Savage, 1998).

Resistance to such disciplinary practices merely demonstrates and reinforces the necessity for discipline. One does not have to visit prisons to witness these mechanisms in use. They are evident in schools, hospitals, factories, banks, insurance companies, and in universities. We would perhaps not normally regard office layouts, timetables, promotion routes and work allocations, for example, as manifestations of power. However, these 'practices' clearly shape our day-to-day activity and interactions, and can thus be regarded as critical elements in the 'field of force relations' controlling and regimenting us, helping to guarantee our ready compliance with social and organizational norms and expectations.

We are confronted daily with this 'web of power' – this 'field of force relations' – which is created and re-created by the cultural practices which we act out and to which we, typically, submit. As Hardy and Clegg (1996, p. 637) put it, 'we are also prisoners in a web of power that we have helped to create'. Those practical and specific institutional, organizational practices condition our thought processes; we accept much of those disciplinary practices as 'natural' and do not question them. These disciplinary practices are thus a positive basis for social and organizational order.

The creation and maintenance of disciplinary practices, in Foucault's perspective, are not processes driven by the plans and intentions of specific individuals. Power here is not equated either with domination by the powerful, or with capitalist exploitation of the working class. (However, it is still possible to argue that disciplinary power can be of value to managers in an organizational context, particularly when it comes to exacting willing compliance with managerial instructions.) The 'field of force relations' is not stable, and is not an inevitable consequence of social or organizational structure. It is instead a shifting network of alliances. Points of resistance and fissure can 'open up' at many points in this network, as old alliances fracture, as individuals regroup, and as new alliances are formed. In other words, this is a conceptualization of power which emphasizes the shifting and inherently unstable networks and alliances in organizations, and across society as a whole (Clegg, 1989, p. 154). In this respect, Foucault's concern with the strategic deployment of power and political tactics is similar to that of Machiavelli.

Foucault's paradigm of disciplinary technology (based on Jeremy Bentham) is the *panopticon*. The panopticon is an architectural structure, a prison, whose cells range around a central watchtower from which the cells' occupants can be surveyed by a single, unseen, observer. Imagine you are an occupant of one of the cells. You are constantly and regularly subject to surveillance, from which you cannot hide or escape. You do not know when you are being observed, but the certainty of surveillance from the watchtower is always with you. How will that knowledge influence your behaviour? You must constantly behave as if you are being watched. You become 'self-surveying'. Your obedience and compliance are assured. As with the operation of bio-power, the structure of the panopticon encourages self-discipline. Here again we see the power of normality and routine in controlling individual behaviour, rather than episodic power. The panopticon can be regarded in two ways. First, this is a practical illustration of disciplinary architecture. Second, the panopticon is a metaphor for the field of force relations, disciplinary power and bio-power, tacitly influencing and constantly controlling our behaviour through our own self-monitoring.

This perspective raises one central question, much debated. Are we trapped in this shifting web of cultural practices? Or, having demystified and understood it, are we capable of 'breaking free', and of transcending or redesigning the web? Foucault uses the expression 'power/knowledge' to address this question. This is a difficult concept to explain in brief; the point is that power and knowledge are inextricably intertwined. The construction and representation of knowledge in society (including knowledge of what is normal and what is deviant) is dependent on the exercise of power. Therefore, 'knowledge is not the antidote of power' (Clegg and Hardy, 1996, p. 695). The generation of more knowledge simply opens further opportunities for the exercise of power, for the control and manipulation of others. Knowledge is not emancipatory in this perspective, but simply a vehicle for perpetuating, albeit in a dynamic and shifting form, the web of power to which we are subject.

Foucault's position may be clarified by contrasting it with more traditional notions of power, as in Table 8.2.

In this brief overview, we appear to have reached some depressing conclusions. We are surrounded by a pervasive web of power. Improved knowledge of power relations is not emancipatory. There is little we can do about this. We may be able to open up 'points of resistance' and change the details, but the field of force relations will in essence prevail.

It is useful to recall that Foucault's is but one, radical alternative, perspective on social and organizational power relations. The value of a

Table 8.2 **Foucault versus traditional concepts of power**

Traditional concepts of power	Foucault's concepts of power
Power is possessed, is accumulated, is vested in the individual.	Power is pervasive, is a totality, is reflected in concrete practices.
Power is in the hands of social and organizational élites; resistance is futile.	Power is to be found in the micro-physics of social life; power depends on resistance.
We are subject to the domination of those who are more powerful than we are.	We construct our own web of power in accepting current definitions of normality.
Power is destructive, denies, represses, prevents, corrupts.	Power is productive, contributes to social order, which is flexible and shifting.
Power is episodic, visible, is observable in action, is deployed intermittently, is absent except when exercised.	Power is present in its absence, discreet, operating through taken-for-granted daily routines and modes of living.
Knowledge of power sources and relationships is emancipatory, can help us overcome domination.	Knowledge maintains and extends the web of power, creating further opportunities for domination.

perspective depends in part on the purpose with which one approaches and adopts it. If you are a social philosopher and historian with a critical interest in the social and political order, then Foucault's perspective is challenging and enlightening. If you are a manager trying to drive a change initiative, then Foucault's views may sound like an esoteric distraction. An episodic concept of power and power relations, therefore, still has considerable relevance and value to those engaged in day-to-day social interaction and interpersonal influence. But this is to enter into a fruitless debate about 'which perspective is correct'. Power is a contested concept around which a number of contrasting perspectives have developed. There is, therefore, value in being able to view this complex and slippery notion from different angles, and to be aware of and be able to draw on the strengths and limitations of different perspectives.

What, then, is the particular relevance of Foucault's position to the contemporary political entrepreneur? First, this perspective forces us to look with a critical and sceptical eye at so-called 'radical' change, and to identify underlying continuities in organization structures and power relations. 'Radical' change may often be a representation, a cosmetic, concealing deep structural continuity despite the rhetoric, despite the new labels suggesting that major upheavals and transformations are afoot. Second, it reminds us that the change driver is part of the field of force relations, changed as well as changing, subject to the influences of power as well as deploying power-political strategies. Third, this is a further reminder that local points of resistance to change can be expected to emerge, and to be e~~1~:+~ 1

Foucault's stance forces us to pay attention to the myria transparent, taken-for-granted, daily routines that continu thinking and behaviour, and that of others. Knowledge emancipatory, but it can be useful. The turf game involves and anticipating the interests and moves of other stakehol knowledge of the forces acting on their thinking and behaviour is invaluable. As Foucault makes clear, the field of force relations is unstable and shifting, and is amenable to challenge and dispute. Knowledge thus opens opportunities to 'fight back' against power. Finding and opening up appropriate points of resistance to power can be achieved proactively. Foucault offers us not simply 'consciousness raising', with respect to the pervasiveness of power, but also an analytical framework, which suggests creative options for action.

The argument of this book might seem to be that Machiavellian managers in the new millennium will enjoy more career success than their ethically constrained colleagues. The evidence does not support this position. For example, Gemmill and Heisler (1972) found in their research in a manufacturing company that managers with a High Mach orientation suffered higher job strain, lower job satisfaction, and experienced less control over their organizational surroundings. A High Mach orientation was not linked with upward mobility. They offer a number of explanations for these findings, including:

A final reason that managers with greater Machiavellian orientations may report more job strain and less job satisfaction arises from the degree to which the organization in which they are employed provides the situational characteristics, outlined by Christie, which are required for the saliency of Machiavellian behavior: (1) opportunity for improvisation in the sense that rewards or outcomes are not tied to objectively defined performance but can be influenced by the manner in which the situation is handled, (2) opportunity for face-to-face interaction, and (3) potential for emotional arousal. To the extent that a large, bureaucratic organization preprograms actions, utilizes standardized rules for allocating rewards, and operates with a norm of impersonality, these situational characteristics would be minimized. When these characteristics are minimized, managers with greater Machiavellian orientations should do no better than managers with lower Machiavellian orientations in terms of achieving desired outcomes. The findings of this study with respect to positional mobility are consistent with this expectation. (p. 60)

So, in a bureaucratic structure, High Mach managers will experience high levels of frustration through lack of opportunity to manipulate and control events and outcomes. But the stable, rule-bound bureaucracy is not the organizational form apparently being developed today. The flat, flexible, fast, fluid and organic organization offers considerable scope for emotional arousal, for direct social interaction, for improvisation. In other words, organizational trends appear to be creating conditions in which the Machiavellian manager will thrive.

It is unwise to speculate in such a highly generalized manner either about organizational trends or about character types. Reality is untidier than this. One of the few confident predictions we can make about the future is that it will probably take us by surprise. Some parts of some organizations will continue to become more fluid, while others will retain bureaucratic characteristics. The existence of a 'Machiavellian character type' is controversial, as Chapter 4 demonstrated. It is more useful to consider instead the *behaviour repertoire* which a Machiavellian approach entails, and which political entrepreneurs can adopt, regardless of their personality profile.

Despite these cautious qualifications, our proposition probably remains sound: that in the flat, flexible and fluid organization, the political entrepreneur has more room for manoeuvre. Foucault would dismiss the notion of 'triggers' of political behaviour as irrelevant. Our behaviour constitutes the field of force relations of which we are a part. Our apparently humdrum activities reflect and maintain the power of the disciplinary practices to which we are subject, particularly in organizational contexts. Political behaviour does not require to be 'triggered'. Zaleznik (1997) distinguishes between 'real work' and 'psychopolitics'. 'Real work' is sane, legitimate, productive. 'Political preoccupations' are unhealthy, diverting, illegitimate. From Foucault's perspective, this distinction is meaningless. Real work and psychopolitics are each inextricably implicated in the other; real work is political behaviour which is real work.

We have argued that the political entrepreneur should be reflective, self-aware, self-critical and self-questioning. Another implication of Foucault's perspective concerns the extent to which we as individuals are active in our own domination, through our uncritical acceptance of taken-for-granted practices, and of current definitions of what is normal and acceptable, and what is not, in our society. Foucault thus encourages a critical, questioning stance towards what we might otherwise regard as 'normal' or 'routine'. We have elsewhere in this book explored what it might mean to argue that the political entrepreneur should act in an ethical manner. One of Foucault's aims was to demonstrate that, while social institutions and organizational practices may appear neutral, their political role in controlling and regimenting individuals is often obscured. Foucault's perspective thus serves to remove that obscurity, opening such practices to challenge and resistance.

The 'right stuff': developing political competence

The field of management development has largely ignored the issue of political competence, and of how such skills and knowledge should effectively be defined and developed. However, various authors have sought to identify the qualities required.

Allen et al. (1979) produced a list of the personal characteristics of effective political actors, based on their study of the views of chief executives, managers and first line supervisors (Table 8.3). These three groups emphasized the significance of different qualities, represented by the ticks in the figure; the starred items indicate the two characteristics rated most strongly by each of the three groups. Chief executives felt that political actors had to be articulate and sensitive, managers that they should be

Table 8.3 **Personal characteristics of effective political actors**

	CEOs	Managers	Supervisors
Articulate	✓ *	✓ *	
Sensitive	✓ *		
Socially adept		✓ *	
Competent		✓	✓
Popular			✓ *
Extroverted			
Self-confident		✓	
Aggressive			✓ *
Ambitious	✓	✓	
Devious			✓
'Organization man'	✓		
Highly intelligent	✓		
Logical		✓	

articulate and socially adept. The most effective political actors in the view of supervisors, however, were popular and aggressive.

Kanter (1989) identifies seven skills which the change agent of the 1990s requires, to perform effectively in the flexible, 'integrative' organization. These include:

1   ability to work independently, without the sanction and support of senior management;
2   the skills of an effective collaborator, able to compete in ways that enhance co-operation;
3   ability to develop high trust relationships, based on high ethical standards;
4   self-confidence, tempered with humility;
5   respect for the process of change, as well as the content;
6   ability to work across business functions and units, to be 'multifaceted and ambidextrous';
7   willingness to stake reward on results and gain satisfaction from success.

This 'person specification' for the change agent seems to be consistent with what is known about flexible, organic organization structures. Kanter speaks of this 'superhuman' change agent, in possession of such wide-ranging expertise, in terms of a 'business athlete'. She argues:

> Our new heroic model should be the athlete who can manage the amazing feat of doing more with less, who can juggle the need to both conserve resources and pursue growth opportunities. This new kind of business hero avoids the excesses of both the corpocrat and the cowboy. Where the former rigidly conserves and protects, the latter relentlessly speculates and promotes. But the business athlete

has the strength to balance somewhere in the middle, taking the best of the corpocrat's discipline and the cowboy's entrepreneurial zeal. Business athletes need to be intense, lean and limber, able to stretch, good at teamwork, and in shape all the time. (Kanter, 1989, p. 361)

Arguing that the effective change agent 'does not have to walk on water', Hutton (1994) does claim that the change agent should be patient, persistent, honest, trustworthy, reliable, positive, enthusiastic, co-operative, confident (but not arrogant), a good listener, observant (of the feelings and behaviours of others), flexible, resourceful, difficult to intimidate, willing to take risks and accept challenge, and able to handle organizational politics. And they should have a sense of humour, a sense of perspective, and be able to admit ignorance and ask for help when appropriate. Hutton accepts that this list, 'may seem daunting', but argues that 'it is not Utopian'. Experience, he also argues, is an effective teacher.

Voss (1992) lists these attributes required to 'play the game' of office politics:

- focus on the job to build your credit;
- skills of observation and listening;
- ability to identify the opinion leaders, the fence-sitters;
- judge personalities and interests;
- ability to develop unobtrusive partnerships based on reciprocity;
- avoid the blatant use of power;
- negotiation skills, and know when to push, when to concede;
- ability to make the boss look good;
- don't alienate superiors, don't say no;
- develop loyal and competent subordinates (who make you look good);
- patience.

Voss notes that developing political 'antennae', building a reputation, and effective influence can take a considerable amount of time, hence his final point.

From their experience of change in a telecommunications company near Manchester, England, Bott and Hill (1994) identify 10 personal qualities required for effective organizational change, under four headings (Table 8.4).

Pettigrew and McNulty (1995) identify some of the personal qualities required to be influential: 'character, wisdom, judgemental competence, feeling more strongly and taking more trouble, strong person in his own right, knowing how to apply experience, a good listener, not too egocentric, awareness' (p. 866), and 'tact and diplomacy, logical argument and persuasion, and respecting the people and norms of conduct on the board' (p. 867).

From a management development perspective, there are two significant problems with these lists of attributes. First, they identify mainly personality traits which resist clear and unambiguous definition; consider, for example,

Table 8.4 **Qualities required for effective organizational change**

Setting an engaging direction	
Focus	The capacity for goal setting and persistence, a determination to stick to targets
Pride	The need to define oneself by association with high standards, and to get recognition
Charisma	Contagious energy and an inclination to work at infecting others with enthusiasm
Fostering independent relationships	
Positivity	Optimism and a tendency to notice the positive in others
Peacemaker	Enjoys conflict resolution, but may prompt conflict to achieve a constructive outcome
Team	Satisfaction from blending individual efforts to get results
Providing a systematic support structure and schedules	
Gestalt	Tendency towards completeness, timeliness, efficiency
Discipline	Developing effective routines, planning and working to plan
A 'doer'	Turns ideas into action, initiator rather than responder
Stabilizing beliefs	
Values	Centre on loyalty, conservation, the work ethic, family, consistency in value expression, perceived as predictable, seen as basis for stability in relationships particularly in the midst of organizational change

Source: Based on Bott and Hill, 1994

how to define 'ability to develop unobtrusive partnerships', 'patience', 'character', 'judgemental competence', 'popular', 'devious', 'peacemaker', 'doer'. The second and related problem is to establish how such qualities could ever be learned, trained or developed. We are left with a position that relies on the accurate identification of inherited personality traits. These specifications thus become interesting lists of selection and promotion criteria, of limited value in a management development context, and of more interest to specialists in psychometric assessment.

Can we identify a management development agenda beyond vague personality attributes? Let us return to our earlier question: 'Has the ground moved?' Whatever characterized the work experience of the change driver in the 1960s, this role now seems to involve dealing with multiple constituencies and perceptions, change which is complex, multi-layered, systemic, integrated, pressured, unpredictable, contested, politicized and shaped by changing management fashions which are supply-driven by American management consultants. What are the implications of this perceptual map of the terrain for the change driver? The following capabilities appear to be

-ificant:

th ambiguity and uncertainty in wide-ranging negotiations, in
ogrammes of change that cut across diverse interests and sub-

- deploying a broad range of political tactics to address conflicts with customers and clients, suppliers, sub-contractors, and other stake-holders, managing a complex blend of cultural and political issues;
- translating project goals into a format that addresses the variety of differently perceived individual, or stakeholder, or constituency interests;
- flexibly incorporating complex and varied sub-cultural work orienta-tions in providing solutions for improved working conditions;
- combining a focus on short-term commercial results with persistence in the pursuit of long-term ideals;
- negotiating and renegotiating change objectives in increasingly visible change programmes – visible in organizational, wider local and perhaps national terms;
- entering the 'social market' for management fashions, and allying with, co-opting and deploying different fashions in pursuit of an 'effective' change agenda;
- blending, balancing and integrating these capabilities in a style that is perceived to be legitimate, that is personally satisfying and self-serving, and that is seen to be consistent with organizational norms (standards, values) and goals.

Evidence suggests that a significant proportion of those responsible for implementing change in their organizations feel that they are not ade-quately recognized, supported, rewarded or developed for their role (Buchanan et al., 1997). The challenge, then, is to establish a development strategy linked to compensation and career management.

The management development agenda seems to have three main components. First, the *skills and knowledge* required to implement change effectively. These appear to be extensive. But these are 'learnable/trainable' competences, and most if not all can be regarded as generic management competences whose significance is increased in a change-driving context. Second, a *behaviour repertoire* that includes the tactics of 'power-assisted steering'. The change driver has to be able to play the turf game, or renounce the role. Using political strategies and 'Machiavellian' tactics does not demand a change in personality. It requires an extended, appro-priate and creatively deployed behaviour repertoire that includes the 'ploys and tactics' identified in Chapter 7. The concept of behaviour repertoire is well established in the field of interpersonal skills development.

However, as Chapter 1 suggested, knowledge of political strategies and tactics seems to be part of the taken-for-granted 'recipe knowledge' of most experienced managers. The final, and most significant, element in the management development agenda concerns a *reflexive practitioner's per-spective* on the role. As Chapter 7 argued, this involves deploying a range of knowledge and experience in a creative, improvisatory, contextually appropriate and self-critical manner. The change driver has to be con-cerned with the relationships between a warrant for political behaviour, the outcomes, the need for appropriate accounting, and the implications for reputation. Can a perspective be learned or trained? Schon argued that this was how professionals, tacitly, already operate.

A loss of innocence?

Our main intention in this book has been to expose to wider scrutiny the phenomenon of political behaviour in relation to organizational change. We seem to be witnessing a trend towards the fluid, unpredictable, 'high-velocity' organizational context. This entails the replacement of stable organization hierarchy and position power with shifting networks and coalitions where expert and referent power carry more sway. Position power is today further weakened by the fact that an autocratic manage-ment style is deeply unfashionable. As we have argued, political skill would seem to be at a premium in this evolving dynamic context.

Evil bastards and dirty tricks

However, it has been suggested to us that some readers may take offence at the argument of this book, at some of the language quoted, at the nature of the incident reports in Chapter 3 and other examples of political strategies and tactics, and perhaps even at one or more of the cartoons used as illustrations. We have perhaps created a surface impression that this book is concerned with 'evil bastards' who play 'dirty tricks'. Clearly our inten-tion is not to offend, but to present the reality of organizational politics as it is experienced by practising managers, to offer insights into the nature of the turf game, and also to offer a working perspective on what appears to be a key dimension of the change management role.

It has also been our intention to challenge commentators who continue to regard organizational politics in uncompromisingly negative terms. The author's nightmare, of course, is that someone else will publish one's argument first. So with trepidation, as the manuscript for this book was nearing completion, we acquired a copy of *Confronting Company Politics* (Stone, 1997). Stone, a psychologist and experienced change consultant, argues that political behaviour has but a single cause, in the individual's attempts to protect their self-image or ego. Stone thus advocates a single management response to company politics – eradication. No. Despite a case woven with existential philosophy, Stone's argument is desperately oversimplified and unrealistic. It ignores the reality of organizational life, and also sidelines the positive dimensions of political behaviour. Denial of the political, we have argued, is an unrealistic and unhelpful posture. Denial can drive discussion of organizational politics 'underground', silencing critics and stifling challenge. This posture in effect serves the interests of the 'evil bastards' (who in Chapter 1 were rather more tactfully described as 'street fighters') by placing them beyond polite discussion and professional debate.

We trust that readers will look below that surface impression and find in this book an argument that links political skill and will to professional, competent, legitimate, ethical management behaviour in general, and to change-driving behaviour in particular. We have argued that the change driver should be a self-critical and reflective *political entrepreneur*. This perspective involves a creative, risk-taking approach to determining the appropriate action to take in context – a perspective that has also been described as 'intuitive artistry'. While politics and dirty tricks may equate on some occasions, we submit that there is nothing illegitimate or evil about our central argument.

Beyond the interpersonal

Political skill is often identified as a sub-category of interpersonal skill. There is substance in this approach, which sections of this book have perhaps reinforced. We have dealt, for example, with issues such as conversation control, impression management, with influencing techniques, and with various approaches to management and leadership style. These are all topics that readily find space on interpersonal skills courses for managers.

However, we have tried to demonstrate that such a simple categorization would be misleading. Political skills involve elements that include, but go some considerable distance beyond, what are commonly understood to be interpersonal skills:

- recognizing the value of different and competing approaches to defining and thus to understanding power and political behaviour in an organizational context;
- understanding the sources and bases of power, personally and for other members of the organization;
- diagnostic capability, in 'reading' the shifting politics of the organization, and the changing motives and moves of other stakeholders;
- understanding of how power can be seen to be embedded in social and organizational structures and systems, and in routine, everyday practices;
- ability to develop power bases through accumulating appropriate resources and expertise;
- understanding the combination of factors which warrant political behaviour in particular organizational settings;
- a behaviour repertoire that includes a range of interpersonal skills, such as impression management and influencing techniques;
- a behaviour repertoire that goes beyond interpersonal skills to include the skill and will to conceive of political strategies and tactics, and to apply these when appropriate;

- an 'intuitive artistry' in deploying one's behaviour repertoire creatively and appropriately to fit the context;
- 'positioning' ability, to take and to switch roles in relation to change appropriately, to maximize personal advantage, to address opposition, and to drive the change agenda;
- understanding the trade-offs in the turf game, and thus calculating (perhaps intuitively) when it is appropriate to 'lose' a play in the game in order to achieve advantage later;
- ability and willingness to construct credible accounts of behaviour, if and when challenged to do so, and to refute the potentially damaging accounts of others;
- ability to construct one's reputation as a skilled political player who acts with fairness and integrity, and to maintain and develop that reputation consistently.

This involves an array of knowledge and capabilities – a depth of expertise – which clearly incorporates interpersonal skills, but which also includes further knowledge, understanding, analytical and diagnostic capabilities, a degree of sensitivity and intuition ('political antennae'), and creative resources.

A loss of innocence

Just before this book went into production, one of us visited a medium-size general hospital, which had 18 months earlier launched a major transformation project. The change agents for this project were not exclusively experienced managers, but had been recruited from across the organization structure: pharmacy manager, ward nurse, radiographer, medical secretary. The discussion turned from the substantive details of change initiatives to their personal learning experiences over this period, and to the skills which they had acquired. One of them summed up this discussion with the expression, 'a loss of innocence'. This is reminiscent of the quote on page 12 from Henry Kissinger, the American diplomat who discovered that you could not convince the President simply with a reasoned case. Driving change in this hospital involved identifying key players and opinion leaders, finding ways to influence or to recruit them, or co-opt their support, or to find ways around their resistance. Their change game was in part focused on the rational and systematic techniques of process mapping and redesign, performance improvements and organization development. But their change game, they had quickly discovered, was also a turf game.

It is our expectation that most experienced managers will readily recognize the issues and arguments of this book, as with those hospital change agents. Political behaviour is a widely experienced organizational phenomenon. It appears to be part of the taken-for-granted 'recipe knowledge' of practising managers. However, it is not so widely discussed, shared openly or analysed in organizational settings, where it remains something of a taboo subject. As we have sought to demonstrate, the discussion to be found in the literature is either remote from the practical concerns of organizational change, or offers oversimplified and unrealistic advice. Some managers may thus feel unnecessarily guilty about playing the turf game to achieve desired results, in career or organizational terms.

This 'loss of innocence' is critical. Honest self-reflection on one's political behaviour and accounts brings them directly into conscious awareness, making them available for analysis, critical judgement and improvement. Avoidance of this reflection and self-knowledge, in an attempt to remain 'squeaky clean' by avoiding organization politics, courts the risk of self-deception. Such an avoidance strategy also puts one at risk of being sidelined by more competent players. This further risks the criticism that one is unskilled and unprofessional in being unable to deal with those players. The choice for some, therefore, may lie between loss of innocence or loss of the change agenda to the street fighters, saboteurs and sub-versives.

The main argument of this book is that the change agent who is not politically skilled will fail. For those who believe that political behaviour is invariably damaging and should be eradicated, progressing a successful management career is probably going to be difficult, in most organizational settings. For those who believe that involvement in the turf game is unethical, the experience of change implementation is likely to be an extraordinarily frustrating one, the level of frustration escalating with the significance of the changes in hand. Honest self-appraisal and self-criticism is more daring, and more rewarding.

In the domain of practical action, as we noted earlier, management is a contact sport. If you don't want to get bruised, don't play. There is little to be gained by complaining about the turf game, its players, its tricks, its strategies, its tactics and its potential damage. Criticism of the existence of organizational politics is likely to have as much impact as criticism of British weather. Organizational politics is an autonomous domain. Political behaviour can be managed, but it cannot be managed away. We hope that we have demonstrated that there is much to be gained by understanding and by engaging with the turf game. Managing change can be a demanding and exhausting role, but it is also extremely challenging and rewarding. The political is one key aspect, which can also be demanding. But we also know that some managers find positive challenge and reward in the turf game, and this may be particularly related to successful organization development and change as well as to personal career success.

Our final advice to the change driver is, therefore: recognize the hypocrisy, shed the innocence, shed the guilt, play the turf game, play to win on one's own terms – and enjoy.

Appendix I
Information sources

It is notoriously difficult to generate rich and detailed empirical evidence in the field of organizational politics, due to the sensitivities surrounding disclosure, as Chapter 3 noted. What information we have tends to be in the form of superficial organizational surveys, on the one hand, or ethnographies of management in general, such as Jackall (1988) and Watson (1994). First-hand accounts from change drivers themselves are rare. The purpose of this appendix is to describe the sources of information, in addition to the literature, on which we drew in the preparation of this book. Readers are invited to compare their own experiences of organizational politics with the argument and examples presented here, and perhaps to feed them back to us, through the email addresses at the front of the book.

Information has been drawn primarily from four main sources:

Management survey

During the first half of 1997, we surveyed 90 middle and senior managers through our Organization Development and Change Forum, based in Leicester. This sample represented a cross-section of management functions: general management, human resources, marketing, project management and consultancy, accounting and finance, public relations. All respondents had experience of, and the majority had management responsibility for, organizational change. Of the 24 organizations represented in this sample, about half were public sector and half private. Full details of survey administration and findings can be found in Buchanan et al. (1997).

Management interviews

Five managers (one female, four male), chosen for their involvement in organizational change, were interviewed for up to one and a half hours each, to collect illustrative material, particularly for Chapter 3. These interviews were tape-recorded, and together generated around 50,000 words of narrative concerning examples of political behaviour – personal and observed, beneficial and damaging. Although the responses across this small group were strikingly consistent in nature, in their acceptance of the need to confront organizational political behaviour, and in similar ways, this sample cannot be regarded as representative. Readers are instead invited to compare their own experiences with these examples and with the overall argument of the book.

Management development

Dave Buchanan works regularly on middle and senior management development programmes covering change implementation issues, and including political issues. One popular element of such programmes involves inviting managers to reveal, in syndicate and then in plenary discussion, the strategies, tactics, moves and ploys which they use (and observe being used by other managers) in 'the turf game'. During the period 1993 to 1997, this discussion was conducted with over 15 management groups, involving approximately 300 participants, in Australia, Britain, Finland and Sweden. About one third of those groups were engaged in executive MBA programmes, and the others were attending either 'company in-house' or public management development programmes.

Action research

Richard Badham has been involved for some time in a series of action research projects with a number of Australian manufacturing companies, where the concern has been to introduce and develop self-managing teamwork. In most organizations, such initiatives represent a radical departure from conventional ways of working, for managers, for supervisors and for shopfloor personnel. These projects have thus offered excellent opportunities to witness the organizational politics of major change initiatives, at first hand, from the perspective of the participant observer, with the researcher as member of the project design and implementation teams responsible for developing cellular and team-based approaches to manufacturing.

Appendix II
The Machiavellian personality

This personality inventory (known as the 'Mach IV' scale) was developed by Richard Christie and Florence Geiss, and can be found in their book *Studies in Machiavellianism* (1970). They claim that scores are a good predictor of how we behave with other people – whether we become emotionally involved, or whether we simply use others to suit our own ends. So, this is a measure of how *Machiavellian* you are in your relations with others. Some people regard this label as a serious insult. How do you feel about this?

Please read each of the following statements carefully, and tick the box at the point on the scale which most closely represents your own attitude.

		Strongly agree	Agree	Neutral	Disagree	Strongly disagree
1	The best way to handle people is to tell them what they want to hear.	❒ 5	❒ 4	❒ 3	❒ 2	❒ 1
2	When you ask someone to do something for you, it is best to give the real reasons for wanting it rather than giving reasons which might carry more weight.	❒ 1	❒ 2	❒ 3	❒ 4	❒ 5
3	Anyone who completely trusts anyone else is asking for trouble.	❒ 5	❒ 4	❒ 3	❒ 2	❒ 1
4	It is hard to get ahead without cutting corners here and there.	❒ 5	❒ 4	❒ 3	❒ 2	❒ 1
5	Honesty is the best policy in all cases.	❒ 1	❒ 2	❒ 3	❒ 4	❒ 5
6	It is safest to assume that all people have a vicious streak and it will come out when they are given a chance.	❒ 5	❒ 4	❒ 3	❒ 2	❒ 1
7	Never tell anyone the real reason you did something unless it is useful to do so.	❒ 5	❒ 4	❒ 3	❒ 2	❒ 1
8	One should take action only when sure it is morally right.	❒ 1	❒ 2	❒ 3	❒ 4	❒ 5
9	It is wise to flatter important people.	❒ 5	❒ 4	❒ 3	❒ 2	❒ 1
10	All in all, it is better to be humble and honest than important and dishonest.	❒ 1	❒ 2	❒ 3	❒ 4	❒ 5
11	Barnum was very wrong when he said there's a sucker born every minute.	❒ 1	❒ 2	❒ 3	❒ 4	❒ 5
12	People suffering from incurable diseases should have the choice of being put painlessly to death.	❒ 5	❒ 4	❒ 3	❒ 2	❒ 1
13	It is possible to be good in all respects.	❒ 1	❒ 2	❒ 3	❒ 4	❒ 5
14	Most people are basically good and kind.	❒ 1	❒ 2	❒ 3	❒ 4	❒ 5
15	There is no excuse for lying to someone else.	❒ 1	❒ 2	❒ 3	❒ 4	❒ 5
16	Most people forget more easily the death of their father than the loss of their property.	❒ 5	❒ 4	❒ 3	❒ 2	❒ 1
17	Most people who get ahead in the world lead clean, moral lives.	❒ 1	❒ 2	❒ 3	❒ 4	❒ 5
18	Generally speaking, people won't work hard unless they are forced to do so.	❒ 5	❒ 4	❒ 3	❒ 2	❒ 1
19	The biggest difference between most criminals and other people is that criminals are stupid enough to get caught.	❒ 5	❒ 4	❒ 3	❒ 2	❒ 1
20	Most people are brave.	❒ 1	❒ 2	❒ 3	❒ 4	❒ 5

Calculate your score by simply adding the numbers beside the boxes that you ticked.

Note your score here:

Your score will lie between 20 and 100. A moderate score is around 60.

Consider yourself a Low Mach if you have a score of 45 or lower.
Consider yourself a High Mach if you have a score of 75 or above.

How do you feel about this result? Is this an accurate reflection of your personality? Do you think you would like to be more Machiavellian, or less, and why?

References

Adams, S. (1996) *The Dilbert Principle*. Harper Business, New York/London.

Adorno, T.W., Frenkel-Brunswik, E., Levinson, D.J. and Sanford, R.N. (1950) *The Authoritarian Personality*, W.W. Norton and Co., London.

Allen, R.W., Madison, D.L., Porter, L.W., Renwick, P.A. and Mayes, B.T. (1979) 'Organizational politics: tactics and characteristics of its actors', *California Management Review*, vol. 22, no. 1, pp. 77–83.

Amburgey, T.L., Kelly, D. and Barnett, W.P. (1993) 'Resetting the clock: the dynamics of organizational change and failure', *Administrative Science Quarterly*, vol. 38, no. 1, pp. 51–73.

Arroba, T. and James, K. (1988) 'Are politics palatable to women managers? How women can make wise moves at work', *Women in Management Review*, vol. 3, no. 3, pp. 123–30.

Astley, W.G. and Sachdeva, P.S. (1984) 'Structural sources of intraorganizational power: a theoretical synthesis', *Academy of Management Review*, vol. 9, no. 1, pp. 104–13.

Bacharach, S.B. and Lawler, E.J. (1981) *Power and Politics in Organizations: The Social Psychology of Conflict, Coalitions, and Bargaining*, Jossey-Bass, San Francisco.

Bachrach, P. and Baratz, M.S. (1962) 'The two faces of power', *American Political Science Review*, vol. 56, pp. 947–52.

Badham, R. (1989) *Computers, Design and Manufacture*, AGPS, Canberra.

Badham, R. (ed.) (1993) 'Special issue: systems, networks and configurations: inside the implementation process', *International Journal of Human Factors in Manufacturing*, vol. 3, no. 1, pp. 3–15.

Badham, R. (1995) 'Managing socio-technical change', in J. Benders, J. de Haan and D. Bennet (eds), *The Symbiosis of Work and Technology*, Frances Pinter, London, pp. 45–58.

Badham, R. and Wilson, S. (1992) 'Beyond the electronic drawing board', *International Journal of Human Factors in Manufacturing*, vol. 2, no. 2, pp. 35–47.

Badham, R., Couchman, P., Moriarty, D., Santiago, B. and Wells, A. (1995) *Team Based Cellular Manufacturing Volumes 1–5*, University of Wollongong, Wollongong.

Badham, R., Couchman, P. and McLoughlin, I. (1997a) 'Implementing vulnerable socio-technical change projects', in I. McLoughlin and M. Harris (eds), *Innovation, Organizational Change and Technology*, International Thomson, London, pp. 146–69.

Badham, R., Couchman, P. and McLoughlin, I. (1997b) *Wombat Plastics: A Case Study*, MITOC Working Paper, University of Wollongong.

Bardach, E. (1977) *The Implementation Game: What Happens After a Bill Becomes a Law*, MIT Press, Cambridge, MA.

Bass, B.M. (1985) *Leadership and Performance Beyond Expectations*, Free Press, New York.

Batstone, E. (1978) *The Social Organization of Strikes*, Basil Blackwell, Oxford.

Beatty, C.A. and Gordon, J. (1991) 'Preaching the gospel: the evangelists of new technology', *California Management Review*, vol. 33, no. 3, Spring, pp. 73–94.

Beatty, C.A. and Lee, G.L. (1992) 'Leadership among middle managers – an exploration in the context of technological change', *Human Relations*, vol. 45, no. 1, pp. 957–80.

Beer, M., Eisenstat, R.A. and Spector, B. (1990) 'Why change programs don't produce change', *Harvard Business Review*, November–December, pp. 158–66.

Benders, J., de Hann, J. and Bennett, D. (1995) *The Symbiosis of Work and Technology*, Frances Pinter, London.

Benfari, R.C., Wilkinson, H.E. and Orth, C.D. (1986) 'The effective use of power', *Business Horizons*, vol. 29, May–June, pp. 12–16.

Bennis, W.G. (1969) *Organization Development: Its Nature, Origins, and Prospects*, Addison Wesley, Reading, MA.

Bennis, W.G. (1984) 'Transformative power and leadership', in T.J. Sergiovanni and J.E. Corbally (eds), *Leadership and Organizational Culture*, University of Illinois Press, Urbana.

Bennis, W.G. and Nanus, B. (1985) *Leaders: The Strategies for Taking Charge*, Harper and Row, New York.

Bensman, J. and Gerver, J. (1963) 'Crime and punishment in the factory', *American Sociological Review*, vol. 28, pp. 588–98.

Berle, A.A. and Means, G.C. (1935) *The Modern Corporation and Private Property*, Macmillan, New York.

Bessant, J. (1991) *Managing Advanced Manufacturing Technology: The Challenge of the Fifth Wave*, Basil Blackwell, Oxford.

Bies, R.S. and Sitkin, S.B. (1992) 'Explanation as legitimation: excuse-making in organizations', in M.L. McLaughlin, M.J. Cody and S.J. Read (eds), *Explaining One's Self to Others: Reason-Giving in a Social Context*, Lawrence Erlbaum Associates, Hillsdale, NJ, pp. 183–98.

Blanchard, K. and Peale, N.V. (1988) *The Power of Ethical Management*, William Morrow and Company, New York.

Bolman, L.G. and Deal, T.E. (1991) *Reframing Organizations: Artistry, Choice and Leadership*, Jossey-Bass, San Francisco.

Bott, K. and Hill, J. (1994) 'Change agents lead the way', *Personnel Management*, August, pp. 24–7.

Bowles, M.L. (1991) 'The organization shadow', *Organization Studies*, vol. 12, no. 3, pp. 387–404.

Brass, D.J. and Burkhardt, M.E. (1993) 'Potential power and power use: an investigation of structure and behaviour', *Academy of Management Journal*, vol. 36, no. 3, pp. 441–70.

Bryman, A. (1996) 'Leadership in organizations', in S.R. Clegg, C. Hardy and W.R. Nord (eds), *Handbook of Organizational Studies*, Sage, New York, pp. 276–92.

Buchanan, D.A. (1994a) 'Principles and practice in work design', in K. Sisson (ed.), *Personnel Management: A Comprehensive Guide to Theory and Practice in Britain*, Blackwell Business, Oxford, pp. 85–116.

Buchanan, D.A. (1994b) 'Cellular manufacture and the role of teams', in J. Storey (ed.), *New Wave Manufacturing Strategies: Organizational and Human Resource Management Dimensions*, Paul Chapman Publishing, London, pp. 204–25.

Buchanan, D.A. (1997) 'The opportunities and limitations of business process re-engineering in a politicized organizational climate', *Human Relations*, vol. 50, no. 1, pp. 51–72.

Buchanan, D. and Boddy, D. (1992) *The Expertise of the Change Agent: Public Performance and Backstage Activity*, Prentice Hall, Hemel Hempstead.

Buchanan, D. and McCalman, J. (1989) *High Performance Work Systems: The Digital Experience*, Routledge, London.

Buchanan, D. and Storey, J. (1997) 'Role taking and role switching in organizational change: the four pluralities', in I. McLoughlin and M. Harris (eds), *Innovation, Organizational Change and Technology*, International Thomson, London, pp. 127–45.

Buchanan, D., Claydon, T. and Doyle, M. (1997) 'Organization development and change: the legacy of the nineties', *De Montfort University School of Business Occasional Paper Series*, November.

Buhler, P. (1994) 'Navigating the waters of organizational politics', *Supervision*, vol. 55, no. 9, pp. 24–6.

Burger, C. (1964) *Survival in the Executive Jungle*, Macmillan, New York.

Burnes, B. (1992) *Managing Change: A Strategic Approach to Organizational Dynamics*, Pitman, London (first edition).

Burnham, J. (1943) *The Machiavellians: Defenders of Freedom*, Books for Libraries Press, New York.

Burns, J.M. (1978) *Leadership*, Harper and Row, New York.

Burns, T. (1961) 'Micropolitics: mechanisms of institutional change', *Administrative Science Quarterly*, vol. 6, pp. 257–81.

Burns, T. and Stalker, G.M. (1961) *The Management of Innovation*, Tavistock, London.

Burrell, G. (1988) 'Modernism, postmodernism and organizational analysis: the contribution of Michel Foucault', *Organization Studies*, vol. 9, no. 2, pp. 221–35; reprinted in A. McKinlay and K. Starkey (eds), *Foucault, Management and Organization Theory*, Sage, London, 1988, pp. 14–28.

Calhoon, R.P. (1969) 'Niccolò Machiavelli and the 20th-century administrator', *Academy of Management Journal*, vol. 12, no. 2, June, pp. 205–12.

Cavanagh, G.F., Moberg, D.J. and Velasquez, M. (1981) 'The ethics of organizational politics', *Academy of Management Review*, vol. 6, no. 3, pp. 363–74.

Chanlat, J.-F. (1997) 'Conflict and politics', in A. Sorge and M. Warner (eds), *Handbook of Organizational Behaviour*, International Thomson Business Press, London, pp. 472–80.

Charlton, R. and Herlihy, R. (1982) 'Organization development in BL Cars: practitioners' observation and prognosis', in A. Kakabadse (ed.), *People and Organizations: The Practitioners' View*, Gower, London.

Christie, R. and Geiss, F.L. (1970) *Studies in Machiavellianism*, Academic Press, New York.

Christie, R. and Merton, R.K. (1970) 'Procedures for the sociological study of the values climate of medical schools', in H.H. Gee and R.J. Glaser (eds), *The Ecology of the Medical Student*, American Association of Medical Colleges, Evanston, IL.

Clegg, S.R. (1989) *Frameworks of Power*, Sage, London.

Clegg, S.R. (1997) 'Power', in A. Sorge and M. Warner (eds), *The IEBM Handbook of Organizational Behaviour*, International Thomson Business Press, London, pp. 481–91.

Clegg, S.R. and Hardy, C. (1996) 'Conclusion: representations', in S.R. Clegg, C. Hardy and W.R. Nord (eds), *Handbook of Organization Studies*, Sage, London, pp. 676–708.

Clegg, S.R. and Palmer, G. (eds) (1996) *The Politics of Management Knowledge*, Sage, New York.

Clemons, E.K., Thatcher, M.E. and Row, M.C. (1995) 'Identifying sources of re-engineering failures: a study of the behavioural actors contributing to re-engineering risks', *Journal of Management Information Systems*, vol. 12, no. 2, pp. 9–36.

Coates, J.F. (1994) 'Organizational politics: a key to personal success', *Employment Relations Today*, vol. 21, no. 3, pp. 259–62.

Cockerell, M. (1996) 'Black arts of the whipping boys', *The Sunday Times*, 17 November, p. 3:9.

Collin, A. (1996) 'Re-thinking the relationship between theory and practice: practitioners as map-readers, map-makers – or jazz players?', *British Journal of Guidance and Counselling*, vol. 24, no. 1, pp. 67–81.

Conger, J.A. (1989) *The Charismatic Leader: Behind the Mystique of Exceptional Leadership*, Jossey-Bass, San Francisco.

Conklin, W. (1993) 'Playing the game of corporate politics', *Communication World*, vol. 10, no. 9, pp. 26–9.

Covey, S.R. (1989) *The 7 Habits of Highly Effective People: Restoring the Character Ethic*, Simon and Schuster, New York © 1989 Stephen R. Covey. Used with permission. All rights reserved.

Covey, S. (1990) *Principle Centred Leadership*, Simon and Schuster, New York.

Crichton, M. (1992) *Rising Sun*, Arrow Books, London.

Cummings, T.G. and Worley, C.G. (1993) *Organization Development and Change*, West Publishing Company, Minneapolis/St Paul (fifth edition).

Dahl, R.A. (1957) 'The concept of power', *Behavioural Science*, vol. 2, pp. 201–15.

Dalton, M. (1959) *Men Who Manage*, John Wiley, New York.

Davenport, T. (1993) *Process Innovation: Re-engineering Work Through IT*, Harvard Business School Press, Boston.

Dawson, P. (1994) *Organizational Change: A Processual Approach*, Paul Chapman Publishing, London.

Dawson, P. (1996) *Technology and Quality: Change in the Workplace*, International Thomson Business Press, London.

Dawson, P. and Palmer, G. (1995) *Quality Management: The Theory and Practice of Implementing Change*, Longman, Melbourne.

Douglas, D. (1993) 'The role of IT in business re-engineering', *I/S Analyzer*, vol. 31, no. 8, pp. 1–16.

Drory, A. (1993) 'Perceived political climate and job attitudes', *Organization Studies*, vol. 14, no. 1, pp. 59–71.

Drory, A. and Romm, C.T. (1990) 'The definition of organizational politics: a review', *Human Relations*, vol. 43, no. 11, pp. 1133–54.

Drucker, P.F. (1990) 'The emerging theory of manufacturing', *Harvard Business Review*, vol. 68, no. 3, pp. 94–102.

Dunphy, D.C. and Stace, D.A. (1988) 'Transformational and coercive strategies for planned organizational change: beyond the OD model', *Organization Studies*, vol. 9, no. 3, pp. 317–34.

Dunphy, D.C. and Stace, D.A. (1990) *Under New Management: Australian Organizations in Transition*, McGraw-Hill, Sydney.

Dunphy, D.C. and Stace, D.A. (1993) 'The strategic management of corporate change', *Human Relations*, vol. 46, no. 8, pp. 905–20.

Dutton, J.E. (1988) 'Understanding strategic agenda building and its implications for managing change', in L. Pondy, R.J. Boland and H. Thomas (eds), *Managing Ambiguity and Change*, Wiley, Chichester, pp. 127–55.

Eccles, R.G. and Nohria, N. (1992) *Beyond the Hype: Rediscovering the Essence of Management*, Harvard Business School Press, Boston.

Eccles, T. (1994) *Succeeding With Change: Implementing Action-Driven Strategies*, McGraw-Hill, London.

Egan, G. (1994) *Working the Shadow Side: A Guide to Positive Behind-the-Scenes Management*, Jossey-Bass, San Francisco.

Eisenhardt, K.M. and Bourgeois, L.J. (1988) 'Politics of strategic decision making in high-velocity environments: towards a mid-range theory', *Academy of Management Journal*, vol. 31, no. 4, pp. 737–70.

Eisendhardt, K.M., Kahwajy, J.L. and Bourgeois, L.J. (1997) 'How management teams can have a good fight', *Harvard Business Review*, vol. 75, no. 4, pp. 77–85.

Feldman, D. and Klitch, N. (1991) 'Impression management and career strategies', in K. Giacalone and P. Rosenfeld (eds), *Applied Impression Management: How Image Making Affects Managerial Decisions*, Sage, London, pp. 67–80.

Ferris, G.R. and Kacmar, K.M. (1992) 'Perceptions of organizational politics', *Journal of Management*, vol. 18, no. 1, pp. 93–116.

Ferris, G.R. and King, T.R. (1991) 'Politics in human resources decisions: a walk on the dark side', *Organizational Dynamics*, vol. 20, no. 2, pp. 59–71.

Ferris, G.R., Buckley, M.R. and Allen, G.M. (1992) 'Promotion systems in organizations', *Human Resource Planning*, vol. 15, no. 3, pp. 47–68.

Fisher, R., Kopelman, E. and Schneider, A.K. (1994) *Beyond Machiavelli: Tools for Coping with Conflict*, Harvard University Press, Cambridge, MA.

Foucault, M. (1977) *Discipline and Punish: The Birth of the Prison*, Penguin Books, Harmondsworth.

Foucault, M. (1979) *The History of Sexuality: Volume 1*, Penguin Books, Harmondsworth.

Frame, J.D. (1991) *The New Project Management*, Jossey-Bass, San Francisco.

Freeman, C. (1982) *Economics of Innovation*, Penguin Books, Harmondsworth.

French, J. and Raven, B. (1958) 'The bases of social power', in D. Cartwright (ed.), *Studies in Social Power*, Institute for Social Research, Ann Arbor, MI.

French, W.L. and Bell, C.H. (1995) *Organization Development: Behavioral Science Interventions for Organization Improvement*, Prentice Hall International, Englewood Cliffs, NJ.

Friedmann, A.L. (1977) *Industry and Labour: Class Struggle at Work and Monopoly Capitalism*, Macmillan, London.

Friis, S. (1988) 'Action research on systems development: case study of changing actor roles', *ACM Computers and Society*, vol. 18, no. 1, pp. 123–38.

Frost, P.J. and Egri, C.P. (1991) 'The political process of innovation', in L.L. Cummings and B.M. Staw (eds), *Research in Organizational Behavior*, JAI Press, Greenwich, CT, pp. 229–95.

Galbraith, J.K. (1974) *The New Industrial State*, Penguin, Harmondsworth.

Gandz, J. and Murray, V.V. (1980) 'The experience of workplace politics', *Academy of Management Journal*, vol. 23, pp. 237–51.

Gardner, W.L. (1992) 'Lessons in organizational dramaturgy: the art of impression management', *Organizational Dynamics*, vol. 21, no. 1, pp. 33–46.

Geddes, M., Hastings, C. and Briner, W. (1990) *Project Leadership*, Gower, London.

Gemmill, G.R. and Heisler, W.J. (1972) 'Machiavellianism as a factor in managerial job strain, job satisfaction and upward mobility', *Academy of Management Journal*, March, pp. 51–62.

Ginzberg, A. and Abrahamson, E. (1991) 'Champions of change and strategic shifts: the role of internal and external change advocates', *Journal of Management Studies*, vol. 28, no. 2, pp. 173–90.

Godfrey, J. (1996) 'Been there, doing that', *Inc. Magazine*, March, p. 21.

Goffman, E. (1959) *The Presentation of Self in Everyday Life*, Doubleday Anchor, New York.

Gouldner, A.W. (1954) *Patterns of Industrial Bureaucracy*, Free Press, New York.

Graham, J.H. (1996) 'Machiavellian project managers: do they perform better?', *International Journal of Project Management*, vol. 14, no. 2, pp. 67–74.

Gray, J.L. and Starke, F.A. (1984) *Organizational Behaviour: Concepts and Applications*, Merril Publishing, Columbus, OH.

Greenleaf, R.K. (1977) *Servant Leadership: A Journey into the Nature of Legitimate Power and Greatness*, Paulist Press, New York.

Greiner, L.E. and Schein, V.E. (1988) *Power and Organization Development: Mobilizing Power to Implement Change*, Addison Wesley, Reading, MA.

Hall, G., Rosenthal, J. and Wade, J. (1993) 'How to make re-engineering really work', *Harvard Business Review*, November–December, pp. 119–31.

Hammer, M. and Champy, J. (1993) *Re-engineering the Corporation: A Manifesto for Business Revolution*, Nicholas Brealey Publishing, London.

Hammer, M. and Stanton, S.A. (1995) *The Re-engineering Revolution – A Handbook*, HarperCollins, New York.

Handy, C. (1993) *Understanding Organizations*, Penguin Books, Harmondsworth.

Handy, C. (1997) 'The citizen corporation', *Harvard Business Review*, vol. 75, no. 5, pp. 26–7.

Hannan, M.T. and Freeman, J. (1984) 'Structural inertia and organizational change', *American Sociological Review*, vol. 49, pp. 149–64.

Hardy, C. (1994) *Managing Strategic Action: Mobilizing Change*, Sage, London.

Hardy, C. (ed.) (1995) *Power and Politics in Organizations*, Dartmouth Publishing, Aldershot.

Hardy, C. (1996) 'Understanding power: bringing about strategic change', *British Journal of Management*, vol. 7, special issue, pp. 3–16.

Hardy, C. and Clegg, S.R. (1996) 'Some dare call it power', in S.R. Clegg, C. Hardy and W.R. Nord (eds), *Handbook of Organization Studies*, Sage, London, pp. 622–41.

Harrison, E.F. (1987) *The Management Decision-Making Process*, Houghton Mifflin, Boston.

Hartley, J., Benington, J. and Binns, P. (1997) 'Researching the roles of internal change agents in the management of organizational change', *British Journal of Management*, vol. 8, no. 1, pp. 61–73.

Helgesen, S. (1990) *The Female Advantage: Women's Ways of Leadership*, Doubleday/Currency, New York.

den Hertog, F., Cobbenhagen, J. and Penning, H. (1994) *Successvol Veranderen*, Kluwer Bedrisfswetenschappen, Den Haag.

Hersey, P. and Blanchard, K.H. (1988) *Management of Organizational Behavior: Utilizing Human Resources*, Prentice Hall, Englewood Cliffs, NJ.

Hickson, D.J., Hinings, C.R., Lee, C.A., Schneck, R.E. and Pennings, J.M. (1971) 'A strategic contingencies theory of intra-organizational power', *Administrative Science Quarterly*, vol. 16, pp. 216–29.

Hiley, D.R. (1987) 'Power and values in corporate life', *Journal of Business Ethics*, vol. 6, pp. 343–53.

Hilmer, F. and Donaldson, L. (1996) *Management Redeemed*, Free Press, New York.

Horkheimer, M. and Adorno, T.W. (1947) *Dialectic of Enlightenment*, Querido Verlag, Amsterdam.

Huczynski, A.A. (1993) *Management Gurus: What Makes Them and How To Become One*, Routledge, London.

Huczynski, A.A. (1996) *Influencing Within Organizations: Getting In, Rising Up and Moving On*, Prentice Hall, Hemel Hempstead.

Hughes, R. (1993) *Culture of Complaint: The Fraying of America*, The New York Public Library/Oxford University Press, New York/Oxford.

Hutton, D.W. (1994) *The Change Agent's Handbook: A Survival Guide for Quality Improvement Champions*, ASQC Quality Press, Milwaukee, WI.

Jackall, R. (1988) *Moral Mazes: The World of Corporate Managers*, Oxford University Press, New York/Oxford.

Jacobs, J. (1969) 'Symbolic bureaucracy', *Social Forces*, vol. XLVII, pp. 413–20.

Jennings, E.E. (1971) *Routes to the Executive Suite*, McGraw-Hill, New York.

Johansson, H., McHugh, P., Pendlebury, A.J. and Wheeler, W.W. (1993) *Business Process Reengineering: Breakpoint Strategies for Market Dominance*, John Wiley, Chichester.

Johns, T. (1995) 'Don't be afraid of the moral maze', *People Management*, 5 October, pp. 32–4.

Johnson, P. and Gill, J. (1993) *Management Control and Organizational Behaviour*, Paul Chapman Publishing, London.

Jürgens, U. (1997) 'Restructuring product development and production networks: learning from experiences in different industries and countries', paper presented at the International Conference on Restructuring Product Development and Production Networks, Science Centre, Berlin, March.

Kakabadse, A. (1983) *The Politics of Management*, Gower Publishing, Aldershot.

Kakabadse, A. and Parker, C. (1984) *Power, Politics and Organizations: A Behavioural Science View*, John Wiley and Sons, Chichester.

Kanter, R.M. (1977) *Men and Women of the Corporation*, Basic Books, New York.

Kanter, R.M. (1979) 'Power failure in management circuits', *Harvard Business Review*, vol. 57, no. 4, pp. 65–75.

Kanter, R.M. (1983) *The Change Masters: Corporate Entrepreneurs at Work*, George Allen & Unwin, London.

Kanter, R.M. (1989) *When Giants Learn to Dance: Mastering the Challenges of Strategy, Management, and Careers in the 1990s*, Unwin, London.

Kanter, R.M. (1997) *Rosabeth Moss Kanter on the Frontiers of Management*, Harvard Business Review Books, Boston.

Kaplinski, R. (1984) *Automation: The Technology and Society*, Springer, Berlin.

Katzenbach, J.R. and the Real Change Team (1996) *Real Change Leaders*, Nicholas Brealey Publishing, London.

Kipnis, D., Schmidt, S.M. and Wilkinson, I. (1980) 'Intra-organizational influence tactics: explorations in getting one's way', *Journal of Applied Psychology*, vol. 65, pp. 440–52.

Kipnis, D., Schmidt, S.M., Swaffin-Smith, C. and Wilkinson, I. (1984) 'Patterns of managerial influence: shotgun managers, tacticians, and bystanders', *Organizational Dynamics*, Winter, pp. 58–67.

Knights, D. and Murray, F. (1994) *Managers Divided*, Gower, Aldershot.

Korda, M. (1976) *Power*, Ballantine Books, New York.

Kotter, J.P. (1985) *Power and Influence: Beyond Formal Authority*, Free Press, New York.

Kotter, J.P. (1990) *A Force for Change: How Leadership Differs from Management*, Free Press, New York.

Kotter, J.P. (1995) 'Leading change: why transformation efforts fail', *Harvard Business Review*, vol. 73, no. 2, pp. 59–67.

Kumar, K. and Thibodeaux, M. (1990) 'Organizational politics and planned organizational change', *Group and Organizational Studies*, vol. 15, no. 4, pp. 357–65.

Kumar, P. and Ghadially, R. (1989) 'Organizational politics and its effects on members of an organization', *Human Relations*, vol. 42, no. 4, pp. 305–14.

Lasch, C. (1979) *The Culture of Narcissism*, W.W. Norton and Co, New York.

Lasch, C. (1984) *The Minimal Self*, W.W. Norton and Co, New York.

Lasch, C. (1995) *The Revolt of the Elites*, W.W. Norton and Co, New York.

Laver, M. (1997) *Private Desires, Political Action: An Invitation to the Politics of Rational Choice*, Sage, London.

Law, J. and Callon, M. (1992) 'The life and death of an aircraft: a network analysis of technical change', in W. Bijker and J. Law (eds), *Shaping Technology/Building Society: Studies in Sociotechnical Change*, MIT Press, Cambridge, MA, pp. 21–52.

Lawler, E.E. (1986) *High Involvement Management: Participative Strategies for Improving Organizational Performance*, Jossey-Bass, San Francisco.

Lawrence, P.R. and Lorsch, J.W. (1967) *Organization and Environment*, Harvard University Press, Boston.

Leary, M.R. et al. (1986) 'Ethical ideologies of the Machiavellian', *Personality and Social Psychology Bulletin*, March, pp. 75–80.

Lee, B. (1997) *The Power Principle: Influence with Honor*, Simon and Schuster, New York. © 1997 Franklin Covey Co., 1-801-975-1776. Used with permission. All rights reserved.

Liden, R.C. and Mitchell, T.R. (1988) 'Ingratiatory behaviors in organizational settings', *Academy of Management Review*, vol. 13, no. 4, pp. 572–87.

McAuley, J. (1996) 'Ethical issues in the management of change', in K. Smith and P. Johnson (eds), *Business Ethics and Business Behaviour*, International Thomson Business Press, London, pp. 221–42.

McCall, M.W. and Kaplan, R.E. (1990) *Whatever it Takes: The Realities of Managerial Decision Making*, Prentice Hall, Englewood Cliffs, NJ (second edition).

McCalman, J. and Paton, R.A. (1992) *Change Management: A Guide to Effective Implementation*, Paul Chapman Publishing, London.

McClelland, D.C. (1970) 'The two faces of power', *Journal of International Affairs*, vol. 24, no. 1, pp. 29–47.

McClelland, D.C. (1975) *Power: The Inner Experience*, Irvington, New York.

McClelland, D.C. and Burnham, D.H. (1995) 'Power is the great motivator', *Harvard Business Review*, vol. 73, no. 1, pp. 126–39.

Maccoby, M. (1976) *The Gamesman*, Simon and Schuster, New York.

McDonough, E. and Griffin, A. (1997) 'Creating systemic NPD capability', paper presented to the International Conference on New Product Development and Production Networks, Berlin, Germany, March.

Machiavelli, N. (1988) in Q. Skinner and R. Price (eds), *Machiavelli: The Prince*, Cambridge University Press, Cambridge.

McKenna, E.P. (1997) *When Work Doesn't Work Anymore: Women, Work and Identity*, Hodder & Stoughton, New York.

McKinlay, A. and Starkey, K. (eds) (1998) *Foucault, Management and Organization Theory*, Sage, London.

McLaughlin, M.L., Cody, M.J. and Read, S.J. (1992) *Explaining One's Self to Others: Reason-Giving in a Social Context*, Lawrence Erlbaum Associates, Hillsdale, NJ.

McMurry, R.N. (1973) 'Power and the ambitious executive', *Harvard Business Review*, vol. 51, no. 6, pp. 140–5.

Madison, D.L., Allen, R.W., Porter, L.W., Renwick, P.A. and Mayes, B.T. (1980) 'Organizational politics: an exploration of managers' perceptions', *Human Relations*, vol. 33, no. 2, pp. 79–100.

Maidique, M. (1980) 'Entrepreneurs, champions, and technological innovation', *Harvard Business Review*, vol. 21, no. 2, pp. 59–76.

Majchrzak, A. and Gasser, L. (1991) 'On using artificial intelligence to integrate the design of organizational and process change in US manufacturing', *AI and Society*, vol. 5, no. 4, pp. 321–38.

Mangham, I. (1979) *The Politics of Organizational Change*, Greenwood Press, Westport, CT.

Mann, S. (1995) 'Politics and power in organizations: why women lose out', *Leadership and Organization Development Journal*, vol. 16, no. 2, pp. 9–15.

March, J.G. and Olson, J.P. (1983) 'Organizing political life: what administrative reorganization tells us about government', *American Political Science Review*, vol. 77, no. 2, pp. 281–96.

Markus, L.M. (1983) 'Power, politics and MIS implementation', *Communications of the ACM*, vol. 26, no. 6, pp. 430–44.

Martin, J. (1992) *Cultures in Organizations: Three Perspectives*, Oxford University Press, New York.

Martin, N.H. and Sims, J.H. (1964) 'Power tactics', in H.J. Leavitt and L.R. Pondy (eds), *Readings in Managerial Psychology*, The University of Chicago Press, Chicago and London, pp. 217–25.

Matejka, K., Ashworth, D.N. and Dodd-McCue, D. (1985) 'More power to ya!', *Management Quarterly*, vol. 26, pp. 33–7.

Mayes, B.T. and Allen, R.W. (1977) 'Toward a definition of organizational politics', *Academy of Management Review*, vol. 2, pp. 672–8; reprinted in C. Hardy (ed.), *Power and Politics in Organizations*, Dartmouth, Aldershot, 1995, pp. 83–9.

Micklethwait, J. and Wooldridge, A. (1996) *The Witch Doctors*, Heinemann, London.

Mills, C.W. (1951) *White Collar: The American Middle Classes*, Oxford University Press, New York.

Mills, C.W. (1959) *The Sociological Imagination*, Oxford University Press, New York.

Mintzberg, H. (1983) *Power in and Around Organizations*, Prentice Hall, Englewood Cliffs, NJ.

Mintzberg, H. (1994) *The Rise and Fall of Strategic Planning*, Free Press, New York.

Moad, J. (1993) 'Does reengineering really work?', *Datamation*, vol. 39, no. 15, pp. 22–8.

Moffat, L.K. and Gerwin, D. (1994) 'Concurrent engineering project teams: an examination of critical success factors', *A Report for the IMS Global Concurrent Engineering Test Case*, Carleton University, Ottawa.

Morgan, G. (1989) *Images of Organization*, Sage, Beverly Hills.

Naisbett, J. and Aburdene, P. (1986) *Reinventing the Corporation*, Warner Books, New York.

Nalebuff, B.J. and Brandenburger, A.M. (1996) *Co-opetition*, HarperCollins Business, London.

Nietszche, F. (1968) *Will to Power*, Vintage, New York.

Nonaka, I. and Takeuchi, H. (1995) *The Knowledge Creating Company: How Japanese Companies Create the Dynamics of Innovation*, Oxford University Press, New York.

Ottaway, R.N. (1983) 'The change agent: a taxonomy in relation to the change process', *Human Relations*, vol. 36, no. 4, pp. 361–92.

Parnaby, J. (1988) 'A systems approach to the implementation of JIT methodologies in Lucas industries', *International Journal of Production Research*, vol. 26, no. 3, pp. 483–92.

Parry, G. (1972) 'The Machiavellianism of the Machiavellians', in B. Parekh and R.N. Berki (eds), *The Morality of Politics*, George Allen & Unwin, London, pp. 114–35.

Pearce, E. (1993) *Machiavelli's Children*, Victor Gollancz, London.

Pearson, A. (1998) 'Jack, joker and king', *The Sunday Telegraph Magazine*, 2 March, pp. 26–35.

Perrow, C. (1970) 'Departmental power and perspectives in industrial firms', in N.Z. Mayer (ed.), *Power in Organizations*, Vanderbilt University Press, Nashville, pp. 59–89.

Peters, T. (1987) *Thriving on Chaos: Handbook for a Management Revolution*, Macmillan, London.

Peters, T. (1994) 'Interview', *Independent on Sunday*, 15 May.

Peters, T. and Waterman, R.H. (1982) *In Search of Excellence: Lessons from America's Best Run Companies*, Harper and Row, New York.

Pettigrew, A.M. (1973) *The Politics of Organizational Decision-Making*, Tavistock Publications, London.

Pettigrew, A.M. (1974) 'The influence process between specialists and executives', *Personnel Review*, vol. 3, no. 1, pp. 24–30.

Pettigrew, A.M. (1977) 'Strategy formulation as a political process', *International Studies of Management and Organization*, vol. 7, no. 2, pp. 78–87.

Pettigrew, A.M. (1985) *The Awakening Giant: Continuity and Change in ICI*, Basil Blackwell, Oxford.

Pettigrew, A.M. (1987) 'Context and action in the transformation of the firm', *Journal of Management Studies*, vol. 24, no. 6, pp. 649–70.

Pettigrew, A.M. (ed.) (1988) *The Management of Strategic Change*, Basil Blackwell, Oxford.

Pettigrew, A.M. and McNulty, T. (1995) 'Power and influence in and around the boardroom', *Human Relations*, vol. 48, no. 8, pp. 845–73.

Pettigrew, A.M. and Whipp, R. (1991) *Managing Change for Competitive Success*, Basil Blackwell, Oxford.

Pfeffer, J. (1981) *Power in Organizations*, Ballinger, Cambridge, MA.

Pfeffer, J. (1992a) *Managing With Power: Politics and Influence in Organization*, Harvard Business School Press, Boston, MA (first edition 1981).

Pfeffer, J. (1992b) 'Understanding power in organizations', *California Management Review*, vol. 34, no. 2, pp. 29–50.

Pfeffer, J. (1994) *Competitive Advantage Through People: Unleashing the Power of the Workforce*, Harvard Business School Press, Boston.

Pichault, F. (1995) 'The management of politics in technically related organizational change', *Organization Studies*, vol. 16, no. 3, pp. 449–76.

Pinchot, G. (1985) *Intrapreneuring: Why you Don't Have to Leave the Corporation to Become an Entrepreneur*, Harper and Row, New York.

Punch, M. (1996) *Dirty Business: Exploring Corporate Misconduct, Analysis and Cases*, Sage, London.

Rabinow, P. (ed.) (1984) *The Foucault Reader*, Penguin Books, London.

Ramsey, H. (1996) 'Managing Sceptically: A Critique of Organizational Fashion', in S. Clegg and G. Palmer (eds), *The Politics of Management Knowledge*, Sage, London, pp. 155–73.

Read, S.J. (1992) 'Constructing accounts: the role of explanatory coherence', in M.L. McLaughlin, M.J. Cody and S.J. Read (eds), *Explaining One's Self to Others: Reason-Giving in a Social Context*, Lawrence Erlbaum Associates, Hillsdale, NJ, pp. 3–19.

Reason, R. (1984) 'Is organization development possible in power cultures', in A. Kakabadse and C. Parker (eds), *Power, Politics and Organization*, John Wiley, Chichester, pp. 185–203.

Rein, I.J., Kotler, P. and Stoller, M.R. (1987) *High Visibility*, Heinemann, London.

Riesman, D. (1950) *The Lonely Crowd: A Study of the Changing American Character*, Yale University Press, New Haven.

Riley, P. (1983) 'A structurationist account of political culture', *Administrative Science Quarterly*, vol. 28, no. 3, pp. 414–37.

Roberts, W. (1995) *Leadership Secrets of Attila the Hun*, Warner Books, New York.

Rosenfeld, P., Giacalone, R.A. and Riordan, C.A. (1995) *Impression Management in Organizations: Theory, Measurement, Practice*, Routledge, London.

Rubin, H. (1997) *The Princessa: Machiavelli for Women*, Bloomsbury, London.

Savage, M. (1998) 'Discipline, surveillance and the "career": employment on the Great Western Railway 1833–1914', in A. McKinlay and K. Starkey (eds), *Foucault, Management and Organization Theory*, Sage, London, pp. 65–92.

Schaffer, R.H. and Thomson, H.A. (1992) 'Successful change programs begin with results', *Harvard Business Review*, January–February, pp. 80–9.

Schilit, W.K. (1986) 'An examination of individual differences as moderators of upward influence activity in strategic decisions', *Human Relations*, vol. 39, no. 10, pp. 933–53.

Schlenker, B.R. and Weigold, M.F. (1990) 'Self-consciousness and self-presentation: being autonomous versus appearing autonomous', *Journal of Personality and Social Psychology*, vol. 59, pp. 820–9.

Schon, D.A. (1963) 'Champions for radical new inventions', *Harvard Business Review*, March–April, pp. 77–86.

Schon, D.A. (1983) *The Reflective Practitioner: How Professionals Think in Action*, Basic Books, New York.

Schumpeter, J. (1968) *The Theory of Economic Development*, Harvard University Press, Cambridge, MA.

Scott-Morgan, P. (1995) *The Unwritten Rules of the Game*, McGraw-Hill, New York.

Servan-Schreiber, J.J. (1969) *The American Challenge*, Penguin Books, Harmondsworth.

Shapiro, E.C. (1996) *Fad Surfing in the Boardroom*, Capstone, Oxford.

Sims, H.P. and Lorenzi, P. (1992) *The New Leadership*, Sage, Newbury Park.

de Sitter, L.U. and den Hertog, J.F. (1990) 'Simple organizations, complex jobs: the Dutch sociotechnical approach', paper presented at the annual conference of the American Academy of Management, San Francisco, August.

Spector, B. and Beer, M. (1994) 'Beyond TQM programmes', *Journal of Organizational Change Management*, vol. 7, no. 2, pp. 63–70.

Stjernberg, T. and Philips, A. (1993) 'Organizational innovations in a long-term perspective: legitimacy and souls-of-fire as critical factors of change and viability', *Human Relations*, vol. 46, no. 10, pp. 1193–219.

Stone, B. (1997) *Confronting Company Politics*, Macmillan Business, Houndsmills, Hampshire.

Strauss, A., Schatzman, L., Erlich, D., Bucher, R. and Sabshin, M. (1973) 'The hospital and its negotiated order', in G. Salaman and K. Thomson (eds), *People and Organizations*, Longman, London, pp. 303–20.

Tannen, D. (1990) *You Just Don't Understand: Women and Men in Conversation*, William Morrow and Company, New York.

Tannen, D. (1995) 'The power of talk: who gets heard and why', *Harvard Business Review*, September–October, pp. 138–48.

Thomas, A. (1993) *Controversies in Management*, Routledge, London.

Thompkins, J.M. (1990) 'Politics – the illegitimate discipline', *Management Decision*, vol. 28, no. 4, pp. 23–8.

Thompson, P. and Davidson, J.O. (1995) 'The continuity of discontinuity: managerial rhetoric in turbulent times', *Personnel Review*, vol. 24, no. 4, pp. 17–33.

Tichy, N.M. and Devanna, M.A. (1986) *The Transformational Leader*, Wiley, New York.

Tinaiker, R., Hartman, A. and Nath, R. (1995) 'Rethinking business process reengineering: a social constructionist perspective', in G. Burke and J. Peppard (eds), *Examining Business Reengineering*, Kogan Page, London.

Tushman, M.L. (1977) 'A political approach to organizations: a review and rationale', *Academy of Management Review*, vol. 2, no. 2, pp. 206–16.

'V' (1991) *The Mafia Manager: A Guide to the Corporate Machiavelli*, St Martin's Press/Griffin, New York.

Veblen, T. (1958) *The Theory of Business Enterprise*, Mentor Books, New York.

Velasquez, M., Moberg, D.J. and Cavanagh, G.F. (1983) 'Organizational statesmanship and dirty politics: ethical guidelines for the organizational politician', *Organizational Dynamics*, Autumn, pp. 65–80.

Voss, B. (1992) 'Office politics: a player's guide', *Sales and Marketing Management*, vol. 144, no. 12, pp. 46–52.

Voyer, J.J. (1994) 'Coercive organizational politics and organizational outcomes: an interpretive study', *Organization Science*, vol. 5, no. 1, pp. 72–85.

Wallace, P.G. (1990) 'Power in practice', *Australian Health Review*, vol. 13, no. 1, pp. 55–62.

Ward, M. (1994) *Why Your Corporate Culture Change Isn't Working – And What To Do About It*, Gower, Aldershot.

Waterman, R.H. (1990) *Adhocracy*, W.W. Norton, New York.

Watson, T. (1994) *In Search of Management*, Routledge, London.

Wellins, R.S., Byham, W.C. and Wilson, J.M. (1991) *Empowered Teams: Creating Self-Directed Work Groups that Improve Quality, Productivity and Participation*, Jossey-Bass, San Francisco.

Westley, F.R. and Mintzberg, H. (1989) 'Visionary leadership and strategic management', *Strategic Management Journal*, vol. 10, pp. 17–32.

Whyte, W.H. (1956) *The Organization Man*, Simon and Schuster, New York, NY.

Wight, M. (1978) *Power Politics*, Penguin Books, Harmondsworth.

Willcocks, L. and Currie, W. (1996) 'Information technology and radical reengineering: emerging issues in major projects', *European Journal of Work and Organizational Psychology*, vol. 5, no. 3, pp. 325–50.

Willcocks, L. and Grint, K. (1997) 'Reinventing the organization? Towards a critique of business process re-engineering', in I. McLoughlin and M. Harris (eds), *Innovation, Organizational Change and Technology*, International Thomson Business Press, London, pp. 87–111.

Wilson, D.C. (1992) *A Strategy of Change: Concepts and Controversies in the Management of Change*, Routledge, London.

Wilson, J.M., George, J., Wellins, R.S. and Byham, W.C. (1994) *Leadership Trapeze: Strategies for Leadership in Team-Based Organizations*, Jossey-Bass, San Francisco.

Womack, J., Jones, D. and Roos, D. (1990) *The Machine that Changed the World*, Macmillan, New York.

Young, M. (1958) *The Rise of the Meritocracy: 1870–2033*, Penguin Books, Harmondsworth.

Zaleznik, A. (1997) 'Real work', *Harvard Business Review*, vol. 75, no. 6, pp. 53–63. (Originally published 1989.)

Zenger, J., Musselwhite, E., Hurson, K. and Perrin, C. (1994) *Leading Teams: Mastering the New Role*, Irwin, New York.

Zugbach, von R. (1995) *The Winning Manager: Coming Out on Top in the Organization Game*, Souvenir Press, London.

Index

Power, politics, and
organizational change

DATE DUE FOR RETURN